LITERARY ESSAYS

BY

WILLIAM G. T. SHEDD, D.D.,

ROOSEVELT PROFESSOR OF SYSTEMATIC THEOLOGY IN UNION
THEOLOGICAL SEMINARY, NEW YORK.

WIPF & STOCK · Eugene, Oregon

Wipf and Stock Publishers
199 W 8th Ave, Suite 3
Eugene, OR 97401

Literary Essays
By Shedd, William G.T., D.D.
ISBN 13: 978-1-57910-286-9
Publication date 10/1/2000
Previously published by Charles Scribner's Sons, 1878

Eng'd by A. H. Ritchie

W. G. T. Shedd

PREFACE.

In a previous volume, entitled Theological Essays, the writer brought together a number of disquisitions upon theological and theologico-philosophical topics; in this, he has collected a series that relate principally to æsthetics and literature. The two volumes thus contain opinions pertaining to a considerable segment of the circle of human knowledge. The reader will find the departments of theology, philosophy, both physical and metaphysical, history, rhetoric, belles-lettres, and fine art, more or less represented. The author is far from claiming that his discussion of such a variety of themes has always been successful. His only object in alluding to this variety in the contents of these volumes is, to call attention to the unity and system which, he is confident, will be found in the method of discussing the subjects. Right or wrong, the opinions themselves spring out of one intuition. The fine art and the theology are kindred to each other; the philosophy and the rhetoric are homogeneous in their spirit and tendency. So far, however, as his own convictions are concerned, the writer finds some reason for confidence in the general correctness of his views, in the fact that they are thus interlocked with each other from the first, and that the growth of his own mind has only interlaced them more and more. The opening essay, upon the true nature of Beauty and its relation to human culture, was composed in 1851, and all of the writer's study of books and observation of man, from that time to the present, has only made him tenfold more certain that the theory of æsthetics then presented is the true one. A moment's glance out upon the present condition of society is more than sufficient to show, that a false idea of Beauty and its functions is fatal, not only to character, but to lofty and noble art. There is little severity in the current culture, and there is little of the ideal or heroic in it, or its products. In again calling attention to the æsthetics of Michael Angelo and Milton, the author believes that he is doing the state some service.

We hear much of moral character, and know well what is meant by it. But there is such a thing as *intellectual* character. There is a virtue of the head, as well as of the heart; a temper of the understanding, as well as of the will. It grows out of high theories; out of exact formulas. Only education of a peculiar type will produce it. It is true, indeed, that intellectual character cannot be divorced from moral. Both develop best together, even as in the human body the brain and the heart concur in a common life. They grow in pairs like Wordsworth's yew trees:

> "Those fraternal Four of Borrowdale
> Joined in one solemn and capacious grove;
> Huge trunks! and each particular trunk a growth
> Of intertwisted fibres serpentine
> Up-coiling, and inveterately convolved."

Still, the imperfect is better than the wholly bad, and it would be well if those who shrink from the severities of religion would remember that there are severities of letters and of art, and, while recoiling from all contact with the doctrines of theology, would resolutely place themselves under the influence of the higher instead of the lower schools of literature. If they cannot begin at the beginning and make their sacrifice to God, let them at least sacrifice to the austerer muses. The elevation of the intellect might be a precursor to that of the heart.

A higher type of intellectuality is greatly needed in our new

America. Strictness and not laxity should characterize our style of thinking, our speculative theories, our judgments, and our tastes. There is imminent danger of the contrary. An easy and indulgent theory of education and refinement is formed among us, and unless counteracted, the only civilization on this Western continent that is worth anything will go to destruction. There is just now a great clamor and demand for "culture," but it is not so much culture that is needed as *discipline*. Twenty years ago, there was among us no formally stated theory like the Epicurean, but there was too much Epicureanism running through society, infusing a debilitating heat, and imparting a hectic flush. But now, the philosophy of Lucretius is distinctly adopted and defended, and the infidel physics organizes the sensual impulse and strengthens the sensual bent of the masses. We are not so sound and healthy a people as we were a generation ago. The debilitation is seen in vices that prevail over the whole extent of the land, and mortice themselves into the frame-work of society so firmly that society must be shocked and racked before they can be torn out. It is seen in the amusements of the people, especially in our large cities, which are fast overflowing their limits, and inundating the country with their fashions and spirit. Amusements are an accurate index of the national stamina, and the frivolous, licentious amusements now so common indicate that the American is undergoing an enervating, debauching process, as the cruel gladiatorial amusements of the Roman indicated that he underwent a hardening, brutalizing process. And it is difficult to say which is worst, in the sweep of years, and with reference to the perpetuity of society—this modern softening of the brain, or that ancient ossification of the heart. The national decay is seen again, in mercantile deceit and breach of trusts, which have become so wide-spread as to inspire foreign and domestic capital with alarm ; causing a general distrust of both individual and national credit, and producing a general stagnation. It is seen in the venality and profligacy of politics, municipal, state, and federal, which has sunk republican government almost to the level of the worst specimens of monarchy in the times of the second Charles, and the French Regency.

A yet worse feature, perhaps, because it stands in the way of reformation, is found in the dislike of stern recuperative theories generally, and the disposition to dilute truth and tone down the austere. The intellectuality of the nation has lost a great deal of its early fibre. In theology, men shrink from thorough statements and absolute punishments, as a weak nerve does from the north wind. In philosophy, even professed students avoid all the deeper problems, and all the strict science. In poetry, those who read and relish Sophocles, Dante, and Milton, are greatly in the minority. And in art, the lofty abstract ideal has well-nigh vanished, so that in much that goes under this name, sense becomes still more sensuous, and flesh still more carnal.

The true course is to look these facts in the eye, and to act accordingly. In 1802, a great poet, English to the bone, and loving his country as he loved his own flesh, denominated England "a fen of stagnant waters," and invoked the stern shade of Milton to raise her up, and give her " manners, virtue, freedom, power." The American Republic needs to-day a similar fidelity, and a similar affection, from all her true sons.

The author has dwelt the longer upon the opening essay in the volume, because it is the key-note to the whole. The tracts upon Rhetoric and Eloquence are in the same line with the æsthetics; affirming the ethical theory of an art very liable to degenerate into intellectual vanity and display. The views presented upon English Studies, Language and Style, Education and mental Discipline, are consonant with the general theory, and illustrate it. The two articles upon the Puritan and the African natures, bring together the extremes of human traits, the temperate and the tropical; and by the sharp contrast may, perhaps, help to a better comprehension of both. The longest essay in the series, is an attempt to form an estimate of the philosophy and theology of one of the most influential intellects of the nineteenth century. It was written in

1852, as an introduction to the complete edition of the writings of Coleridge published by the Messrs. Harper, and is by their kind permission republished in this form. At the time of its production, and for years previously, there had been various and discordant opinions, especially in theological circles, respecting the correctness and value of Coleridge's views. The writer has seen no reason to alter the general estimate which he made in his early life. The points upon which he then agreed, and upon which he then dissented, stand the same with him now. With the exception of a modified view of the doctrines of atonement and inspiration, he believes the matured and final opinions of Coleridge to be in harmony with the evangelical system, as constructed and adopted in England and America. The present state of sentiment in the reading and cultivated classes, makes the philosophical opinions of Coleridge more valuable than ever. He was the first Englishman at the beginning of the century, to combat the materialism of Hartley, Priestley, and the French Encyclopædists; and at the close of the century, the distinctions which he laid down, and the positions which he maintained, are still the best answer to the revived materialism of their successors.

The closing article upon the Confessions of Augustine directs attention to a form of religious experience that is deeply interesting to the believer, and not less so to the psychologist. No intellect outside of the circle of inspiration has, on the whole, influenced the human mind so greatly as the North-African father. Theology has moved mankind, both pagan and Christian, more than has philosophy, or science, or art. Man's religion is, after all, the principal feature in his history. It explains peace, and it explains war. A great theologian is therefore a prime mover; and Augustine was eminently such. He shared his influence, in his own day, in the patristic church, with others; but subsequently, he became the dominant and controlling spirit. The theology of the entire Middle Ages was chiefly, though imperfectly, moulded by Augustine. Anselm and Aquinas were his reverent pupils; and neither of the Scotuses would have ventured formally to oppose him. The theology of the Reformation was confessedly founded upon the Augustinian. Luther listened to Augustine, when he would listen to no other father, and to no schoolman. Calvin, next to the written word of God, fortifies his positions by Augustine; and wherever in the wide modern world Calvinism has directly gone, or exerted any indirect influence, the thinking and experience of the son of Monica has reappeared. The Roman Catholic still claims him. Petavius, and Bellarmine, and Möhler, all endeavor to prove their orthodoxy, by agreement with the great anti-Pelagian. The roots of all this vast intellectual influence lay in that wonderful experience so powerfully described in the Confessions. At a time when the forces of history are being investigated, and the phenomena of the religious life are being examined even by the skeptic, here is fertile matter for thought and study.

UNION THEOLOGICAL SEMINARY
NEW YORK, Sept. 4, 1878.

CONTENTS.

	PAGE
THE TRUE NATURE OF THE BEAUTIFUL AND ITS RELATION TO CULTURE	1
THE INFLUENCE AND METHOD OF ENGLISH STUDIES	37
THE ETHICAL THEORY OF RHETORIC AND ELOQUENCE	79
THE CHARACTERISTICS AND IMPORTANCE OF A NATURAL RHETORIC	123
THE RELATION OF LANGUAGE AND STYLE TO THOUGHT	149
SCIENTIFIC AND POPULAR EDUCATION	187
INTELLECTUAL TEMPERANCE	207
THE PURITAN CHARACTER	229
THE AFRICAN NATURE	245
COLERIDGE AS A PHILOSOPHER AND THEOLOGIAN	271
THE CONFESSIONS OF AUGUSTINE	345

THE TRUE NATURE OF THE BEAUTIFUL, AND ITS RELATION TO CULTURE.*

GENTLEMEN OF THE LITERARY SOCIETIES:

COMING as I do in the most beautiful season of the year, into the midst of some of the most beautiful scenery on the continent, and from the midst of scenery differently but equally beautiful; coming in mid-summer into the valley of the River from the valley of the Lake; you will not be surprised that my subject has connections with the environment in which I wrote and in which I speak. Surrounded, both while thinking and while giving utterance to my thoughts, by Beauty; composing and speaking in the midst of a material nature saturated and suffused with this element; it will not appear forced or unnatural if I find in it, the theme of our reflections at this hour.

It is not my purpose however to surrender myself, or to lead others to surrender themselves, to the extreme influence and impression of this quality, and to fall into a vague and rhapsodic train of thought or feeling. On the contrary my aim will be purely and perhaps intensely practical, and I hope with the aid of your own after-

* A discourse at Amherst College, August 13, 1851.

thought to make the particular aspect of the general subject of Aesthetics that will be exhibited, contribute to scholarship, and thorough education.

The specific theme then, to which I would invite your attention, is: *The true theory and relative position of the Beautiful, with reference more particularly to culture and to character.* In investigating this subject, I think we shall find it one for the times, and the class of men addressed. If I am not mistaken we shall find, in a false theory of Beauty, and, as a consequence, in the false position which it holds as a source and instrument of culture, the root of some of the radical defects, and false tendencies, of the educated class. For if this class need any one thing more than another, it is a rational, sober, and severe estimate of the *essential* nature of the Beautiful, and especially of the relation which it sustains to the True and the Good. In our age there is danger that culture will go the way that Grecian and Roman culture went, and from the same cause; an undue cultivation of the aesthetic nature, to the neglect of the intellectual and moral. There is always danger lest the most influential class in society, the literary and cultivated portion, form and shape themselves by Beauty more than by Truth, by Art more than by Philosophy and Religion.

If we accept the Platonic classification, all things in the universe arrange themselves under these three terms: the Beautiful, the True, and the Good. These three ideas cover and include all that can possibly come before the human mind as a worthy object of thought and action. On them, as a foundation, the human mind has built up its most permanent and grandest structures, and with them, in some one or other of their manifold aspects the human mind is constantly occupied. The idea of the Good lies at the bottom of all religion, and of all inquiries connected with this chief concern of man. The idea of the True lies at the bottom of all science, and of the scientific tendency in individuals and nations. The idea of the Beautiful underlies all those products and agencies of the human soul that address the imagination; all art, and all literature in the stricter signification of the term, as the antithesis of science. This classification, the work of the most philosophic brain of antiquity, at once so simple and so comprehensive, may therefore well stand as the condensation and epitome of all thought, and the key to all the varieties in human culture and national character.

But what is the order in which these ideas stand?— Which is first and which is last in importance? Which is most necessary and absolute in its nature? Which is the substance, and which is the accident? The answer to these questions, the theory upon this point, according as it shall be, is either vital or fatal. It will determine the whole style and character of human culture, both individual and national. If Beauty is placed first, in speculation and in life, and Truth and Goodness are regarded as subordinate, a corresponding style of education will follow. If the True and the Good are recognized as the substance, and the Beautiful as the property and shadow, another and entirely different style will result. Here, therefore, the inquirer stands at the point of divergence between the two principal species of civilization and culture of which human history is made up; that of luxury, enervation, decline, and fall, on the one hand, and that of severity, strength, growth, and grandeur, on the other. At this point, also, he stands upon the line which divides the lower from the higher forms of literature; the lower from the higher products of art itself; the more shallow and erroneous, from the more profound and correct, systems of philosophy and religion. Here is the summit-level and ridge whence the streams flow due east and due west, never to mingle in a common ocean. For if history teaches anything, it teaches that according as a nation and a national mind starts from the one or the other of these ideas, as a point of departure and as the guiding thought in its career, will be its style of development.

The true theory of Beauty subordinates it to the True and the Good. Any estimate of it, that sets it above these two eternal and necessary ideas, is both incorrect and unphilosophical. The closer we think, and the nearer we get to the essence of these three conceptions, the more clearly shall we perceive that while Truth and Goodness appear more and more absolute and necessary, Beauty, *in comparison with them*, appears more and more relative and contingent. The human mind can never, in its own thinking, annihilate the True and the Good; i. e. it cannot conceive of their non-existence. It cannot abstract them from the Divine nature and from the created universe, and have anything substantial left.— These *must* be.

> If *these* fail,
> The pillared firmament is rottenness
> And earth's base built on stubble.

But not so with Beauty. The mind can abstract it from the nature of God, and if Truth and Goodness still remain, there is still something august, something awe-inspiring, something sublime, left. The mind can think it away from the universe of God, but if that universe is still filled with the manifestations of wisdom and excellence, it is still worthy of its architect. It is indeed true that Beauty has a real and immanent existence, both in the being of God and in creation; but the point we are urging is, that it is there as *subordinate* to these moral elements, and these higher ideas. It is indeed true that from eternity to eternity Beauty is a quality in the nature of the First Perfect and the First Fair, and from this fountain has welled up and poured over into the whole creation of God like sunset into the hemisphere, but it has been only as the accompaniment and adornment of higher and more august qualities. The Beautiful is not, as some teach, either the True or the Good; neither is it more absolute and perfect than these. These are the substance, the eternal essence, and it, *in relation to them*, is the accident. The Beautiful indeed inheres in the True and the Good, and it forever accompanies them, even as light, according to the fine saying of Plato, is the shadow of God; but it is not therefore to be regarded as the highest of all ideas, or as the crowning element in the universe.

For where does Beauty reside? Where is its seat? Always in the *form*, as distinguished from the substance. When the human soul swells with the feeling, it is impressed not by the truth and substantial reality of an object, but by something that in comparison with this is secondary and accidental. When, for example, the sense for Beauty is completely filled and deluged by a sun-set or a sun-rise, the essential meaning of this scene is not necessarily in the soul. That which this scene is for Science, its truth for the pure intellect, is most certainly not in the mind; for the poetic vision and the scientific vision are contraries. And that which it is for Religion may be, and too often is, alien to the soul; for this feeling for the Beauty that is in the sun-rise, is by no means identical with the feeling for the Goodness that is there. In every instance it is the form and not the substance, it is the beauty and not the truth, that addresses the aesthetic nature, while in every instance it is the substance and not the form, it is the true and not the beautiful, that addresses the intellectual and moral natures.

And why should it not be so? If, as we have seen, the Beautiful is a subordinate quality; if it is only the glittering garment of the universe; to what part of man's nature should it appeal, but to that luxury rather than necessity of the human soul, the aesthetic sense. And so it is. Over against that Beauty which the Creator has poured with lavish, I had almost said indifferent hand, over his creation, he has set a portion of man's nature, whose function it is to drink it in, and as He never intended that this mere decoration of his works should engross the soul to the exclusion of the wisdom and goodness displayed in them, so He never intended that the sense for the Beautiful should absorb and destroy the sense for the True and the Good.

We shall see still more clearly the correctness of this theory of the Beautiful, by considering for a moment the nature and influence of that department which is based upon this idea, viz: Fine Art. The aim and end of Art is fine form, and nothing but fine form. I do not forget that in every work of Art there is a truth at the bottom, and that the power of a painting or a statue is dependent upon the *meaning* everywhere present in it. Still this significant thought at the base, this intellectual expression in the product, is not that which *constitutes it a work of Art*. It is the beauty of this thought, the fine form of this idea, which is the end of Art, and which renders its products different from those of Science. For if Art were merely and purely an expression of truth, how would it differ from Science, and why would not every subject that had meaning in it be a fit one for the artist?

Art, it is true, has a significance, and it is high and ideal in proportion to the depth and fulness of the idea it embodies, yet it differs from Science and Religion by employing both the True and the Good as *means* only. Its own sole *end* is Beauty, to which it subordinates all else. It embodies Truth and Virtue only that it may exhibit the beauty in them, and addresses the intellect and heart only that it may reach the imagination. After all its connection with the substance, Art is still formal. And this is no disparagement to it. It is no undervaluation to draw sharp lines about a department of human effort, and strip off what does not essentially belong to it. Fine Art has its own proper and important vocation, and Science and Religion have theirs, and each is honored by being strictly defined, and rigorously confined to its own aim, end, and limits.

Now such being the nature of Fine Art, considered as a department of human effort and an instrument to be employed in educating the human mind, what must be its influence if left to itself; if unbalanced and uncompleted by other departments? What style of culture will the idea of the Beautiful originate in the individual and national mind, when severed from the ideas of the True and the Good? The answer to this question is to be found in history. One of the great historical races, in the plan of Providence, received its training and development under the excessive and exorbitant influence of Beauty, and for a moment I invite your attention to an examination of the results.

The Greek mind was eminently aesthetic, and the Greek nature was controlled by a too strong and intense tendency to the Beautiful. If the human mind is truthful and solemn anywhere, it is so within the sphere of religion; but we may say of the Greek, as was said of one of the most genial of modern errorists by one of the most profound of modern thinkers, that he was more in love with the beauty of religion than its truth. The Greek religion was the worship of Beauty, and the whole life of the people; private and public, literary and political; was formed by this idea to an extent and thoroughness never witnessed before or since. But the Greek mind, with all the charm and influence it has exerted upon the modern mind, and will continue to exert to the last syllable of recorded time, had one great and radical defect. The True and the Holy did not interest it sufficiently. These ideas did not mould it and form it from the centre. Hence the Greek nature was not a deep and solemn one. It never felt, unless we except the heroic period in its history; a period that is hardly historic; the influence of that which is higher than Beauty, and which has an affinity with a more profound part of the human constitution than the aesthetic sense.

The truth is, that as the intellectual and moral nature of man is his highest endowment, so the True and the Good, as the highest ideas, are its proper correspondent. When, therefore, as in the case of the Greek, a relatively inferior portion of the soul became superior, and a relatively inferior idea became ultimate and engrossing, it was not possible that the highest development of human nature should take place, or the highest style of culture should be originated. The influence which the Greek mind has exerted upon the modern world, great as it has been, and beneficial as it has been, has nevertheless not been of the absolutely highest order, unless we set the aesthetic above the intellectual and moral, Art before Science and Religion, and the culture springing from the form above that springing from the substance.

Far be it from me, on such an occasion and before

such an audience, to undervalue classical education. I have not the slightest sympathy with that Jacobinism in literature which would throw aside the study of the ancient classics, and shut out the modern mind from the beauty, and symmetry, and cultivating influence, of Greek and Roman letters. Still it should be remembered that no single literature can do everything for the human intellect. On the contrary, each and every literature that is historic has one particular function to perform. In the education of the modern mind, classical literature has its own peculiar office to discharge, and this is, to infuse that beauty and symmetry which it possesses in so high degree into modern thought; to furnish a fine Form for the modern Idea. For it must not for a moment be supposed that the modern mind is to go back to the ancient for the substance of literature. The Christian world cannot go back into the Pagan world in search for the True and the Good, but it ever must go back there for the Beautiful. For the sphere of cognition, and consequently of reflection and feeling, in which the ancient mind moved, was narrow and contracted, compared with the "infinite and sea-like arena" on which the modern careers. Not that minds may not be found in the ancient world of equal depth, grasp, and power, with any that have adorned modern literature, but the materials on which they were compelled to labor fell far short of that which is the subject of modern effort, in depth, richness, and compass. The range of thought and feeling, in which the ancient mind moved, in respect to the great subjects pertaining to man's origin and destiny, was "cabined, cribbed and confined," compared with that vast expanse in which it is the privilege of the modern to think and feel. The Christian Revelation, while it imparted more determinateness and significance to those doctrines of natural religion upon which Plato and Aristotle had reflected with such truthfulness and profundity, at the same time lodged in the mind of the modern world an amount of new truth, that widened infinitely the field of human vision, and the scope of human reflection. We have but to compare Homer, Aeschylus, and Virgil, with Dante, Shakspeare, and Milton, to see how immensely the range of the human mind was augmented by a Divine Revelation. In these latter instances, it moves in a region large enough for it, and feels the influence of those "truths deep as the centre" with which it is connected by origin and destiny; while in the former instances, though the vague yearnings, and obscure anticipations, and unsatisfied longings, evidence the heaven-born nature of the human spirit, yet they serve only to reveal still more clearly the helplessness of its bondage, and the closeness of its confinement to this "bank and shoal of time." *

But although the Christian Religion so widened the sphere of human thought and feeling, and so deepened and spiritualized the processes of the human mind, and so enriched it in the material for literature, it indirectly diminished its artistic ability, and rendered it less able to embody its conceptions. This very opulence in the material, and this very elevation of the theme, embarrassed the mind. For in proportion to the richness and intrinsic excellence of the thought, does the difficulty increase,

---

* Hence that undertone of melancholy in the more serious portions of classical literature, (as the Histories of Tacitus, and the Morals of Plutarch) unrelieved by any notes of hope or triumph struck out by the knowledge, and the prospect, of the final consummation. The gloom of Dante is far different from the gloom of Aeschylus; for while, like his, it springs from the consciousness of the life-long conflict between good and evil, it is illumined by the knowledge of the final issue. In the case of the Pagan the gloom is made thicker by the total ignorance of the great hereafter.

of putting it into a form worthy of it. The problem of Art, in every instance, is to attain an exact correspondence between the matter and the form; to embody the idea in just the right amount of material, so that the idea shall not overflow and drown the form, nor the form overlay and crush the idea. Hence, among other qualities, the *cleanness*, the *niceness*, of a successful work of Art. But this problem, it is plain, becomes more difficult, in proportion as the idea, or guiding thought, is more profound or significant in its nature. For by reason of its depth and expanse it becomes vastly more comprehensive and pregnant, and less capable of being brought within the limitation of Art, within the bounds of a form. The nearer the subject-matter approaches the infinite; the more vast and unlimited the idea in the mind; the greater the difficulty of exhibiting it in the finite shapings of Art.

Now the ancient mind had these advantages. In the first place the material, the truth, upon which it labored, was far more wieldy and compassable than that which is presented to the modern mind, and in the second place it was (especially in the instance of the Greek) a much more artistic mind, in and of itself. The result, consequently, was a far closer correspondence between the substance and the form, and hence a much more successful solution of the problem of Fine Art, than has ever been attained by any other people.

The modern mind therefore, the Christian world, while it cannot go back into the Pagan world for the substance of literature, for the True and the Good, must ever go back there for the form, for the Beautiful. And it was precisely because the European mind, in the fifteenth century, felt the need of this aesthetic element in culture, which it was conscious of not possessing, that it betook itself to classical literature. At that period, when the human mind was waking up from the dormancy of the middle ages, and was beginning to feel the fresh impulses of the Christian Religion, it was filled, to overflowing, with ideas and principles, thoughts and feelings. Its powers and energies were being almost preternaturally roused by this influx of new truth, the natural tendency of which is to stir the human soul, preconformed as it is to its influence, to its inmost centre. But this season of mental fermentation was no time for serene contemplation, and beautiful construction. The whole *materiel* for a new literature was originated; but originated in a mind agitated to its lowest depths by the energy and force that was pouring through it, and which for this very reason was not master of itself, or of the material with which it was laboring. *Form*, rounded symmetrical finished *Form*, was needed for this Matter, and hence the modern betook himself to the study of that literature preeminent above all others for its artistic perfection. The study of the serene and beautiful models in which Grecian thought embodied itself tamed the wildly-working mind of the Goth, and imparted to it that calm, artistic, *formative* power by which the intellectual chaos was to become cosmos.*

* It is indeed true, that in the higher forms of Greek literature there is a remarkable depth and seriousness of sentiment which seems to militate against the position taken. Here the Beautiful is more in the back-ground, and the True mainly in the fore-ground. But it should be remembered that the real nature and tendency of the Greek appears far more in the lighter forms of the literature, and especially in that wilderness of works of Art that covered all Greece, than in the deep-toned poetry of Homer and Aeschylus, or the profound sentiment of Plato and Thucydides. This portion of Greek literature derived its tone and matter from that elder period; that heroic age; when the national mind was impressed, as the elder mind always has been, more by the essential than the formal, more by Truth than by Beauty.

But if the literature of the Greeks is predominantly aesthetic, and performs this aesthetic function in the system of modern education, the national character was still more so. The student of Grecian history, especially of the internal history of the Greeks, is struck with the disparity between the national character and the national literature; between the products of the Greek mind, or rather of a few choice Greek minds, and the Greek himself. The more the student becomes acquainted with that extremely imaginative and extremely tasteful, but too lively and too volatile, race of men, the more does he wonder that so much depth and truth of sentiment should be found in the literature that sprang up among them; the more does he wonder that the native bent and tendency of the national mind did not overrule, and suppress, all these higher elements. It is only on the supposition that the great men of Greece were above their race, and breathed in a more solemn and meditative atmosphere than that sunny air in which the Athenian populace lived, that he can account for the remarkable difference between the profound, severe, and moral, spirit of the Greek tragedy, and the fickle, gay, and altogether trifling temper of the Ionic race.

Whatever this excessive tendency to the Beautiful may have wrought out for the Greeks, in some respects, it is certain that it contributed to the enervation and destruction of all strong character in the nation. That Ionic race, instead of following indulgently and extravagantly, as they did, their native bias, ought to have subjected it to the most severe education and restraint. Those two other ideas which dawned in such solemnity and power upon the intellect of their greatest philosopher, ought to have rained down influence upon them. Those more serious and awe-inspiring objects of reflection, the True and the Good, ought to have dawned upon the popular mind in a clearer light and with a more overcoming power. How different, so far as all the grand and heroic elements of national character are concerned, were the Greeks of that golden age of ancient Art, the age of Pericles, from the Romans of the days of Numa! We grant that there is but little outward beauty, in that naked and austere period in Roman history, but there is to be found in that *character*, as it comes down to us in the legends of Livy and has been reconstructed in the pages of Niebuhr, the strongest, and soundest, and grandest, and sublimest, nationality in the Pagan world. And this was owing to the fact that the early Roman was intellectual and moral, rather than aesthetic. I am speaking, it will be remembered, of a Pagan character, and my remarks must be taken in a comparative sense. Bearing this in mind, we may say that the strength and grandeur of the national character of the first Romans, sprang from the fact that it was moulded and shaped mainly by the ideas of Truth and Virtue. The aesthetic nature was repressed, and, if you please, almost entirely suppressed, but the intellect and the moral sense were developed all the more. Hence those high qualities in their national character; courage, energy, firmness, probity, patriotism, reverence for the gods and the oath; qualities that were hardly more visible in the ancient, than they are in the modern, Greek.

And this brings us to the more distinct consideration of what we suppose to be the influence of Fine Art, when it becomes the leading department of effort, and the chief instrument and end of culture, for the individual or the nation. The effect of the Beautiful upon the human soul, when unmixed, uncounteracted, and exorbitant, is enervation. And this, from the very nature of the element itself. We have seen that it cannot be placed upon an equality with the other two elements that enter into the constitution of the universe. It cannot be regarded as so substantial and so necessary in its nature, as the True and the Holy. It is only the property and decoration of that which is essential and absolute. It is only the form. It consequently does not address the highest faculties of the human soul, and if it did, could not waken or generate power in them. When, therefore, it is made to do the work of the higher ideas; when it is compelled to go beyond its own proper sphere, the aesthetic nature, and to furnish aliment for the intellectual and moral nature; it is set at a work it can never do. The intellect and moral sense demand their own appropriate objects ; they require their correlatives, the True and the Good; they cry out for the substance and cannot be satisfied with the form, however beautiful. When therefore Beauty is selected as the great idea, by which the individual or national mind is to be moulded, the result is of necessity mental enervation. The human intellect cannot, any more than the human heart, be content with mere form. Like the heart, it cries out, in its own way, for the living God; for Truth and Goodness, the most essential qualities in the Divine nature; for Wisdom and Virtue, the most essential elements in the moral universe He has made. And what is there in the very process of Art itself, when it is isolated from the other and higher departments of human effort, that goes to render man more intellectual ? The very vocation of Art is to sensualize ; using the term technically and in no bad sense. Its processes, so far as they are merely artistic, are not spiritualizing, but the contrary. The vocation of Art is to bring down an idea of the human mind; a purely intellectual, purely immaterial, entity; into the sphere of sense, and there materialize it into colors, and lines, and outlines, and proportions, for the sense. The very calling of Art, as a department of effort, is to render sensuous the spiritual. And the fact that it does this, in the case of all high Art, in an ideal manner; that in the genuine product, the idea shines out everywhere through the beautiful form; does not conflict with the position. If, therefore, in a general way and for the purpose of characterizing the departments, we may say that in Science and Religion the mental process is spiritualizing, we may affirm that in Art the process is sensualizing. If in the analysis and synthesis of the True and the Good, the mind passes through an increasingly intellectual process, in the embodiment of the merely Beautiful, it passes through an exactly opposite one. If Philosophy and Religion tend to render the mind more intellectual, Fine Art tends to render it more material and sensuous by fixing the eye on the form.

Now such an influence as this upon the human mind and character, if unbalanced and uncounteracted, is enervating. There may be, and generally has been, great outward refinement and a most luxurious elegance thrown over the culture that originates under such influences, but it is too generally at the expense of strength and virtue and heroism of character. However high the aims of the individual or the nation may have been in the outset, history shows too plainly, that the nerve was soon relaxed and the mind slackened all away, at first, into a too luxurious, and finally, into a voluptuous culture. When the Artist, by the very theory and metaphysical nature of his vocation, is compelled to keep his eye on Beauty, on Fine Form, on the sensuously Agreeable, he must be a strong and virtuous nature that is not mastered by his calling. If he can preserve an austere tone; if he can even keep himself up on the high ground of an abstract and ideal Art, and not sink into a too ornate and licentious style; we may be certain that there was great moral stamina at bottom.

But speculation aside, let us appeal to history again. What does the story of Art in modern times teach in relation to the position that the unmixed, unbalanced, effect of the Beautiful, is mental enervation? The most wonderful age of Art was that of Leo X. The long slumber of the aesthetic nature of man, during the barbarism and warfare of those five centuries between the dismemberment of the Roman empire and the establishment of the principal nations and nationalities of modern Europe, was broken by an outburst of Beauty and Beautiful Art, as sudden, rapid, and powerful, as the bloom and blossom of spring in the arctic zone. Such a multitude of artists and such an opulence of artistic talent, will probably never be witnessed again in one age or nation. But did a grand, did even a respectable, national character spring into existence along with this bloom of Art, this shower of Beauty? We know that there were other influences at work, and among others a religious system whose very nature it is to carnalize and stifle all that is distinctively spiritual in the human soul; but no one can study the history of the period, without being convinced that this excessive and all-absorbing tendency of the general mind of Italy towards Beauty and Fine Art contributed greatly to the general enervation of soul. Most certainly it did not work counter to it. Read the memoirs of a man like Benvenuto Cellini; an inferior man it is true, but an artist and reflecting the general features of his time; and see how utterly unfit both the individual and national culture of that period was for any lofty, high-minded, truly historic, achievement. The solemn truths of Religion, and the lofty truths of Philosophy, exerted little or no influence upon that group of Italian artists, so drunken with Beauty. They possessed little of that intellectual severity which enters into every great character; little of that strung muscle and hard nerve which should support the intellect as well as the will. — And therefore it is that we cannot find in the Italian history of those ages, any more than in the Italian character of the present day, any of that high emprise and grand achievement which crowds the history of the Teutonic races, less art-loving, but more intellectual and moral. — These races and their descendants have sometimes been charged with a destitution of the aesthetic sense, and the inferiority of their Art, compared with that of Italy, has been cited as proof of their inferiority as a race of men; but it is enough to say in reply, that these Goths, educating themselves mainly by the ideas of the True and the Good, have given origin to all the literatures, philosophies, and systems of government and religion that constitute the crowning glory of the modern world. The Italian intellect was enfeebled and exhausted by that unnatural birth of Beauty upon Beauty. Ever since the fourteenth century, it has been wandering about in that world of fine forms, like Spenser's knight in the Bower of Bliss, until all power of intellect is gone.

Every truly great and grand character, be it individual or national, is more or less a *severe* one; a character which, comparatively, is more intellectual and moral, than aesthetic.* This position merits a moment's examin-

---

* According to the etymology of the old Grammarians, favored by Doederlein, the severe is the *intensely true.* Doederlein i. 76, præferendum censet vett. Gramm. sententiam qua *severus* cognationem habeat oum *verus*;
. . . . . ita ut *se*, ex more Gr. *a* priv., intensivam vim contineat.
— *Faccioluti's Lexicon in loc.*

ation. And in the first place, look into political history and see what traits lie at the bottom of all the best periods in national development. Out of what type of mind and style of life has the venerable, the *heroic*, age always sprung? Are men enervate or are they austere, are they aesthetic or are they intellectual and moral in culture, during that period when the national virtue is formed and the historic renown of the people is acquired?

The heroic age of Greece, as it comes down to us in the Homeric poems, was a period of simplicity and strictness. The Greeks of that early time were intellectual men, moral men, compared with the Greeks of the days of Alcibiades. Turn to the pages of Athenæus, and get a view of the in-door life and every-day character of a still later period in Grecian history, and then turn to the corresponding picture of the heroic period contained in the Odyssey, mark the difference in the impression made upon you by each representation, and know from your own feelings, that all that is strong, and heroic, and simple, and grand, in national character springs from a severe mind and a predominantly moral culture, and all that is feeble, and supine, and inefficient, and despicable, in national character, springs from a luxurious mind and a predominantly aesthetic culture.

And how stands the case with Rome? Which is the venerable period in her history? Is it to be sought for in the luxurious and (so far as Rome ever had it) the aesthetic civilization of the empire, or in the intellectual and moral civilization of the monarchy and republic? All the strength and grandeur of the Roman character and of the Roman nationality lies back of the third Punic war. Nay, if Rome had been conquered by Carthage, and had gone out of political existence, its real glory, its proper historic renown, would have been greater than it is. If in the idea called up by the word Rome, there were wanting, there could be eliminated, the physical corruption and the luxurious but merely outward refinement of the empire, and there were left only the stern virtue, the sublime endurance, and the moral grandeur, of the monarchy and republic, the idea would be more sublime in history and more impressive in contemplation. And whence originated that Sabine element, that tough core, that hard kernel, in the Roman character, that lay at the centre and kept Rome up, during her long agony of intestine and external conflict? It had its origin among the mountains, amid the great features of nature, and it was purified by the privation and hardship of a severe life in the forests of central Italy, on that spine of the Ausonian peninsula, until it became as sound, sweet, and hard, as the chestnuts of the Appenines upon which it was fed. Intellectual and moral elements, and not an aesthetic element, were the hardy root of all the political power and prosperity of Rome.

There is no need, even if there were time, to cite instances corroborating the view presented, from modern political history. The Puritanism of Old England and of New England will readily suggest itself, to every one, as the one eminently austere national character, with which the power and glory of the English and Anglo-American races, and the highest hopes of the modern world, are vitally connected. It will be sufficient to say, that the more profound is our acquaintance with political history, the more clearly shall we see that all that is powerful, and permanent, and impressive, in the nations, nationalities, and governments of the world, sprang directly or indirectly from a nature in which the aesthetic was subordinate to the intellectual and moral, and for which the True and the Good were more supreme ideas than the Beautiful.

Furthermore, the position taken holds true in the sphere of literature also. The great works in every instance are the productions of a severe strength; of "the Herculeses and not the Adonises of literature," to use a phrase of Bacon. When the aesthetical prevails over the intellectual and moral, the prime qualities, the depth, the originality, and the power, die out of letters, and the mediocrity that ensues is but poorly concealed by the elegance and polish thrown over it. Even when there is much genius and much originality, an excess of Art, a too deep suffusion of Beauty, a too fine flush of color, is often the cause of a radical defect. Suppose that the poetry of Spenser had more of that passion in it which Milton mentions as the third of the three main qualities of poetry; suppose (without however wishing to deny the great excellence of the Fairy Queen in regard to intellectual and moral elements) that the proportion of the aesthetic had been somewhat less, would it not have been more powerful and higher poetry? Suppose that the mind and the culture of Wieland and Goethe had been vastly more under the influence of Truth, and vastly less under that of Beauty; that the substance, instead of the form, had been the mould in which these men were moulded and fitted as intellectual workmen; might not the first have come nearer to our Spenser, and might not the latter have produced some works that would perhaps begin to justify his ardent but ignorant admirers in placing him in the same class with Shakspeare and Milton; a position to which, as it is, he has not the slightest claim.

As a crowning and conclusive proof of the correctness of the view presented, I will refer you to only one mind.

I refer you to John Milton, one of those two minds which tower high above all others in the sphere of modern literature. If there ever was a man in whom the aesthetic was in complete subjection to the intellectual and moral, without being in the least suppressed or mutilated by them, that man was Milton. If there ever was a human intellect so entirely master of itself, of such a severe type, that all its processes seem to have been the pure issue of discipline and law, it was the intellect of Milton. In contemplating the grandeur of the products of his mind, we are apt to lose sight of his mind itself, and of his intellectual character. If we rightly consider it, the discipline to which he subjected himself, and the austere style of intellect and of Art in which it resulted, are as worthy of the reverence and admiration of the scholar as the Paradise Lost. We have unfortunately no minute and detailed account of his every-day life, but from all that we do know, and from all that we can infer from the lofty, colossal, culture and character in which he comes down to us, it is safe to say that Milton must have subjected his intellect to a restraint, and rigid dealing with its luxurious tendencies, as strict as that to which Simon Stylites or St. Francis of Assisi subjected their bodies. We can trace the process, the defecating purifying process, that went on in his intellect, through his entire productions. The longer he lived and the more he composed, the severer became his taste, and the more *grandly* and *serenely* beautiful became his works. It is true that the theory of Art, and of culture, opposed to that which we are recommending, may complain of the occasional absence of Beauty, and may charge as a fault an undue nakedness and austerity of form. But one thing is certain and must be granted by the candid critic, that whenever the element of Beauty *is* found in

Milton, it is found in absolute purity. That intense refining process, that test of light and of fire, to which all his materials were subjected, left no residuum that was not perfectly pure. And therefore it is, that throughout universal literature, a more absolute Beauty and a more delicate aerial grace, are not to be found than appear in the Comus and the fourth book of Paradise Lost.

But we are not anxious on this point of Beauty, especially in connection with the name of Milton. Sublimity is a higher quality, and so are Strength and Grandeur; and if Beauty does not come *in the train*, and *as the mere ornament*, of these, it is not worth while to seek it by itself and for its own sake. And much will be gained when education, and culture, and authorship, shall dare to take this high stand which Milton took; shall dare to pass by Beauty, in the start, and to aim at deeper elements and loftier qualities, in the train, and as the ornament of which, a real Beauty and an absolute Grace shall follow of themselves.

Returning then to the intellectual character of Milton, let me advise you to study that character until you see that the strict, and philosophically severe theory of the Beautiful and of Art lies under the whole of it. Milton had no affinities for excessive sensuous Beauty. He was no voluptuary in any sense. So far as the sense was concerned he was abstemious as an ascetic, and so far as the soul was concerned he knew no such thing as luxury. He devoted himself to poetry, an Art which, glorious as it is, yet has tendencies that need counteraction, which tempts to Arcadian and indulgent views of human life and human character, and which, as literary history shows, has too often been the medium through which dreamy and uncontrolled natures have communicated themselves to the world. But as a poet, he constructed with all the truth of Science and all the purity of Religion. The poetic Art, as it appears in Milton, is spiritual and spiritualizing.*

If this element of severity is entirely wanting in a man; if he is entirely destitute of austerity; if his nature is wholly and merely aesthetic, constantly melting and dissolving in an atmosphere of Beauty; whatever else may be attributed to him, strength and grandeur cannot be. We do not deny that there is a sort of interest in such natures, but we deny that it is of the highest sort. If a man is born with a beautiful soul, and it is his tendency (to use a Shaksperean phrase) " to wallow in the lily beds;" to revel in luxurious sensations, be they wakened by material or immaterial Beauty; unless he subject his mind to the training of higher ideas, and of a higher department than that of Fine Art, his career will end in the total enervation of his being. This tendency ought in every instance to be disciplined. The individual in whom it exists, ought to superinduce upon it a strictness and austerity that will check its luxuriance, and bring it within the limits of a severer and therefore purer taste.

The least injurious and safest form which an undue aesthetic tendency can take on, is a quick sense for the Beautiful in nature. But even here, an unbalanced, uneducated, tendency is enervating. That dreamy mood of young poets, that dissolving of the soul in "the light of setting suns," must be educated and sobered by a stern discipline of the head and heart, or no poetry will

* We may say of Milton, in reference to the highly ideal character of his Art, as Fuseli has said of the same feature in Michael Angelo; "he is the salt of Art." He *saves* it from its inherent tendency to corruption, by a larger infusion of intellectual and moral elements than exists in the average productions of the department.

be produced that will go down through all ages. It is not so much a deep tendency as a transient mood of the soul, and needs the infusion of intellectual and moral elements, in order that it may become "the vision and faculty divine." Turn to a great collection, like Chalmers' British Poets, and observe how large a portion of this mass of poetry is destitute of the power of producing a *permanent* impression upon the human imagination; how little out of this great bulk is selected to be read by the successive generations of English students; how small a portion of it, compared with the whole amount, is profoundly and genuinely poetic; and at the same time notice how very much of it was evidently composed under the influence which the Beautiful in nature exerts upon an undisciplined, and uneducated, aesthetic sense, and you will have the strongest possible proof of the enervating, enfeebling, influence of this quality when isolated from the intellectual and moral. — The mind needed a deeper culture, and a discipline wrought out for it by higher ideas, that could *use* and *elaborate* these obscure feelings, these dim dreams, this blind sense, for the purposes of a higher and more genuine Art. It is often said, we know, that science is the death of poetry; that the study of the Kantean philosophy injured the poetry of Schiller, and the study of all philosophies the poetry of Coleridge; that the charm, and the glow, and the flush, and the fulness, and the luxuriance, and the gorgeousness, were all destroyed by the acid and blight of science. But we do not believe this. These poets might have written more, had their imagination not been passed through these severe processes of the intellect, they might have been more fluent, but that they would have written more that will have a *lasting* poetic interest remains to be seen. Their Art is all the higher, for the check and restraint imposed upon their poetic nature. And who will not say, to take a plain example, that if the young soul of Keats could have been corded with a stronger muscle, and overshaded with a severer tone of feeling and sentiment; that if a more masculine culture could have been married with that genuinely feminine soul; a higher poetry and a still purer Beauty would have been the offspring of this hymeneal union?*

And this brings us to the more positive side of the subject. Thus far we have spoken in a negative way of what the Beautiful is not, and of what it cannot do for the human soul and human culture. We now affirm that only on the theory which subordinates Beauty to Truth can the highest style of Beauty itself be originated, and that only when the department of Aesthetics is subordinate to those of Philosophy and Religion, does a genuinely beautiful culture, either individual or national, spring into existence. Without this check and subordination, the aesthetic quality will destroy itself by becoming excessive. The more staple elements that must enter into and substantiate it, will all evaporate; as if the warm organic flesh should all turn into the fine flush of the complexion; as if the air and the light and the foliage and the waters, all the *material*, all the *solidity*, of a beautiful landscape, should vanish away into mere crimson and vermilion. For, as we have already observed, true Beauty in a work of Art, is conditioned upon the presence in it of some intelligible idea. There must be some truth and some expression, in order to the existence of the pure quality itself. Beauty cannot stand alone. There must be a meaning underneath of which

---

* If the school of Tennyson needs any one thing, it is an austerer manner.

it is the clothing. There must be an intellectual conception within the product, to which it can cling for support, and from which it derives all its growing, lasting, highest charm for a cultivated taste. Hence it is, that as we go up the scale, Beauty actually becomes more ideal, more and more intellectual and moral. It undergoes a refining process, as it rises in grade, whereby the sensuous element, so predominant in the lower products of Art, is volatilized. There is more appeal to the soul and less to the sense, as we go up from the more florid and showy schools of painting, e. g., to the more ideal and spiritual. The same is true of the Beautiful in nature. As we ascend from the inferior to the higher vegetation, we find not only a more delicate organization, but a more delicate Beauty. The gaudy and coarse coloring gives place to more exquisite hues, in proportion as *mind;* in proportion as the *presiding intelligence* of the Creator; comes more palpably into view. In the words of Milton, all things are

> more refined, more spirituous, and pure,
> As nearer to Him placed, or nearer tending,
> Till body up to spirit work.
> So from the root
> Springs *lighter* the green stalk ; from thence the leaves
> More *aery ;* last the bright consummate flower
> *Spirits odorous* breathes ; flowers and their fruit,
> Man's nourishment, by gradual scale sublimed
> To *vital spirits* aspire, to *animal,*
> To *intellectual.**

And all things grow more highly beautiful as we keep pace with this upward step in nature, until we pass over into the distinctively spiritual sphere, and reach the

---

* Par. Lost. v. 475.

crown and completion of all Beauty; the beauty of character, or the "beauty of holiness." Observe that all along this limitless line we find a growing severity; that is, an increase of the intellectual or moral element. Sensuous beauty is displaced, or rather absorbed and transfigured, by intellectual beauty; the ideas of the True and the Good more and more assert their supremacy, by employing the Beautiful as the mere medium through which *they* become visible, even as light, after traversing the illimitable fields of ether without either color or form, on coming into an atmosphere, into a medium, thickens into a solid blue vault.

A reference to the actual history of Fine Art will also verify the position here taken. As matter of fact, we find this spiritualizing process; this advance of the substance and this retreat of the form; going on in every school of Art that grew more purely and highly beautiful, and in the soul of every artist who went up the scale of artists. That school which did not grow more ideal, invariably grew more sensuous and less beautiful, and that artist who did not by study and discipline become more strict and pure in style, invariably sunk down into the lower grade. All the works of Art that go down through succeeding ages with an ever-growing beauty as well as an ever-towering sublimity; all the great models and master-pieces; owe their origin to a most exact taste and a most spiritual idea. The study of the great models in every department of Art, be it painting, or sculpture, or poetry, will convince any one that the imagination, the artist's faculty, when originating its greatest works imposes restraints upon itself; in reality is rigorous with itself. If the artist allows his imagination to revel amid all the possible forms that will throng, and press, through this wonderfully luxuriant and productive power, if he suffers it to waste its energy in an idle play with its thick-coming fancies; if, in short, he does not preserve it a *rational* imagination, and regulate it by the deeper element and higher principle inherent in it, his productions will necessarily be in the lower style. It is for this reason that the artist betakes himself to study. He would break up this revelry of a lawless, uneducated, imagination. He would set limits to a vague and aimless energy. He would wield a productive talent that lies lower down; that works more calmly and grandly; more according to reason and a profounder Art. The educating process, in the case of the artist, is intended to repress a cloying luxuriance and to superinduce a beautiful austerity; to substitute an ideal for a material beauty. Hence we see that the artist, as he grows in power and high excellence, grows in strictness of theory and severity of taste. His products are marked by a graver beauty, and the presence of a purer ideal, as he goes up the scale of artists.

As an example, we may cite the instance of Michael Angelo. For grandeur, sublimity, and power of permanent impression, he confessedly stands at the head of his Art, and although in regard to beauty, Raphael may dispute the palm with him, and by some may be thought his superior, yet no one can deny that (as in the case of Milton) whenever this element does appear in "the mighty Tuscan," it is of the most absolute and perfect species.*

* Winckelmann, looking from his point of view, which was that of classic Art merely, has expressed a disparaging opinion in regard to Angelo, so far as the Beautiful is concerned, and seems to have laid the foundation for the superficial and too general opinion, that in respect to this quality he was by nature greatly inferior to Raphael. But the able editors of his works justly call attention to the fact, that Winckelmann is wrong in judging of modern Art in this servile way, and allude to a scarce and but little known poem of Angelo's, in which a most delicate and feminine appreciation of beauty

Yet all his productions are characterized by an austere manner. The form is always subservient, and perhaps sometimes somewhat sacrificed, to the idea. And, at any rate, the man himself, compared with the Italian artists generally, compared with Raphael especially, was a spiritual man both in culture and character. We confess that we look with a veneration bordering upon awe upon that grand nature, abstinent, abstract, and ideal, in an age that was totally sensuous in head and heart, and in a profession whose most seductive and dangerous tendency is to soften and enervate. By the force of a strong heroic character, as well as a hard and persevering study both of Art and of Nature, he counteracted that tendency to a sensuous and a sensualizing beauty, which we have noticed as the bane of Art, and in that nerveless age, so destitute of lofty virtue and stern heroism, stands out like the Memnon's head on the dead level of

---

is apparent. "In this poem," say they, "the great Michael Angelo reveals himself in a manner that appears striking and wonderful to such as have known him only from his paintings and statues. Heartfelt admiration for beauty, love too deep to be disclosed to its object, a gentle touching sadness wakened by the sense of an existence that cannot satisfy an infinite affection, and a melancholy longing, growing out of this, for dissolution and freedom from the bonds of earth, form the ground-tone of this warmly-glowing poem, in which Angelo gives an expression of the feminine element in his great and mighty nature, that is all the more lovely from the fact that the masculine principle is the prevailing and predominant one in his works of Art."—*Winckelmann's Werke von Meyer und Schulze*, iv. 43, *and Anmerk*. p. 262.

Consonant with this are the following remarks of Lanzi. "We may here observe that when Michael Angelo was so inclined, he could obtain distinction for those endowments in which others excelled. It is a vulgar error to suppose that he had no idea of grace and beauty; the Eve of the Sistine Chapel turns to thank her Maker, on her creation, with an attitude so fine and lovely that it would do honor to Raphael."

History of Painting, (*Roscoe's Trans.*) i. **176.**

the Nile, grand and lonely, yet with "elysian beauty and melancholy grace."

And, in this connection, I cannot refrain from calling your attention to that greatest of American artists, who is at once a proof and illustration of the truth of the general theory advanced. No man will suspect Allston of an underestimate of the Beautiful. In the whole catalogue of ancient and modern artists, there is not to be found a single one in whose mind this element existed in more unmixed and absolute purity: — beauty

> chaste as the icicle
> That's curded by the frost from purest snow,
> And hangs on Dian's temple.

But this spirituality was the fruit not only of a pure nature, but of a high theory. He recognized and felt the supremacy of the True and the Good, over the Beautiful. The reader of his lectures on Art, is struck with the religious carefulness with which he insists upon the superior claims of Truth over those of mere Art, and the earnestness with which he seeks to elevate and spiritualize the profession which he honored and loved, by making it the organ and proclamation of Truth and Holiness. By this, we think the fact can be explained that he produced so little, compared with the exhaustless fertility of the Italian artists. His ideal was so high, the Beautiful was so *spiritually* beautiful for him, that color and form failed to embody his conceptions. His uniform refusal to attempt the representation of Christ, a far too common attempt in Italian Art, undoubtedly rested upon this fact. It was not because his intensely spiritual mind had a less adequate idea of the Divine-Man, than that which floated before the Catholic imagination, but because there beamed upon his ethereal vision, a FORM of such high and awful beauty as could not be put upon a material canvas. It was because he saw so much that he did so little.

But, Gentlemen, there is a still more practical and important side to this whole subject. The department of Art sustains a relation to the growth and development of the human mind, and human society. Like all other departments of human effort, it should therefore be subservient to the great moral end of human existence, and if there were no other alternative, it would be better that the aesthetic nature, and the whole department of Art, and the whole wide realm of the Beautiful, should be annihilated, than that they should continue to exist at the expense of the intellectual and moral, of the True and the Good. We are not at all driven to the alternative, if there be truth in the general theory that has been presented, but if we were, we acknowledge boldly that we would side with the Puritan iconoclast and dash into atoms the Apollo Belvidere itself. Rather than that the department of Art should annihilate Philosophy and Religion; rather than that an enervate beauty should eat out manly strength and severe virtue from character; rather than that a sensualizing process should be introduced into the very heart of society, though it were as beautiful as an opium dream; we would see the element struck out of existence, and man and the universe be left as bald and bare as granite. We honor therefore, that trait in our ancestors, (so often charged upon them as a radical defect in nature, and so often tacitly admitted as such even by some of their descendants), which made them afraid of Fine Art; afraid of music and painting and sculpture and poetry. They dreaded the form, but had no dread of the substance, and therefore were the most philosophic of men. They dreaded the material, but had no dread of the ideal, and therefore were the most intellectual of men. They dreaded the sensuous, but had no dread of the spiritual, and therefore were the most religious of men. The Puritan nature owed but little, comparatively speaking, to aesthetic culture. It was not drawn upon and drawn out, as some natures have been, by Literature and Art, for in the plan of Providence its mission was active rather than contemplative; but we do not hesitate to say, that the contents and genius were there, and that even on the side of the imagination, that nature, had it been unfolded in this direction, would have left a school and a style of Art, using the term in its widest acceptation, second to none. And as it is, we see its legitimate tendency and influence in the poetry of Milton. The Miltonic style of Art is essentially the Puritan Art; beautiful only as it is severe and grand; the Beautiful superinduced upon the True and the Holy.

Gentlemen:

In the opening of my discourse, I alluded to the fact, that the style of civilization and culture peculiar to the individual or the nation is determined by the theory, which is consciously or unconsciously assumed, of the nature and relative position of the Beautiful; and at the close of it, I would call your attention to it again. My aim is not iconoclastic. My aim, in all that I have said, has been, not to destroy or in the least to disparage the department of Aesthetics, but to establish and recommend a high and strict and philosophic theory of it, for the purpose of putting it in its right place in the encyclopædia, and thus of promoting its own true growth, and what is of still more importance, the growth of the human mind. Called upon to address scholars, I desire to do something that will contribute to high-toned culture, high-toned thinking, and high-toned character. And I know of no better way, on such an occasion as the present, than to bring out distinctly before the youthful and recipient student, a philosophic, precise, and lofty, theory in regard to that whole department of Art, so fascinating to the young mind and so liable to be employed to excess by it. Depend upon it, Gentlemen, the older you grow and the riper scholars you become, the more exact will be your tastes and the more austere will be your literary sympathies. You will come to see more and more clearly, that neither music, nor painting, nor sculpture, nor architecture, nor poetry, can properly be made the main instrument of human development; that the human intellect and heart demand ultimately a "manlier diet;" that you must become powerful minds and powerful men, mainly through the culture that comes from Science and Religion. You will never, indeed, lose your relish for the Beautiful; on the contrary, you will have a keener and a nicer sense for it, and for all that is based upon it; but you will find a declining interest in its lower forms. — Schools of Poetry and of Art that once pleased you, will become insipid, and perhaps offensive, to your purer taste, your more purged eye, your more rational imagination. There will be fewer and fewer works in the aesthetic sphere that will throw a spell and work a charm, while the deep and central truths of Philosophy and Religion will draw, ever draw, your whole being to themselves, as the moon draws the sea.

And in this way, you will be fitted to do the proper work of educated men in the midst of society. I have alluded to the downward movement, the uniform decay, of the ancient civilizations. History teaches one plain and mournful lesson; that man cannot safely be left to his luxurious tendencies, be they of the sense or the soul. There must be austerity somewhere. There must be a strong head and a sound heart somewhere. And where ought we to look for these but in the educated class? In whom, if not in these, ought we to find that theory of education, that style of culture, and that tone of intellect, which will right up society when it is sinking down into luxury, or hold it where it is if it is already upright and austere? Educated men, amid the currents and in the general drift of society, ought to discharge the function of a warp and anchor. They, of all men, ought to be characterized by strength. And especially do our own age and country need this style of culture. Exposed as the national mind is to a luxurious civilization; as imminently exposed as Nineveh or Rome ever were; the Beautiful is by no means the main idea by which it should be educated and moulded. As in the Prometheus, none but the demi-gods Strength and Force can chain the Titan. Our task, gentlemen, as men of culture, and as men who are to determine the prevailing type of culture, is both in theory and practice to subject the Form to the Substance; to bring the Beautiful under the problem of the True and the Good. Our task, as descendants of an austere ancestry, as partakers in a severe nationality, is to retain the strict, heroic, intellectual, and religious spirit of the Puritan and the Pilgrim, in these forms of an advancing civilization. In order to this; in order that the sensuously and luxuriously Beautiful may not be too much for us; strength and reserve are needed in the cultivated classes. They must be reticent, and, like the sculptor, chisel and re-chisel, until they cut off and cut down to a simple statuesque beauty, in Art and in Literature, in Religion and in Life.

THE INFLUENCE AND METHOD OF ENGLISH STUDIES.*

THAT the philological structure and history of the English language is a branch of investigation very greatly neglected by all to whom this tongue is vernacular, will hardly be questioned. If one examines the public or private libraries of this country, he finds them better supplied with works in almost every other department of knowledge, than with those that relate to the origin and early progress of the literature of the Englishman and Anglo-American. How little is known of the lexicographical labors of Junius, Lye, and Spelman; of the critical researches of Hearne, Ritson, Pinkerton, Tyrwhitt, Wright, and Price; and even of the histories of Warton, and Ellis. The publications of the Camden and Percy societies rarely make their way over the Atlantic. The small but increasing stock of Anglo-Saxon literature, well edited by scholars like Conybeare, Thorpe, Bosworth, Kemble, and Cardale, and still more, the Anglo-Norman literature brought to light by Michel and other French scholars, is a terra incognita to many whose explorations in classical and oriental regions have been extensive and accurate. Notwithstanding the genial and thorough criticism of Coleridge, Hazlitt, and Schlegel, it can hardly be affirmed that

* Reprinted from the Bibliotheca Sacra, April, 1856.

the literature of the Elizabethan era has made that profound impression upon the thinking and composition of the present age which its intrinsic merits entitle it to. That hearty and idiomatic, yet flowing and graceful, style of English, which is one result of the study of this portion of the language and literature, is confined to a comparatively small circle of writers. The common English diction of the day, has been formed more by the age of Queen Anne, than by that of Shakspeare and Bacon. The orator, reviewer, and paragraphist, puts on the "learned sock," not of Jonson the dramatist, but of Johnson the moralist, and the pompous and measured diction of Gibbon is preferred to the more natural and flexible, but not less finished and musical phrase of Hooker.

The critical study of the English language and literature, as a special discipline in the general system of modern education, is consequently a topic that needs to be frequently and earnestly discussed, in order that a proper interest may exist in reference to it. The readers of this journal will bear testimony, that, from time to time, attention has been directed to this department of inquiry; and it is in the line of these preceding efforts that we would labor, and move forward.

The English language is the language into which we are born, and the English literature is the literature in which we are brought up. From the beginning of our existence, onward, through all the several ages of life, and through all the multiplied experiences of head and heart, we are continually receiving and propagating that fine and volatile influence which emanates from the national language and literature, upon every individual of the nation. A literature, therefore, in which we have an interest by virtue of our very birth and origin, and which penetrates so pervasively our daily life, has claims upon our best powers, in order that we may come to apprehend, with a distinct consciousness, its *peculiar* character and worth, and thereby experience more and more of its *specific* influences and impressions. For the objection that meets us, whenever we recommend the analytic study of a vernacular tongue, viz. that we are recommending a superfluity, inasmuch as the mother tongue is imbibed with the mother's milk, vanishes the moment we remember that the purpose of study, in nearly all instances, is to substitute a clear knowledge for an obscure one. There is meaning and truth in the Platonic dictum, that learning is reminding. One of the principal processes in mental cultivation consists in acquiring a distinct perception of that by which we are spontaneously, and therefore unreflectingly, influenced or actuated. What the common mind sees as in a glass darkly, the educated mind sees face to face. The most of men are the creatures of the moulding and shaping ideas that are mercifully inlaid in their mental constitution, and of those institutions and permanent circumstances amidst which they live; and, inasmuch as these ideas are ideas of reason, and these institutions and permanent circumstances are arrangements of divine providence, no practical injury results to the individual, even when he surrenders himself to their influence and actuation, without philosophic reflection upon their nature and qualities. The citizen, for example, will suffer no injury, who yields himself up most implicitly and obediently, to the moral or the civil law, without analyzing the contents of this idea, or becoming metaphysically aware of its vast implication. Let him allow the principle and spirit of law to take possession of his whole being, and suffer all his faculties and energies to be absorbed in this august and beneficent power, and he wil-

experience no detriment, intellectually or morally, even though he reflects but little upon the nature of the agencies by which he is moulded. In like manner, the individual may surrender himself to the influence of the literature and civilization of the nation to which he belongs, and, if these be truthful and sound, his comparative unacquaintance with what is constantly pressing upon him, and shaping and forming him, on all sides, will not prevent his being rightly shaped and formed. He is under and within a divine constitution, and, whether consciously or unconsciously, must feel its power, and receive its influence. But while this is said, it must not be inferred that *philosophic reflection* upon that which exerts an influence upon us, whether we will or not, is of no worth; that *analytical study* into the nature and qualities of that which actuates us, whether we think or not, is superfluous and unnecessary. Powerful as ideas, principles, and institutions are, even in relation to the unthinking man; and at times, for instance in political revolutions, they are as powerful as fire in gunpowder, and accompanied with nearly as little distinct knowledge; they yet receive a vast accession of power, when their operancy is accompanied with the clear intuitions of reason, and the lucid perceptions of self-consciousness.

These remarks upon the general relation of analytic study and philosophic reflection to that which is innate in our mental constitution, or intrinsic to those permanent circumstances which exert a constant and unperceived influence upon us, independent of our reflection, apply with full force to subjects so close to us, and influences so spontaneous and irresistible, as those of our own mother tongue and our own native literature. For although none can help speaking their vernacular, and feeling more or less of the influence of the literature embodied in it, yet only those few feel its selectest influence and drink in its most essential spirit, who pass beyond the every-day use of the language to the critical and philological study of it. It is indeed true, that, whether the Englishman or the Anglo-American has studied his national language and literature, or not, he has, nevertheless, been so moulded and affected by it, that, if those elements in his culture which have come in from this source, should be withdrawn, it would lose its most vital if not its finest constituent; still he cannot feel, and he has not felt, the freshest, heartiest, healthiest, and most effective influence from this source, unless, by study and reflection, he has made himself unusually conscious of the intense power of the English language, and the vast wealth of the English literature. But in order to this intimate acquaintance, something more is needed than that easy and passive perusal of the current literature of the present period, which, in the case of one's native language and literature, so often passes for study. The full power of the English language cannot be adequately apprehended short of an acquaintance with it in *all* the periods of its history. The life of a language, like the soul of a body, is all in every part; and its highest intensity must therefore be sought for by a laborious and patient study of the language, back, through all its change and growth, to the lowest root.

There is a special reason for this close and minute study of our vernacular, founded on the fact that, speaking it, and writing it, and thinking in it, as we do continually, we unavoidably acquire a moderate knowledge of it, which we are too willing to regard as philological and thorough. In the case of a foreign tongue, we are compelled to the lexicon and the grammar, because we cannot *understand* it without such study; and hence we inevitably acquire, in a greater or less degree, a critical knowledge of it. But it is not so in the case of our own language. The majority of words we have some acquaintance with, without any study on our part. It is true that this acquaintance is not close and accurate, like that which springs from etymological and careful analysis; but it is sufficient for all the purposes of practical life, and of an easy, passive perusal of books.

The only remedy for this superficial knowledge is to be found in the study of the language in all its periods, and especially in those elder forms which have passed out of use, and which, consequently, sustain something of the relation of a foreign tongue to the modern Englishman. Not that these earlier forms are really alien to us, like the French or the Latin tongues, for they still have an existence in the heart and pith of the English of the present day; but they require, in order to their being understood by the modern reader, a minute philological study, like that expended upon the Greek and Latin, which brings the mind into close and invigorating contact with them. For, to carefully trace a word, through its whole history, up to the root from which its true force and significance are, in the majority of instances, derived, is the only sure way of imbuing the mind with the spirit of a language. By this slow analysis, the power of the word is brought out and felt.

The same remarks hold true respecting the scope and riches of our national literature. He who is conversant with it in only one or two of its periods, can have but a meagre conception of its opulence. The national mind finds a full expression only in the totality of the national literature. Like the individual mind, it passes through great varieties of being; through a great multiplicity of moods; through various stages of development; and therefore its complete expression and manifestation must be sought for in the *whole* literature to which it has given origin. It often happens that the earlier literature of a people contains elements not to be met with in any of the after periods of its history. The national mind often shows a phase, in some one particular period, which centuries of existence would not bring round again. Should the English nation, for example, continue in existence, and the English mind continue to undergo change and development until the end of time, it is not probable that another period would occur in its history, in which the drama would reach such a height of life and power, and such a breadth and depth of passion, as characterize the Elizabethan drama. And can we ever expect the re-appearance of the fresh, hale, and lifesome spirit of " merrie England," as it appears in Chaucer? The beautiful vanishes and returns not again in the same form. Each age has its own excellences; and not until we have passed all the ages in review, can we know and feel the endless variety and opulence of a national mind.

With these general remarks upon the neglect, and the importance of the philological study of the English language and literature, we proceed to consider the quality of the influence which flows from this particular branch of discipline, and to indicate the best method of pursuing it.

I. The first effect of a thorough acquaintance with English literature, is the *vivification of the culture that flows into the modern mind from the classic world*, and the prevention, thereby, of a dry and artificial classicality. This undoubtedly was the purpose aimed at, by those who constructed the modern system of education. A department of instruction in the English language and literature is established in all those institutions which propose to impart a symmetrical and complete discipline, in order that the youthful student, while in the flexile process of education, may be in communication with the modern mind and the modern world, as well as with the ancient mind and the classic world. Those who planned that system of liberal instruction by which the modern scholar is trained up, selected the vernacular tongue of the pupil himself, as one of the concurrent branches of knowledge to be pursued in order to a harmonious mental development, because it furnishes an element needed in modern culture, and derivable from no other source. They "yoked," as has been said of the education of Leibnitz, "all the sciences abreast," that the mind might be subjected to the widest possible intellectual influence, and, by binding the ancient and the modern world together, threw in upon the modern scholar the combined influence of both.

The difference between the ancient and the modern mind is exhibited in the following extract from Coleridge, with remarkable comprehensiveness and conciseness. " The Greeks," he says, " idolized the finite, and therefore were the masters of all grace, elegance, proportion, fancy, dignity, majesty ; of whatever in short, is capable of being definitely conveyed by defined forms or thoughts ; the moderns revere the infinite, and affect the indefinite as a vehicle of the infinite ; hence their passions, their obscure hopes and fears, their wandering through the unknown, their grander moral feelings, their more august conception of man as man, their future rather than their past, in a word, their sublimity." * But this native difference has been still more increased by the influence which Christianity has exerted upon the modern world, and the new

---

* Works, Vol. IV., p. 29. Harper's Ed.

species of development that has been introduced thereby. Consequently it is only a particular and peculiar element of culture, and not the entire culture itself, which the modern is to derive from the cultivated pagan. It is the form only, and not the matter, of literature, that is to be furnished by the Greek and Roman. The Christian world cannot go back to the pagan for ideas and thoughts. The humblest modern mind that lives within the pale of revelation, moves in a sphere of thought and feeling infinitely transcending that of the loftiest heathen sage. It is not, therefore, for information and for living force, that the modern devotes himself, as he has ever since the revival of classical learning, to the study of the beautiful models of Greece and Rome. The function of classical discipline is æsthetic.

On the other hand, the modern mind is full of matter, and overfull of force. It is not naturally master of itself or its materials. Its vitality and energy require direction and a serene flow. The Goth needs to become an artist. Hence the coöperation of the Pagan with the Christian in the process of modern education; a coöperation that will be beneficial, only so long as the former is confined to its proper function of refinement, and justifiable, only in proportion as the latter does not permit its vigor and vitality to be killed out by the seductive grace of the former. *Upon the due proportion and the right mingling of the æsthetic element derived from classical literature, with the philosophical and theological elements derived from the world of modern Christian thought, depend the harmony and perfection of modern education.* For if the form and the grace become predominant to the neglect of the idea and the thought, the vitality and the force, culture becomes formal, artificial, and spiritless. It will not even make the impression of the model itself, to which it has been so servile. It will exhibit the symmetry, and finish, and elegance of the works of the Grecian and Roman mind, in the manner of a mere copyist, and with none of the genuine classic feeling and spirit. The peculiar vigor and energy which characterize modern literature, and which must characterize it, in order that it may produce a permanent impression upon the modern mind, will be wanting in the productions of such an unvivified classicality, and they will be out of place in the midst of all the motion and energy of the modern world.

For proof of this, we need only look at those periods in the history of literature, which were marked by an exclusive devotion to classical studies, to the neglect of modern thought. The eighteenth century was a period in English literary history characterized by excessive classicism. The elder literature of England was greatly neglected and undervalued, by the literary men of this period.* The English mind during this century having almost no communication with the modern European mind, contented itself with a by no means genial and reproductive, but servile and mechanical, study of Greek and Roman models. Much is said of the influence of French models, and canons of criticism, upon this period in English literary history; but what were the French models themselves, but cold copies of the classic age, with no modern

---

* The estimate in which Shakspeare was held by a mind like David Hume, is an example in point. The criticisms of Johnson, meritorious as his services in other respects were in regard to the earlier English literature, display little profound sympathy with the elder English spirit, as one feels on passing from them to the English and German criticism of the present century. The endeavor of Addison, in the Spectator, to awaken an interest in Milton and the Old Ballads, though more appreciative and genial than that of any other critic of the eighteenth century, was on the whole a failure, so far as the popular mind of that day is concerned.

new-born life in them; and what were the canons of criticism but the substantially correct rules of ancient art *mechanically* applied, and that too under totally different circumstances, and amidst entirely foreign relations? For as Schiller truly remarks: "The French, wholly misapprehending the *spirit* of the ancients, introduced upon the stage a unity of place and time, *according to the common empirical sense of the terms*, as if in the drama there could be any other place than mere ideal space, and any other time than the mere progress and sequence of the action." *

The truth is, the literary men of such periods started from the wrong point of departure. Instead of generating within themselves the stuff and material of literature, and employing classical culture as a formal or instrumental agency, in order to the symmetrical and finished presentment of it, they isolated themselves from the great process and movement of modern thought, violently threw themselves back into the ante-christian world, and sought the matter, where they should have sought only the form, of literature. The result ought not to surprise us. For a genuine literature, one that is destined to live in other ages, and to impress other nations can originate only in the midst of present actual realities; only in the stir and throng of daily interests and feelings; only in the most intense and concentrated nationality. The training, the elaboration, the stimulation, may be brought from foreign climes, and from all ages, but the central root must grow up out of native soil. All the modern endeavors to revive the Pagan culture have failed, because they were attempts to find the principle and substance of literature in a stage of human history that has

* Ueber den Gebrauch des Chörs in der Tragödie.

had its day, and which cannot, therefore, furnish anything beyond the artistic and the formal. A return to the culture and poetic polytheism of the classic world, such as Shelley strove for, and Schiller yearns after in his poem entitled, *Die Götter Griechenlands*, would be as impossible and irrational, as would be the attempt to reconstruct the fauna, or reanimate the flora, of the primitive geological periods.*

The proper method of counteracting the tendency to formalism, which seems to be as natural in literature as it is in morals, is, not to give up the study of the great ancient masters and models of form, but, along with this study, and coincident with it, to pursue with equal thoroughness and diligence, the study of modern literature. And inasmuch as, in most instances, a selection must be made from the several literatures that are comprised within this denomination, there are strong reasons for the selection of that of England.

In the first place, the English literature is the most universal and generic in its character of the literatures of modern Europe. It may be regarded as the one, among them all, in which the distinctive peculiarities of the modern mind have found the most full and forcible expression. For the English race itself is the most comprehensive of any. It is a mixture and cross of all the best of the modern stocks. At the bottom of it lies the Celtic, a portion of that great Scythian people which was the first to move westward from Central Asia, the cradle and birthplace of the human family. Judging from the

---

* The history of the efforts of the New Platonics to revive Paganism in its religious aspects is equally instructive with these attempts to revive it in its literary phase, and ought to be pondered by that circle of religionists, of the present day, who seem to be repeating that futile endeavor.

relics of it, still to be found among the mountains of Wales, the highlands of Scotland, the bleak and uncultivated district of Britanny in France, and in the eloquent and impetuous Irishman, it was a race eminently fitted to constitute the ground-work of a national character. Bold, fearless, and possessing an indomitable love of freedom, as the Commentaries of Cæsar evidence, the Briton still lives in the modern Englishman; and, by a singular yet natural coincidence, gives his name to England itself, whenever the elements of power and empire are sought to be made prominent. For they are "*Britons* who never will be slaves;" and it is *Britannia* who

> needs no bulwark,
> No tower along the steep,
> Whose march is o'er the mountain-wave,
> Whose home is on the deep.

Into this living and solid root was then grafted one of the very finest shoots of the great Germanic race—the Anglo-Saxon. The second wave of Asiatic emigration thus rolled over upon the first, and mingled with it. Widely-differing national characteristics, originating in the same centre of the world, but separated by centuries of rude and savage, yet real and thorough development during the various fortunes of emigration and warfare, of conflict with man and with material nature, were thus commingled in the Saxonized Briton. And, lastly, into the nation and character thus formed, an infusion of the Roman nature was introduced by the invasion and armed occupancy of the land by the Normans.

Constituted in this manner, the English mind became an exceedingly comprehensive one. Containing the qualities and characteristics of all the principal races that have made Europe their home, with the exception of the Sclavonic, a race which, perhaps, is to play an important part in the future history of the world, but which, as yet, has had no development, and, until recently, has been a mere cipher in European history—containing, we say, such widely-different and yet substantial characteristics, the English mind is the most adequate representative of the Universal-European or Modern Mind.

But, in the second place, besides this peculiar conformation of the English race and mind, there is still another feature in its history which contributes to render the study of it, and its productions, of more worth than that of any other of the literatures of modern Europe. We allude to the peculiar and powerful influence which the Christian religion has had upon its formation and development. We have already alluded to the fact that one great cause of the difference between Ancient and Modern culture, civilization, and literature, is to be traced to the influence of divine revelation. Christianity imparted a depth and spirituality to the thought and feeling of the modern world, which could not arise under the predominantly sensualizing tendency of paganism, and those literatures which imbibed its spirit most deeply and purely, other things being equal, are most worthy of attention. For they harmonize best with the tone and spirit of the modern world; they best prepare the scholar to enter vividly and with a vital consciousness into the career and movement of modern society; they afford more that awakens and strengthens and nurtures the individual mind; they are less liable to be exhausted of their contents and to be outgrown and left behind in the progressive development of human nature. But of all the literatures of modern Europe, the English felt the influence of Christianity in its purest form. The literatures of Southern Europe grew up under the influence of a nominal Christianity that had in it far more of the sensualism of paganism than the spirituality of the gospel. The effects of it are to be seen, this day, in the nerveless, emasculated national character, and the feeble, decaying, dying literature. The English mind and heart, on the contrary, have in the main, been exposed, age after age, to the spiritualizing influences and discipline of the Christian religion. Even those periods in English history when a false Christianity prevailed, only served to make the recoil more violent, and to subject the nation to a still purer and still more spiritual form of truth. The rich, healthy genius and strong sense of England have, for a longer and less interrupted period than has been the case with any other people, been slowly, and from the centre, unfolding themselves under the cultivating, elevating, humanizing influences of the Christian religion.

In the English literature, then, by virtue of the comprehensive representative character of the English mind, and the strength, depth, and purity of the influence exerted upon it by the Christian religion, is the modern student to find the most effectual preservative against that literary formalism which an unbalanced, and in reality ungenial study of classical literature is sure to produce. The modern scholar ought to be a man of power and of impression. He ought also to be a man of well-proportioned, symmetrical, elegant culture. But he is more likely to be the latter, if he is already the former, than he is to be the former, if he is, first, the latter. For, wherever there is matter and power to start with, there *may* be beauty, and grace, and elegance. The same degree of careful effort devoted to the artistic and formal finish of a work *after*, instead of before, the proper diligence and care have been devoted to its material origination within the mind, will elaborate it into a high beauty and an exquisite grace, that are absolutely beyond the power of one who has not thus begun at the beginning; who has not first gendered the work in his own soul.

In the thoughtful opulence and the throbbing life of the English literature, the modern student should, then, seek for mental wealth and power; for that vigorous and masculine principle that will vivify all his other culture from whatever source it come. In so doing, he is going to Ophir for gold, to the gorgeous East for barbaric pearl, to the very heart of nature for the forces of life. For let him bring before his mind, for a moment, the series of productions in the several departments of literature, which the English mind has been originating and throwing off with freedom, and force, and wonderful variety, during the last half millennium; let him remember the wisdom of Bacon, and Hooker, and Burke; the satire of Hall, of Butler, of Dryden, of Swift; the humor of Chaucer, of Goldsmith, of Sterne, of Lamb; the brilliancy and art of Pope; the magnificence and architecture of Milton; the sweetness, and fluency, and flushed beauty, of Spenser; the meditativeness of Wordsworth, and the intensity of Byron; let him think, lastly, of that wonderful being in whom all these qualities existed in their prime and purity, and found their full expression in the immense range and expanse of the Shaksperean drama, in the portraiture of the whole human being in its myriad minds and moods: let the modern student recall all this, and feel its full impression, and believe that, in pursuing the close and thorough study of English literature, he is pursuing the study of the richest and the most thoughtful, the most vigorous and the most vitalizing literature of the modern world.

II. The second principal effect of English studies is seen in the *excellence of the style of thought and expression that results from their prosecution.*

The mode of thinking induced into a mind by a course of education is a matter of the highest importance. If it cannot be said that it is of as great moment *how* the mind thinks, as *what* it thinks, it can be asserted with positiveness, that the *matter* of its thoughts is very closely connected with the *manner* of them, and, in this respect, the style of thinking becomes worthy of attention and cultivation.

By the *style of thinking*, is meant the particular and peculiar manner in which thought is produced in the mind when left to its spontaneous, unwatched workings. This peculiar manner undoubtedly has its lowest foundation in the peculiar structure of the individual mind; but it is also modified, and, to a certain extent determined, by the class of minds and kinds of thought, in other words, by the species of literature, with which it is familiar. Besides, so far as the style of thinking is founded upon, and determined by, the structure of the human mind itself, it is a correct one, and all deviations therefore, in the wrong direction, must be traced to external influences. For the mind itself is well made, and when its laws and constitution are perfectly obeyed, nothing, either in its mode of action, or in its products, requires emendation or correction.

When, however, a mind is exposed to the influence of other minds, whose way of thought is unnatural, affected, artificial, extravagant, or whatever the bad quality may be, it is very liable to be drawn into the same false manner. Especially is this true, in case there be in the individual mind a bent of the same general character. In this case, the student, while in the plastic process, and before he has reached "the years that bring the philosophic mind," is extremely liable to attach himself to some school in letters, in which the false mode of thought has embodied itself in all probability in dazzling glare, and with a species of imposing power difficult to be resisted. Falling in, as it does, with his own particular tendency, it is no wonder that his whole intellect is taken captive by it, and he acquires a fixed style of thinking, in which the most glaring faults of his model appear.

But the age, as well as the single individual, always has a style of thinking that is peculiar to itself, and this also exerts a controlling influence upon the individual. For that must be an extremely intense and determined individuality that can keep itself out of the great main current and tendency of the age in which it lives, and, in strong contrast, exhibit a style of thinking purely suigeneric. Such individualities, when genuinely original, become the creators of new schools in literature, and of new eras in art. The great mass of men, however, naturally share in the general intellectual characteristics of the age in which they live, and no one can rid himself of the faults of his age, unless he carefully study and imbibe some of the better characteristics of other periods. If he contents himself with the literature of the present, and suffers himself to be the mere creature and copy of its good and bad qualities alike, he will not attain the best development of his own mind, and will help to perpetuate what is defective in the existing type of thought and culture.

The influence of English studies, and especially of the study of the earlier English, in reference to the point under consideration, is most excellent. For, if we were called upon to mention the distinguishing characteristic of these elder writers, we should mention the sincerity and thoroughness of their mental processes. They never write for merely momentary effect, but absorb themselves, with great self-forgetfulness, in the subject of their reflections. They had, it is true, one advantage over writers of the present day: they composed before criticism (either as theory or practice) became a constituent part of the national literature, and hence wrote without restraint. But, aside from this, the elder English mind was a singularly thoughtful and even-tempered one. When stirred deeply, it proved itself to be a mind full of powers and energies, as the political history of England shows. But this force was under the control of strong English sense, and of that more profound faculty which is the parent of ideas and the discoverer of laws. This temperance of intellect, this moderation of soul, invariably accompanies depth and richness of thought, and manifests itself in a grave and commanding style of reflection and expression. Turn, for example, to the poetry of Spenser and Milton, to the philosophy of Bacon, to the history of Raleigh, and notice the entire absence of that quality so much strained after by the modern belle-lettrist, the striking and the startling. The charm lies not in individual passages—and hence no compositions suffer more when judged of by "elegant extracts" from them—but in the continuous and continual flow of the main current of thought, which pours onward in gentleness, in quietness, and in broad, deep strength. This same characteristic is seen in every department of literary composition. Even in autobiography, where the writer would be specially tempted to throw a brilliant hue over his own personal history, the same sedateness and balance of judgment is exhibited. The Memoirs of Lord Herbert of Cherbury, for example, contain the history of one of the most rare and accomplished gentlemen, as well as one of the most learned and thoughtful students, of the age in which he lived. They also contain an account of chivalrous adventures,

> of most disastrous chances,
> Of moving accidents, by flood and field;
> Of hair-breadth scapes i' the imminent deadly breach.

And yet the narrative is equable and tranquil, the language mild, melodious, and flowing; and the coloring over the whole, not glaring and showy, but sober, suffused, and rich. Indeed, what Heminge and Condell, the editors of the first edition of Shakspeare, say of this author, applies to the early English writers generally: "As he was a happy imitator of nature, so he was a most *gentle* expresser of it. His mind and hand went together; and what he thought, he uttered with that easiness, that we have scarce received from him a blot in his papers."

These characteristics in the mode of thought and expression arose from the singular sincerity and gravity of the English character and mind, in these earlier stages of its history. By sincerity we mean the pure outgoing or *issue* of the mind, unmodified by any outward references. As has been already remarked, the Englishman of this period had not the fear of the critic before his eyes. English literature, therefore, though it suffered undoubtedly for the want of a sound philosophic criticism, and was somewhat lacking in those excellent qualities, conciseness and perspicuity, which the sharp analysis of a later day has superinduced upon it, did, nevertheless, attain to a sweet fluency, and rich copiousness, and sober gravity, and wise thoughtfulness, that have never been surpassed. Again, the author of these periods did not write for all grades and capacities of intellect. He was not a society for the diffusion of useful knowledge among all classes of men, but he was a retiring, studious person, who thought as he listed, and wrote without much regard to an immediate sensation, for a "fit audience though few." Far be it from us to speak disparagingly of the useful knowledge diffused so widely at the present day, or of that body of sound and useful literature which has been called into existence by the wants of the people. In reference to all the solid characteristics and qualities of literature, it is more worthy of the name than much of the so-called polite literature and belles-lettres of the times. Like the elder literature of which we have been speaking, it is an honest and sound production. It came into being owing to a felt want, and it meets a felt want of an intelligent, sound-hearted body of men, and therefore it is to be respected by every one who respects the human mind. Still, the somewhat insulated position of the earlier English writers, by freeing them from all side influences and by aims, gave them an opportunity to free their mind as slowly, as lengthily, as copiously, as thoroughly as they pleased. They were at liberty, in the retirement of their closets, and addressing a limited public of similar cultivation with themselves, to pay no attention to time, place, or circumstances, in the development of a subject. That short method, rapid movement, and striking statement in which we of the present excel them, and which is a necessary quality in oratory, is not to be found in them. We must look to modern English literature for the best specimens of oratorical composition.

The whole influence of such a thoughtful and sincere literature upon the mind is educating in the highest degree. The reader is not violently excited by a rapid series of single striking thoughts and images, which, in the phrase of De Quincey, "can hardly have time to glance, like the lamps of a mail coach, before his hurried and bewildered understanding," but he is gradually penetrated and permeated by warm currents of rich and genial reflection. He acquires, insensibly, the same temperate and composed style of thinking; learns to *commune*, long and patiently, with the subjects that come before his mind; and, like these his teachers and models, finds all themes wonderfully fertile. For, along with this simplicity, there is a remarkable copiousness in the literature of which we are speaking. Instead of being made poor by this freedom and prodigality, these minds, like a living fountain, only became more ebullient the more they were drawn from. Call to mind, for example, the wonderful fertility of the English mind in the Elizabethan age. What an immense amount of rich and weighty thought, that was rich and weighty enough to come down to our day, and which will have a permanent interest for the human mind in all time, was originated during the fifty years between 1575 and 1625. During this short fifty years, English literature was enriched by the productions of Spenser, Sidney, Raleigh, Bacon, Hooker, Shakspeare, Jonson, Beaumont and Fletcher, Chapman, Marlowe, Webster, Middleton, and Ford. The catalogue reminds one of the dazzling treasure vault of Marlowe's rich Jew of Malta:

>Infinite riches in a little room,
>Bags of fiery opals, sapphires, amethysts,
>Jacinths, hard topaz, grass-green emeralds,
>Beauteous rubies, sparkling diamonds,
>And seld-seen costly stones of so great price,
>As one of them, indifferently rated,
>And of a caract of this quality,
>May serve, in peril of calamity,
>To ransome great kings from captivity.

This fertility of the English mind was, at once, the cause and effect of the prevailing style of thinking at that period. The striking, startling, brilliant mode, which has reached its acme in the modern novel, not drawing upon the meditativeness and *reserve* of the intellectual character, is utterly incompatible with such a *union of quantity with high quality*, as appears in this Elizabethan literature. On the contrary, that calm and composed method which characterized these men, and which is worth toiling after, is most conformed to the nature of the human mind, to that "large discourse of reason which looks before and after," and consequently may be presumed to be, more than any other one, the mode in and through which the contents of the mind may be discharged in richest abundance and with least self-exhaustion.

In this connection, it is worthy of notice that the principle here advanced holds good in other departments besides that of letters. The highest and most productive genius in Fine Art is also the calmest and gravest. Raphael died at the early age of thirty-seven, yet he filled all Europe with master-pieces before he died. And into each one of these works he threw, with all the prodigality of nature herself, a world of life, motion, and expression. Many of his pieces are groups, and groups within groups; and yet each individual in them is itself a study. His creative talent finds no parallel but in Shakespeare himself; and there is certainly no distant similarity between that universality and wealth of artistic power which projected itself in the paintings of Raphael and that which embonied itself in the vastness of the Shaksperean drama. But Raphael's genius was mild and serene. His temperament bordered upon the feminine; and his activity as an artist was deliberate, equable, and sustained. Indeed, the history of literature, generally, shows that ages of great productive power have not been marked by violent and spasmodic action. The intellects of that wonderful age, the age of Pericles, were grave and tranquil in their nature and actings. So equable and calm was their intellectual manner, that the Greek prose of this period, especially that of Plato, is rhythmic and sweetly musical, and their thought is so utterly destitute of everything startling or glaring, that the modern student, brought up, as he has been, amid the animation, and brilliancy, and sensation of the present age, must school himself, and acquire a classic taste, a taste for *Platonic* beauty, before he can feel its hidden charm.

But while this feature in the elder English mind and literature is brought out, it is necessary to guard against the notion that this calmness was accompanied with dulness, that the body of thought thus originated is destitute of vitality and energy. The life and the power run very deep, and they are felt with tremendous force, by that mind, and only that mind, which by a genial and somewhat reproductive study, has adopted the same style of thinking. For when the student has once sunk down into the element, and the depth, where these minds think, and can repeat their processes, he knows of a vitality and an energy not to be found nearer the surface. The literature of which we are speaking, is in no sense languid or lifeless. The minds that produced it were deeply earnest, inspired with a serious purpose, and at no rare intervals glowing with enthusiasm. Nay, they seem to have found their most congenial sphere in the drama; the department of all most aloof from coldness, tameness, and lifelessness. The subject-matter in which they seem to have taken the liveliest pleasure was human passion; and that this most vivid part of human nature found a powerful painter in them, the Elizabethan drama is a proof. For if we look through universal literature, we cannot find anything more passionate than this drama. Saying nothing of its immense range and expanse, it being nothing less than the whole human consciousness, an infinite canvas which would seem to require an infinite rather than a finite power to fill up; saying nothing of its vast extent, nowhere do we find such an intensity of life, breath, and motion; and this too at every point, and in every part and particle. Take the play of Hamlet, for example. We do not find the violent, volcanic energy of a modern melodrama, or of a modern French novel; but he must be stone-dead in the depths of his being who does not find beating throughout this *organism* the deep life of nature and reality, and beating with a stronger pulse the more he knows of it. Take again, a play like the " White Devil," of Webster, and see with what terrible strength the fundamental passions of human nature are shown working. Notice the rousing effect of the play upon the mind. This production of this same reserved and thoughtful period is intensely passionate. It has a most profound affinity with the human imagination, and raises storms of feeling and passion in the mind of the reader.

The truth is, the literature of this period is alive *all through*, and hence the depth and calmness of its life. The more that is known of it, the more will it be felt to be a powerfully educating instrument. No literature imparts a more distinctive and highly determined character to the culture of one who studies it; and this not for one stage of the intellectual life, but for all stages. It is characteristic of a less reserved and more striking mode of thinking, that it seizes with violence upon the mind at a particular period, and takes possession of it altogether during this period. It exerts a greater influence than it has a right to, because no one style is absolute and perfect enough to justify this monopolizing of all the powers and capacities of the human soul, to the exclusion of all other forms of literature, or modes of thought. Even in the case of the higher and more perfect species of literature of which we are speaking, the influence exerted is not to the exclusion or at the expense of that of other excellent species, such as the classic, for example, but in coincidence and harmony with it. It is therefore an unfavorable sign in relation to the character of a mode of thought, or a school in letters, if the mind, during one particular period in its history, and especially if it is an unripe one, become so absorbed in it as to be dead to all other forms. A reaction must come eventually, and the favorite author will become as intensely repulsive, as he was once intensely attractive.

But the influence of the literature under consideration is eminently catholic and liberalizing. The mental tendency produced by the study of it does not in the least unfit the student for a genial appreciation of other forms. Nay, we affirm that it is one of the very best preservatives against narrowness in criticism, and bigotry in literary feeling. The calm, self-possessed, thoughtful spirit, which reigns in English literature, taken as a whole, tends to extirpate all exclusive sympathies, and to render the intellectual affinities more comprehensive and far-reaching. Whenever we meet a mind, one of the deep bases of whose culture has been laid in a thorough apprehension and genial admiration of English thought in its best forms, we meet one of enlarged and catholic views of literature generally. Such an one is far better qualified to sit in judgment upon a false and exaggerated mode of thinking, than he who is wholly involved in it can be. The admiration which he feels towards a dazzling school or author is far more correct, because it is far more moderate and intelligent, than that of a servile disciple. He is not blind to its faults, and therefore best knows the actual worth of its excellences.

And more than all, and better than all, the style of

thinking produced by the study of the literature in question is essentially permanent in its character. By this is not meant, that it is a stiff and rigidly fixed style, incompatible with mental freedom; a style that is a mechanical, rather than a vital process, and keeps the thinker constantly running in his old ruts. The style is permanent, in the sense of being broad enough, and calm enough, to make room for all the modifications that may be introduced into it by the growing culture of the student, *without changing or deranging the ground-work*. The mind has not been committed, so to speak, to intensity of any sort, to any violent manner, but is impartial, grave, and judicial in its tone and temper. Hence it is not compelled, in order to change at all in its style of thought or expression, to change altogether and take on some entirely new form of intensity or mental violence, thus going through a round of particular and transient manners, or rather *mannerisms*, but never acquiring any one permanent and standard style. For it is noticeable, that a constant hankering after the most intense and striking form is destructive of all true form. An intellectual restlessness is produced in this way, that keeps the mind in a ceaseless chase after the novel and the startling, in neither of which can it ever find permanent satisfaction and rest.

The truth of these remarks may be seen by a reference to the style of the modern journalism. The journal must be striking and brilliant, or it is nothing. That repose and reserve of manner which appears in the treatise, in the methodical organized product that makes a positive addition to the sum of human knowledge, is death to the journal. Hence the journalist must be ever on the alert for forms of expression, and turns of periods, and peculiarities of manner, that will make a sensation in distinction from an impression. He is compelled to lead an intense,

excited, unnatural intellectual existence, and to find ever
new, and ever changing forms for it. But how little of
standard style, of finished, noble form, is there in the current journal literature! There is not mental repose long
enough to allow the mind to settle into one permanent
manner. The production of fixed form, the crystalliza
tion, is prevented by the perpetual jar and agitation.

Such then, we conceive, is the influence of English
studies upon the style of thinking. They induce a calm,
grave, sincere, profound, exhaustive, and commanding
manner of mind. And inasmuch as it is the great end of
education to enable the mind to think its very best thought,
and to express it in its very best manner, the great worth
of this literature for educational purposes becomes apparent. It is a powerful organ and instrument of culture.
It is to be recommended to the modern student, as an
extremely influential means of bringing out into full action
his best capacity. If there be any literature that can stir,
and stimulate, and elicit, while at the same time it nurtures and enriches, it is the English. And it *is*, whatever
may be our theory on the matter, the literature to which
we betake ourselves when we wish to feed our mind with
sweet and wholesome food; when we wish to have its best
powers roused; when we wish to think for our own satisfaction, or to give out thought for others. If we are
scholarly now, we keep Milton, and Shakspeare, and
Chaucer, and Bacon, and Hooker, by us; and if we shall
continue to be scholars, these minds will continue to mould
and educate our minds. For this literature is home-bred,
and, apart from its intrinsic excellence, speaks in our own
tongue, and addresses our own nationality, and our own
individuality. To feel its influence, we need only to keep
a healthy English spirit, and a sound English heart
within us; we have but to open our mouths, and draw

in the fresh bracing element and atmosphere we were born for.

III. In our discussion thus far, we have devoted almost exclusive attention to the elder English writers; and it might, perhaps, be inferred that we would discard the productions of the later authors, and do them injustice. This would be a mistaken inference: for, although we believe that if a line were drawn between the literature preceding, and that succeeding, Milton, the weightier and more precious portion would lie on the further side of it, we would not say one word that could possibly lead to the neglect of any portion of a literature that we desire to have studied as a sum-total. From his contemporaneous position, and immediate relation to it, however, the modern will not be likely to undervalue modern English authorship; while, on the other hand, there is much need of effort and urgency to prevent him from remaining as ignorant of Chaucer, and even of Spenser, as if, instead of being the "wells of English undefiled," they belonged to a foreign literature. The purpose, therefore, of the remainder of this discussion will be, to give some practical directions respecting the best method of pursuing English Studies philologically and critically.

One principal reason why the language and literature of England, which really forms the connecting link between the student and the great modern world into which he is soon to enter and become a constituent part, has exerted so little comparative influence in the system of public instruction, and in connection with classical, mathematical, and philosophical discipline, lies in the fact that it has not been made the subject of *etymological* study and *philological* analysis. No language, no literature, as we remarked in the outset, can exert a thoroughly educating power, unless the mind works its way into it by the study of its individual words and radicals; unless its force and life are felt through the slow process of decomposing and recombining its rudimental elements. The first practical recommendation therefore is this: Select an old English author from a period so remote that his language and style shall be so strange and unknown, as to require close glossarial and grammatical study in order to a bare understanding of him. The common error is, to select a writer, Milton or Shakspeare, for example, so near to our own time as to require but little study of this sort in order to reach his general meaning. But, in reality, such authors as these should be *studied* only after a preparatory discipline of the sort we are recommending. The wonders of their English style can be appreciated only by one who has analyzed the language in its roots, and has acquired a knowledge of its history; only by one who has traced words up to their origin, and down again, through all their changes and uses; only by one who has investigated the various styles of thinking to be found in the literature as a whole, and knows, in some good degree, all the various types and manners the national mind has taken on. For these great masters are highly national in their literary character, and their productions contain the concentrated essence of the general English mind and heart, and the general English culture. In order to their profound apprehension, a very extensive knowledge of English literature is required; and the truly philosophic study of them cannot be commenced, even, without much previous preparation. The student must, then, select Chaucer to start with. He must go back of the prolific and somewhat familiar sixteenth century, across the almost totally sterile and barren fifteenth century, and plant himself in the very heart of the fourteenth. In this way, he will have put a gulf between his present knowledge of English and that knowledge which he proposes to acquire, over which he cannot pass without some more earnest and thorough study than is implied in an easy and passive perusal of a form of English like that of Shakspeare or Spenser. He will be made aware that the Englishman of 1350 used a form of English that is, to a great extent, unintelligible to the Englishman of 1850; and yet a form which thorough philological study will show is not so wholly different from that employed by himself, as he might imagine in his present ignorance of it. Increasing acquaintance with it will evince that, after all, it is genuine, hearty, idiomatic English, and has a most close and vital affinity with the best portion of his own vocabulary, and with the raciest, heartiest trains of thought in his own mind.

An additional reason for selecting Chaucer is found in the fact that in his works the English language first appears in a tolerably fixed form. Previous to Chaucer, it had been passing through those intermediate stages which marked the transition from the pure Saxon to the English proper. Hence, the literature of the nation may be said to have sprung into existence with him. For, Layamon's translation of Wace, the metrical Chronicles of Robert of Gloucester and Robert Mannying, and the Vision of Piers Plowman—the principal productions that mark the progress of the language and literature of England during the two centuries between 1150 and 1350—all bear evident marks of immaturity and instability. While the range of thought is trivial and mean,* the form of the language and the character of the style indicate that the national mind, during this period, was uncultivated and unformed. It was feeling the effects of the Norman conquest. For, although the Norman was more cultivated than the Saxon

* *This* remark is not true of the Vision of Piers Plowman, which is a vigorous and lively picture of life and manners.

whom he conquered, still the Saxon *serf* could derive to himself but little of the culture of his Norman lord. The relation existing between the two parties precluded any civilizing and cultivating influence of one upon the other. Only in proportion as the Saxon recovered his rights and political freedom, did he profit by the culture which his conquerors possessed. During the two centuries of which we are speaking, the English nation was slowly recovering its freedom, and the English mind was slowly emerging from the ignorance and barbarism of a servile condition. The literary productions of this period, although they must receive, sooner or later, the careful study of every one who wishes to obtain a complete knowledge of the English language and literature, are crude in their matter, inelegant and even barbarous in their form. There is the same objection, therefore, to commencing with them that there is to commencing with the Saxon, in order to a complete knowledge of English. They are too naked and bald for the mere beginner. They are not thoughtful and attractive enough to waken the interest of the student, in the first period of his English studies. They need to be examined in the light thrown back upon them from a succeeding age, and under the interest excited by their seen relation to forms of English that have already been studied and mastered. For it is plain that the natural method for the Englishman to pursue, in the study of his mother tongue, is retrogressive. He should work his way back, from the present form of the language, step by step, until he reaches its heart and root. Instead, therefore, of leaping from the last and newest form to the first and oldest; from the present English to the Saxon of Beowulf or Caedmon; he should study, one by one, the intermediate forms, until, by a natural and imperceptible progress, he arrives at the beginning. All that is needed is, that he study the subject by distinctly-marked periods; that he investigate authors who are sufficiently far apart to enable him to see and realize that the language has undergone a great change.

As one of the first steps, then, in English study, let Chaucer be taken up as an author to be studied critically and for years to come. This is a better method than merely to peruse a history of the language and literature, like those of Warton and Ellis, and there stop. It is true, that such histories afford a selection of extracts from the principal writers of each period, from which some general notions and views may be formed; but they are the last works to be put into the hands of a beginner. He who has already mastered the few leading authors of the different periods may make use of them, as an aid in epitomizing and generalizing his knowledge. For, by this independent and accurate study of individual authors, he has obtained a clew that will lead him through the maze and perplexity of a historical series, and leave him in possession of distinct and well-methodized information. But without this clew and previous preparation, the vast amount of material contained in such a history as that of Warton will only confuse and overwhelm the mind, leaving it full of obscurity and vagueness. In selecting a particular author, and devoting the whole attention to him for the time being, the student has only a single end in view. He is busied with one individual mind, and in endeavoring to penetrate into its nature and spirit his own mind moves in one straight line, and all his acquisitions are simple and homogeneous in their character. And if the author whom he selects be worthy of such an undivided attention; especially if he be one in whom the general culture and spirit of his age found expression; the knowledge acquired is not only thorough, but extensive. For such minds are very broad as well as deep, and there need be no fear of becoming narrowed by such exclusive study of one writer. That close and undivided attention which the Greeks, in all ages of their history, devoted to their Homer, contributed, as much as any one thing, to the liberal and expanded feeling so characteristic of Greek literature. The Greek, unlike the Englishman, did not allow the dialect or the poetry of the father of his national literature to become strange or obsolete. His works were familiar alike to the educated Greek of the Attic and Alexandrine periods. In the words of Heeren: "The dialect of Homer remained the principal one for epic poetry, and had an important influence on Grecian literature. Amidst all the changes and improvements in the language, it prevented the ancient from becoming antiquated, and secured it a place among the later modes of expression."* And had the Englishman been as careful to prevent the language and works of the English Homer from becoming obsolete and unknown, the English language and literature would have been different from what it now is, by a very important modification. If that stream of sweet, fresh, and limpid thought had been kept running, for four centuries past, into the great main volume of English thought, there would be more of nature and less of art in it. If that simple, expressive, nervous, and (notwithstanding all that has been said to the contrary by critics who had not *imbued* themselves with Chaucer) that melodious diction had come along down as a familiar form of the language, the English of the present day would be a higher type of the language than it is.

Another reason for selecting Chaucer, and making him the subject of exclusive and close study for a long

---

* Ancient Greece. Chapter VI. Bancroft's Translation.

time, is found in the fact, that in this way alone can he be understood and appreciated. To read a few extracts from his works in a compendium, in connection with a few extracts from all the other leading writers of England, is not the way to a worthy and fruitful knowledge of him. Indeed, the first effect of Chaucer upon the modern is to repel; and it is only the first effect that is experienced upon the perusal of extracts. The immediate impression of an old writer upon an uncultivated mind, generally, is that of disappointment. The unschooled reader finds nothing but strangeness of diction, excessive simplicity of sentiment bordering upon triviality, pathos that is bathos, and a verse from which no ingenuity can extract either melody or harmony. All this is true, in its full extent, of Chaucer. Even such clear heads and sensible minds as Dean Swift and Alexander Pope saw no poetry or charm in him; if their burlesques and travesties of him afford, as they unquestionably do, any index of their real opinion. But it is the effect of the critical and prolonged study of Chaucer, to so imbue the mind with his matter and manner, that his truthfulness, and charm, and power, as a poet, are felt vividly and fully. Perhaps the point upon which the sceptic would hold out longest in relation to him would be his verse; it being an unquestioned assertion, in some very respectable schools of criticism, that it is destitute of both melody and harmony. But we do not hesitate to affirm, that when the student has by long continued intercourse become *familiar* with him; when his antique strangeness has worn off, and the ear has become accustomed to certain variations from the modern custom in pronunciation; when, in short, he has so cultivated himself, that Chaucer is to him what he was to the ear and the poetic feeling of his own age, we affirm that more melodious and harmonious verse is not to be found in the literature. It can be read longer, and not weary the ear, than the verse of Scott or Moore can be; because the melody is ever subordinate to the harmony; because the sentiment is natural, and the measure undulates with the sentiment. But such a genial and truthful apprecia tion of Chaucer is not the work of a day. The scholar must gradually grow into it, and grow up to it. Time alone imparts the sense and vernacular feeling of his excellence.

When this author has been completely mastered, the student is prepared for those still earlier and ruder forms of English, of which we have spoken. Once at home in the English of Chaucer, the passage to that of the metrical chronicles and scripture paraphrases is easy and natural; and when these have been studied, the few remains of Saxon that are left furnish the matter for the final study in this direction.*

The second practical recommendation respecting the best manner of pursuing the study of the English language and literature is this : Select from leading periods in the history of the literature those productions in which the power of the great minds found its fullest expression,

---

* An English Chrestomathy is a desideratum. Beginning with selections from Gower's Confessio Amantis (1415), followed by most of the Canterbury Tales (1390), then with extracts from Langland's Piers Plowman (1360), from Lawrence Minot (1340), from the hybrid form of the language in Robert de Brunne's Chronicle (1339), and Robert of Gloucester's (1280), from Layamon's translation of Wace (1165), and ending with specimens of the Saxon in all its periods ; such a reading book, provided with a full glossary, and a brief Anglo-Saxon Grammar, would do great service towards imparting an etymological and critical knowledge of English. For the study of Saxon alone, the life of Alfred, by Pauli, in Bohn's Antiquarian Library, which is supplemented by a very correct edition of the text of Alfred's Orosius, together with a glossary and a concise Anglo-Saxon Grammar, furnishes a very convenient apparatus.

and regard them as models to be studied. As examples, may be cited such productions as Bacon's Advancement of Learning, the first book of Hooker's Ecclesiastical Polity, Milton's Speech for the Liberty of Unlicensed Printing, Locke's Conduct of the Understanding, Burke's Reflections on the French Revolution.

Productions like these are eminently English. They are highly characterized by the solid sense, the strong understanding, and the thoughtful spirit of England. These qualities, it is true, are characteristic of all genuine products of the English mind, but they are found in their greatest energy, only in the productions of leading minds. With these, therefore, the student should imbue himself. He may peruse the second-rate writers without being greatly affected by these characteristics, but he cannot meditate upon such treatises as the above mentioned, without becoming more thoroughly English in the process. The importance of a national spirit in culture cannot be overestimated, and to this point we would direct attention for a moment. The individual mind is not individual merely; it is also national in its structure. It partakes of the peculiarities of the particular race of mankind to which it belongs. As the state is in the individual, as really as the individual is in the state, so the nation is in the individual, as really as the individual is in the nation. By virtue of a political nature and element in his constitution, the individual contains the groundwork and inward reality of the commonwealth of which he is outwardly a member; and by virtue of a national and idiomatic element in his mind, the individual contains the groundwork and inward reality of the nation of which he is outwardly a member. In neither case could any conceivable heightening of the *merely and strictly individual*, possibly produce the *national*. No degree, however intense, of private

4

and individual feeling could possibly produce patriotism. Private interest and private feeling spring out of the individual in the man, and public interest and public feeling spring out of the state in the man. Both natures coexist in one subject, in harmony when human nature is in a normal condition, and in antagonism when it is not; but each has its distinct characteristics, and forms the basis of a distinct activity.

These remarks hold true in relation to literature, as well as politics. In respect, therefore, to culture and to authorship, the national is, or should be, in the individual. While the individual opens his mind and heart to all that is true and genial in the productions of foreign minds, he should retain his own nationality in its most independent and determined form. The Englishman should think like an Englishman, and compose like an Englishman.

Now the thoughtful, and ever repeated, perusal of such products of the great English minds as have been specified above, contributes to strengthen and develop that which is national and idiomatic in the individual intellect. And in the present influx of foreign literature, of foreign modes of thought and expression, the conservative influence of these great English masters and models should be felt more than ever. It is only by a more profound acquaintance with these, that the good elements in other literatures and other national minds can be assimilated, and the bad rejected. An ardent attention to French literature, for example, would induce an excessive materialism, and an ardent attention to German literature a hyper-spiritualism, in the English mind and literature, if each were not counteracted by the sober sense and calm reason of our own thinkers.

The influence of German literature upon the student, in this connection, merits a moment's consideration. At this late day, no respectable scholar will deny that this literature ranks among the very first, as a source of knowledge and an instrument of culture. Probably none exerts a more profound influence upon the stuff and substance of literature, upon thought itself, than this. Eminently speculative and thoughtful, it seizes with a strong grasp upon the laws of thought, and habits of thought, and style of thought, and exerts a wonderfully modifying, moulding, and internally revolutionizing power. But it cannot safely be made the principal instrument of education. It must be kept in check and subordination by others. Its strong spiritualizing tendency must be counteracted by opposite tendencies; and this in order that this very spiritualizing tendency itself may do its best work. For this bias, if left to run on indefinitely, results, as the history of some of the most interesting schools of philosophy and literature shows, in the sheerest and merest materialism. Any tendency if excessive, annihilates itself by turning into its own contrary. And the Englishman, especially, is liable to this result. If his large roundabout sense and sober reason are once overmastered by the tendency and influence in question, he becomes the most ultra of spiritualists. The wines and luxury of the south of Europe entering into the strong and coarse nature of the northern tribes generated an intoxication and a debauch, at which the Southron himself stood aghast. When Caliban feels the fumes, the drunkenness is absolute.

In furnishing a proper counteraction to this tendency, and to all other foreign tendencies, and thus preserving the true nationality of the scholar, the works in question are invaluable and indispensable. They are by no means destitute of speculation, but they are remarkable for their sobriety and sense. Even when they verge strongly in the direction of materialism, they are valuable aids; especially in the reference now under consideration. Take, for example, the treatise of Locke on the Conduct of the Understanding, the best tract yet written upon education. It is less a model product of the English mind than some others in the list, because it sprang from a root that had too strong a tang of earth; because it grew out of an extravagantly sensuous system of philosophy, and a culture corresponding thereto. But it furnishes a most excellent and efficacious corrective to a wan and bloodless hyperspirituality. If the Englishman or Anglo-American has weakened himself by too much dreaming over such interesting, but, after all, somewhat effeminate products, as those of the German Novalis, or the French Chateaubriand and Lamartine, or the English Tennyson, let him transfuse into his veins the blood of John Locke. If he has become thin and pale in the process, let him feed upon the pulp and brawn of as masculine a mind as ever lived.

The preservation of nationality, in all respects and relations, is of the highest importance in this age of the world, when the ease, and frequency, and intimacy of intercommunication are erasing some lines that ought to be scored still more deeply rather than obliterated. The extinction of nationality, like the extinction of individuality, would be the death of all the great interests of the human race. The confusion of tongues, and the origination of many languages, though primarily a curse, yet like the curse of labor, brings many blessings in its train. The formation of nations and of languages has unquestionably contributed to a more profound and exhaustive development of the *fallen* human soul, than could have been attained without it. And the further progress of the race in art, in science, in literature, in philosophy, and in religion, is dependent upon the preservation, and the quickening collision, of this variety in unity. The moment a mind loses its nationality, it loses its charm and power for other minds; even for that other mind in which it has servilely sunk its own nationality.

By this thoughtful and prolonged perusal of the products of the master-minds of the literature, the student will preserve and strengthen what is national and idiomatic in his mental structure, while at the same time he will more genially appreciate, and heartily relish, what is national and idiomatic in other literatures. And, what is not less important, he will be storing his intellect with the best sense and reason of the nation to which he belongs; he will be planting the seeds and germs of all noble and ennobling truths, thereby preparing himself to be an original and influential thinker and author in his own day and generation. For the words of Chaucer are as true now as ever:

>   Out of the olde fieldes, as men saithe,
>   Cometh all this newe corn fro yere to yere;
>   And out of olde bookes, in good faithe,
>   Cometh all this newe science, that men lero.

THE ETHICAL THEORY OF RHETORIC AND ELOQUENCE.*

THE proper product of Rhetoric is Eloquence, and the purpose of a rhetorical education is to produce an eloquent thinker, and an eloquent writer or speaker. So far as it comes short of this, therefore, Rhetoric comes short of its true end.

Hence it becomes important to inquire, first of all, into the essential nature of Eloquence itself; and, particularly, to define it in such a manner as to detect all false products, and preclude all specious methods and models. For nothing exerts a more injurious influence upon the taste, the studies, and the mental habits of an educated man than a false idea of Eloquence. All educated men desire to be eloquent, and at times make greater or less effort to be so. An eloquent man is, universally, an object of admiration and of imitation. The idea of Eloquence is, consequently, one that exerts a highly formative and modifying influence upon both individual and national culture. When an educated man has been seized by this idea, when he has become possessed with the desire and the aim to influence public opinion by free and fluent speech, how wonderfully are all his thoughts, and feelings, and acquire-

* Published in 1859, as an introduction to the writer's translation of Theremin's Die Beredsamkeit eine Tugend.

ments pressed into the service of it. If he has the true idea, he almost invariably becomes eloquent; if he has the false idea, he invariably becomes over-ornamented, and glittering, and degenerates into inflation, and bombast, — so energetic and influential is the idea itself, whether truly or falsely apprehended. It enters the mind with an interest and influence peculiar to itself, and works there with all the potency of a plastic principle. The thought of becoming a philosopher, or a poet, or an artist, or a man of science, when once formed, indeed exerts a controlling influence upon the whole intellectual life; but the thought of becoming an eloquent man, a man who " wields at will the fierce democracie and shakes the arsenal," exerts an overmastering influence, so that the mind either becomes the most passionate of the passionate, or else the feeblest of the feeble, according to the truth or falsity of its idea of Eloquence, and its ideal of an Orator.

I. In proceeding to discuss *the true nature and essential properties of Eloquence*, it is deserving of notice, that nearly as many definitions have been given of Eloquence, as of Poetry, and so far as a perfectly exhaustive definition is concerned, with about the same success. Perhaps no one definition that shall include all the essential qualities of what are strictly *vital* products of the human mind can be given. We must be content to reach the inward nature of Poetry, and of Eloquence, by approximations; by several definitions, each of which contemplates some particular aspect of the subject, and specifies some peculiar characteristic omitted by the others. The more mechanical and common products of the human understanding may often be clearly comprehended in a single conception, and fully defined in one statement; but its rarer, richer, and more living productions, such as

OF RHETORIC AND ELOQUENCE. 81

Poetry, and Eloquence, being more mysterious in their origin, are more difficult of comprehension, and consequently of definition. We may lay it down as a general rule that in proportion as a product takes its origin in the more salient, impulsive, and original agencies of the mind; in proportion as it is less the work of mere experience, and trial, like a product of useful art, or of mere memory and classification, like a manual of science; in proportion as its nature is living, and its origin is fresh, will it be more difficult to bring it within the limits of a concise and full definition. Like the definition of life itself, the definition of Poetry, and Eloquence, must be an approximation only.

Socrates, according to Cicero,* was wont to say that all men speak eloquently when they have a thorough knowledge of their subject. The duty and office of Rhetoric, and hence of Eloquence, according to Bacon,† is to apply reason to imagination for the better moving of the will. Style, says Buffon—by which he means an eloquent style—is the man himself: a definition corresponding with the remark of Pascal, that a simple and natural style, the eloquence of nature, enchants us for the reason that while we are looking for an author we find a man. Eloquence, says D'Alembert, ‡ is the ability to cause a sentiment with which the mind is deeply penetrated to pass with rapidity into the souls of others, and imprint itself there with force and energy. Eloquence, says Campbell, § adopting the definition of Quintilian, is that art or talent by which the discourse is adapted to its end, and the end of discourse is to move the will.

* De Oratore, I. 14.
† Advancement of Learning, Book II.
‡ Reflections sur l'élocution oratoire.
§ Philosophy of Rhetoric, Book I. Chap. 1.

If we examine these definitions we shall find that they all presuppose a common nature and properties in Eloquence, and are all of them approximate definitions of it. Neither of them is sufficient of itself to exhaust the subject; perhaps all of them together are insufficient; but they all look one way, and give the mind of the inquirer one general direction. They all teach or imply, that *truth* is the substance, and principle, of all genuine Eloquence, —*truth clearly perceived, deeply felt, and strongly expressed*. Men are eloquent in proportion as they thoroughly know their subject, says Socrates. Eloquence is truth all aglow and practically effective in a human soul; it is reason in the forms of the imagination in order to influence the will; says Bacon. It is the coöperation of the understanding with the imagination and the passions, in order to carry the will, say Quintilian and Campbell. Eloquence is truth felt and transferred to others; it is the transfer of the orator's consciousness into the auditor's consciousness; says D'Alembert.

All these definitions teach that actual verity is the substance of Eloquence, and that through the transformation which it undergoes by passing through an earnest and eloquent mind its final effect is to carry the whole man, head, heart and will, along with it. This *capture* of men's minds, this mental *movement* in speaker and hearers, this *streaming* of thought and feeling to an outward end, seems to be inseparably connected, in all these definitions, with Eloquence as different from other forms of discourse. While in the essay, the historical narrative, or the philosophical disquisition, the thought more or less moves in a circle, returning back upon itself, and thus forming a wider expanse, in the oration, the thought is ever rushing onward in a deep narrow channel, like a river to the main. We are speaking, of course, of an ideal or perfect oration;

and bearing this in mind, we may say that in proportion as the mind of the orator is improgressive in its action, it ceases to be eloquent in its action and influence. A mind that is continually eddying; that is inclined to *dwell* long, either upon a particular thought, or upon the expression of it, either upon a bright idea, or a beautiful figure; must break up this habit, and overcome this disposition, before it can create that strong rushing current, that overwhelming, overbearing torrent in a discourse, which under the name of δεινότης the Greeks regarded as the height of Eloquence. By this term, which was applied particularly to the eloquence of Demosthenes, the Greeks intended to denote that overpowering *vehemence*, in the exercise of the mental powers, which results from a clear consciousness of the truth and the right, united with a glowing fiery interest for it. This vehemence of soul, this onward sweeping rush in a channel which the mind has worn into a subject, and which it is continually wearing deeper, is preclusive of all retrograde movements, and of all stationary attitudes. Even if the subject calls in a great amount of argumentative or explanatory matter, this *current* draws it all into its own volume, so that it accelerates rather than impedes its mighty flow. "In his oration for the crown," remarks one,* "Demosthenes must have had as cumbrous a satchel as any bearer of the green bag in our courts of law. He brings forward a great mass of testimonies, written and oral laws of Athens, decrees of foreign towns and of the Amphictyonic council, and records of history, all exhibited and discussed with the utmost force and clearness. But through the whole process, there is an under-current and moving power of passion and eloquence that carries us forward to a final and unavoidable result.

* Marsh's Remains: Tract on Eloquence.

It is as though we were embarked upon a mighty river. All is animation and energy around, and we gaze with a momentary reverie upon the deep and transparent waters beneath. But even while we admire, the current grows deeper and deeper, and we are unconsciously hurried onward with increasing and irresistible power."

An eloquent mind, then, is a mind under motion. It is a mind moving forward, under the influence of clear knowledge and deep feeling, with constantly accelerated motion, and constantly increasing momentum, to a final end, which is always a practical one. Eloquence itself, then, is thought with an impulse in it, thought with a drift and rush in it. Eloquence is, as we instinctively denominate it, a *flood*.*

Without dwelling longer upon these definitions, and others that have been given of Eloquence, we proceed

---

* "Hazlitt," says De Quincey, "was not eloquent, because he was *discontinuous*. No man can be eloquent whose thoughts are abrupt, insulated, and (to borrow an impressive word from Coleridge) non-sequacious. Eloquence resides not in separate or fractional ideas, but in the relation of manifold ideas, and in the mode of their evolution from each other. It is not enough that the ideas should be many, and their relations coherent; the main condition lies in the *key* of the evolution, in the *law* of the succession. The elements are nothing without the atmosphere that moulds and the dynamic forces that combine. Now, Hazlitt's brilliancy is seen chiefly in separate splinterings of phrase or image which throw upon the eye a vitreous scintillation for a moment, but spread no deep suffusions of color, and distribute no masses of mighty shadow. A flash, a solitary flash, and all is gone." This remark of De Quincey applies with force to an American writer whose rhetorical care and effort are unquestionably great, but misapplied. Emerson, much more than Hazlitt, is discontinuous and fractional. His literary work is a mosaic, and not a growth. It illustrates the remark of Buffon, that " it is from the fear of losing isolated fugitive thoughts, and from the desire of introducing, everywhere, striking traits, that there are so many compositions formed of inlaid work, and so few that are founded at a single cast. Nothing is more opposed to warmth of style."

now to a consideration of that particular one, upon which Theremin founds his rhetorical system. Eloquence, says Theremin, is a *virtue*. This definition differs from the others that have been quoted, more in appearance than in reality. It does not, as its author remarks, differ essentially from the definition given by the elder Cato, and handed down to us with approbation by Quintilian; and it coincides with the general doctrine taught by the more profound writers upon Eloquence, in all ages,—all of whom have recognized the moral element as the essential one in this species of intellectual products. Stated, however, in this brief and epigrammatic form, Eloquence seems to become identical with morality, and the author in one place actually speaks of Rhetoric as a part of Morals.* By this, however, it is conceived, he did not mean to imply that Eloquence is merely and only a moral virtue, and is sufficiently defined when it is put into the list of virtues, along with temperance, or honesty, or veracity. Perhaps the real meaning of the author would be more precisely expressed, by saying that Eloquence is an *intellectual* virtue. It has a common origin with the moral virtues, in the resolute action of the moral force or character of the man, and, so far as the point of *ultimate origin* is concerned, may therefore be denominated virtuous, or of the nature of virtue. The theory of Theremin is, that all true Eloquence springs from integrity and strength of character; that the principle and the power by which the several faculties of the mind concerned in the production of Eloquence are actuated and guided is the voluntary principle and power, and hence that the product, in its *ultimate* and *essential* nature, must be moral Let us explain in detail, that the theory may be under

* Book I., Chap. xiv.

stood. In the production of an eloquent oration, the understanding, and the imagination are employed. By the first mentioned faculty, truth simple and abstract is presented to the understanding of the hearer. By the second, this same truth is taken out of this abstract and intellectual form, and put into an imaginative form for the imagination of the hearer. Now, it is plain that the excellence of the oration depends upon the presence in it, of some power or principle that shall swallow up into the unity of its own life all these separate processes of the understanding and imagination, and thereby become that vehement and terrible energy which, we have seen, according to the Greek definition, is the reality and vitality of Eloquence. The unity of the oration, moreover, depends upon the proportionate and harmonious exercise of these diverse faculties. Any excess in the functions of the understanding, e. g., will be to the injury of those of the imagination. The oration, in this case, must either lose its unity, or else give up its oratorical character and pretensions, and be converted into a philosophic essay. And any excess in the action of the imagination will unduly repress that of the understanding, and convert the oration into a poem.

Now, that power by which each of these faculties is to be concentrated and governed, so that there shall be an even force and a just proportion in their co-working, is the *will* of the orator. He is to repress an undue tendency to ratiocination, by moral determination. He is to repress an undue poetic tendency, by moral determination. And let it not be thought that only a slight and feeble exercise of the self-controlling power is needed in the origination of this so-styled virtue of Eloquence; that but little moral energy and stern force of character is required in order to the highest eloquence. How often does it happen that the oration degenerates (for in this reference it is degeneration) into the abstract essay, or the over-ornamented prose-poem, solely because there was not enough of moral strength, not enough of will, in the orator, to compel all his acquisitions, and all his tendencies, into subservience of that practical end, the actuation of his hearers, which is the ultimate end of Eloquence. Oftentimes, as much self-control is needed to mortify a strong logical propensity, in order that it may not damage or destroy a rhetorical process, as is needed in order to mortify a lust of the flesh. And still more often, as much force of character is needed to restrain a luxuriant imagination, in order that it may not clog and stop the onward movement of the oration by excessive illustration and ornament, as is needed in order to restrain an animal passion. In short, that vanity, that self-feeling, which would draw off the orator from the *practical end* of his discourse to the undue display of his logic, if his mind is predominantly philosophic, or to an undue employment of the poetic element, if his nature is predominantly imaginative, requires for its conquest and extirpation, precisely the same *kind* of moral force, force of will, that is needed in the suppression of vice, or in the formation of any of the strictly so-called virtues.

Now, it is in this reference that Eloquence is styled a virtue. So far as the principle from which it proceeds, and the impulse by which it is impelled, are concerned, Eloquence is ethical, rather than philosophic, or æsthetic. It is the position of Theremin, that Eloquence is more strictly of the nature of virtue, than of the nature of science, or of the nature of art. Its essential quality and properties, he contends, are more properly ethical, than scientific, or artistic. Neither a scientific nor an artistic talent can become the living fountain of Eloquence,

Only a moral force can. Although both a philosophic and an artistic process properly and necessarily enter into that complex mental action of which Eloquence is the product, yet neither of them is the *fundamental* process. We must look for this in the moral process which springs out of the character of the orator; which involves his earnestness, his sincerity, his honesty of conviction, his consciousness of the truth, and his love for it. These moral elements must first exist, or there can be no Eloquence. In the same sense, then, that the orator, according to Cato and Quintilian, is a *good* man, is Eloquence a virtue. Not that every good man is eloquent, or that every virtue is *ipso facto* Eloquence (though we often say of the virtues, as they shine out in human character, that they are eloquent); but no man is eloquent who is destitute of moral force of character, and no discourse is eloquent that is not prevaded with a moral earnestness that is higher than any mere scientific talent or æsthetic feeling.

The truth which there is in Theremin's definition may be seen, again, by considering the difference between an Oration and a product of Fine Art. According to the theory of Theremin, Eloquence is not strictly a fine art. It is no more one of the fine arts because it contains an æsthetic element, than it is one of the sciences because it contains a philosophic element. It is taken out of the department of mere and pure art, by the *practical and outward end* which it has in view. For if there is anything settled in the theory of art, it is, that an æsthetic product has no practical end out of itself. Art, as such, has no utility, or morality. Its productions exist for themselves, and not for any object other than themselves. We must not go beyond them, and look for a practical or beneficial influence exerted by them upon the minds of men, in order to decide whether they are excellent in their kind or not. Hence art cannot become religion, or even morality. If a painting or a statue is beautiful, we cannot deny its *artistic* excellence. Whether it is useful, or whether it is moral, are questions for philosophy and religion, but not for art. The artist, unlike the philanthropist, or the orator, works for his own gratification solely. His work has no end but the embodiment of a beautiful idea. As an artist *merely*, he is indifferent to the practical effects that may result. The work of art is addressed solely to the æsthetic sense. If it were addressed to the cognitive powers, solely, it would be a scientific work. If it were addressed to the moral or religious nature, solely, it would be a religious work.

It is true, indeed, that a work of art may make a moral impression, and as matter of fact the highest works in this department invariably do. It is true that the Apollo may elevate the soul of the beholder, and the Madonna may soften and humanize it, but neither of them, *as works of art*, owed their origin to any such practical and moral aim. Fine art is its own end. It is self-sufficing, self-included, and irreferent. If it has ever contributed to the intellectual or moral improvement of man, this was a happy accident, and not a predetermined and foreseen result.

But that morality which thus stands in no inward and necessary connection with art constitutes the very essential principle of Eloquence. The oration, unlike a painting or a statue, aims to exert a moral influence upon a moral agent. It seeks to work a change, more or less deep and extensive, in the state of man's active powers, employing his cognitive and imaginative faculties as mere means and media. The orator cannot, like the artist, isolate himself from all outward circumstances, and find the goal of his efforts in the serene and complacent embodiment of his idea in a form of beauty, without troubling himself in the least about the influence he may exert. The orator is a man of moral influence, and of moral impression, upon moral agents, or he is nothing. If, then, the term virtue denotes, generally, a product of the *will*, and not of the intellect merely, or the imagination merely, is not Eloquence a virtue? If that agency of the soul be virtuous, or of the nature of virtue, which has an outward aim; the aim, viz., to exert a legitimate influence upon the character and actions of men; is not Eloquence a virtue? Is not this earnest, moral, and practical product of the human mind much more properly denominated a virtue than an art?

To place the definition given by Theremin in another aspect, we may say that Eloquence is a virtue of the intellect as *modified* by the will. When the understanding merely follows its own structure and laws; when its action is *constitutional* merely, and unmodified by any reference to an auditor, or to an outward impression upon other minds; the product is logic, and this action of the understanding is scientific. When the imagination merely follows its own nature and law, the product is poetry, or some other work of fine art, and this action of the imagination is æsthetic. In both of these instances, the intellectual faculty is left to the guidance and impulse of its own mechanism. The will exercises no modifying influence in either case, and consequently there is no moral element, nothing virtuous or of the nature of virtue, in these species of intellectual activity. It is true that the subject matter of both philosophy and art may be moral, but the mental process itself cannot be so characterized. It is a purely constitutional process, not deriving its quality in the least from the voluntary power, from the

OF RHETORIC AND ELOQUENCE.

character of the individual, or even being in the least modified by it. The process in the one case is purely logical or scientific, and in the other purely artistic.

But Eloquence has a different origin from either science or art. It results, not from the isolated action of a particular faculty, like the understanding, or the imagination, but from the interpenetration and coöperation of these intellectual powers, under the sway and actuation of the voluntary force. The *degree* in which each faculty shall work, as we have already remarked, is fixed by the self-determination of the orator, and the acme of Eloquence is seen in the rush, in one resistless volume, of all the cognitive and imaginative powers in the unity of the moral will. The combined action of these powers, in this instance, unlike their isolated action in the production of the philosophic essay, or the poem, is moral, and therefore of the nature of virtue. The will interpenetrates the logical and imaginative processes in the mind of the orator, and thus renders them ethical. Eloquence, in this aspect, is seen to be the virtuous action of the human *intellect*, as distinguished from that virtuous action of the isolated human will, to which the term "virtue" is more strictly and commonly applied. There is voluntary action in both cases, and hence the epithet "virtuous" belongs to both; but in the case of a virtue, commonly so called, the action is confined to the will itself, while in the case of Eloquence it is action of the will *in* and *by* the powers of understanding and imagination. The virtue of patience, e. g., is the product of the isolated action of the will, just as logic is the product of the isolated action of the understanding. Patience is the product of the will operating upon *itself*, subduing its own restiveness, and therefore is simply a particular habit of the will. But the virtue of Eloquence is the product of the will as it operates upon, and in, other mental faculties, for the purpose of exerting an influence upon the will of others. Eloquence is reason and imagination wrought into a living synthesis by the vitality of a will, by the force of a strong, deep, and earnest *character.*

There is less difficulty, therefore, in understanding this definition of Theremin, and in adopting it, if we do not take the term " virtue " in its more limited and common signification, but in its widest sense, as denoting a product into which the moral strength of the individual, his force of character, enters as the fundamental quality. And such we suppose to be the essential nature of Eloquence. If we are required to locate it, we think there are fewer objections to placing it within the province of practical ethics, than in that of abstract science, or in that of æsthetic art. As Theremin affirms, that theory will be most successful, will explain most phenomena and exert the most beneficial influence upon the student, which assumes that the practical and moral element in Eloquence is the fundamental and dominating one, and that the philosophic and æsthetic elements are subsidiary to this. We know that the ancients, from whom it is not generally safe to differ upon subjects like the one which we are considering, regarded Eloquence as one of the fine arts, and assigned it a place in the list along with poetry, and painting, and sculpture; and the modern world has generally acquiesced in their classification. And yet the rhetorical treatises of Aristotle, of Longinus, of Cicero, and of Quintilian, contain much that is irreconcilable with this theory. Unconsciously, the doctrine that Eloquence is at bottom neither speculatively philosophic, nor imaginatively æsthetic, but practically moral, creeps into these treatises, and exerts a modifying influence throughout. And it is the merit of Theremin, as it seems to us, that he has *systematized* this ethical view of Eloquence; that he has organized these materials scattered here and there through all the best treatises on the subject, and wrought them into the unity of a consistent theory. Instead of defining Eloquence to be a fine art, and then, under the instinct and impulse of good sense and sound feeling beating off and away from the definition, until it is perfectly apparent that there has been a mistake in the outset, and that Eloquence has received a wrong *location*, this author affirms distinctly that it is not a fine art, but that it is (for want of a better term) a virtue. Starting with this position as the basis of his theory, he is not troubled, as were the ancient rhetoricians, by a conflict between his theory and its detailed unfolding and application. He is not *compelled* to those statements respecting the necessity of character, of integrity and sincerity and earnestness, in the orator, the necessity of subjecting everything in the oration to a practical outward end, and of subordinating philosophy and art themselves to the moral purposes of Eloquence, which are irreconcilable with the definition that makes Eloquence a fine art. On the contrary, these statements which suggest themselves so unconsciously, and spontaneously, as actually to override the false theory that has been assumed by the rhetorician, are merely *corroborations* of the ethical theory of Eloquence. As they grow out of it, so they return back into it; like vigorous shoots which by inarching are made to contribute to the vigor and strength of the parent stock.

The truthfulness of the ethical theory of Eloquence is still farther evinced, and illustrated, by a consideration of its influence upon the Orator. Here its excellence and value appear in plain view. Here is the place of its triumph. For even if an opponent should be able to make a stand, while discussing the nature of the theory itself, and to raise objections that are forcible, and difficult to remove, yet when its practical application and practical influence come into consideration, the defender of the theory may speak with boldness and confidence. He really has the entire history of the department in his favor. All those forcible and impressive statements, in ancient and modern treatises upon rhetoric, which lay emphasis upon the moral element in Eloquence, and in the orator himself,—statements that fall glowing from the mind of the theorist, when, having for a moment left his speculative theory behind him, he speaks more from the common feeling, and the common sentiment, of mankind at large upon this subject,—all such statements, we say, come thronging in upon the mind, when it is considering the practical influence of the theory in question. The advocate of the ethical theory feels that all these statements legitimately belong to *him*, and to him alone ; that they are but the practical and informal enunciation of his own speculative and formal theory. When he hears Quintilian define the orator to be " an *upright* man who understands speaking," he thinks he hears a concrete annunciation of the abstract position that "Eloquence is a virtue," and believes that, in the establishment of his theory, he has only applied an affirmation to oratory itself, which long ago was applied to the orator. Supported thus, as he is, by the spontaneous and unbiassed opinions of theorizers themselves, he is the more confident in his belief that the actual application of the ethical theory of Eloquence will only serve to verify it, and its practical influence to recommend it, in the very highest degree.

1. The influence of the ethical theory of Eloquence is most excellent, in the first place, upon *the studies of the Orator*.

It is the natural tendency of that theory of Eloquence

which defines it to be a fine art strictly, to isolate oratory from the real sciences, and the solid acquirements of the orator. The eye is too intently fixed upon form, and the secondary properties of discourse, because it is assumed that the *ultimate* end of Eloquence, like that of any other fine art, is Beauty. The studies of the orator, consequently, will take their main direction from this theory, and he will bestow undue attention upon those departments of human knowledge, and those species of literature, which have more affinity with the idea of the Beautiful, than with the ideas of the True and the Good. These higher ideas will be made to take a secondary place in his mind, and his culture will be characterized more and more by superficiality, and lack of vigorous strength. He will become more and more interested in works of art, and the lighter forms of literature, and less and less interested in science, philosophy, and theology.

But the natural tendency of that theory of Eloquence which regards it as essentially moral rather than æsthetic; which sets up for it an outward and practical end, and does not for an instant allow it an *artistic* indifference in respect to an outward and practical impression; which connects Eloquence far more with the ideas of the True and the Good than with the idea of the Beautiful,—the natural tendency, and strong direct influence, of *such* a theory of Eloquence is to promote the graver and higher studies in the orator. The more profound and central powers of the mind will be continually exercised, and thus the foundation for a powerful and impressive mental activity will be laid. Such an orator, like Pericles of old, will study and meditate upon the dark problems of philosophy and religion, and while, like the patron of Phidias and the decorator of Athens, he will not by any means be indifferent to beauty and to art in their proper place, he will yet derive that commanding and overwhelming eloquence, that Olympian power attributed to the great Grecian, from these loftier themes, these more profound departments of human inquiry and effort.*

2. Again, the influence of that theory of Eloquence which regards it as ethical, rather than either scientific or æsthetic, is most excellent, in respect to *the models of the Orator.*

The general influence of the ethical theory of Eloquence upon the *taste* is to render it strict and pure. The orator whose mind has been moulded by it, naturally selects models from the very highest range of oratory, and thereby feels the very choicest influence of the department. His models, consequently, are few in number, but they are such as can never be outgrown and left behind in his onward progress. A single model like Demosthenes contains, for the mind that is prepared for it by a strict and high theory of Eloquence, more educational power than myriads of inferior models. Such a model is a standard and permanent one. But in order that the first-class models may be apprehended and appreciated, a severe taste must have been engendered in the student. He must have been so disciplined by a high theory that he has acquired an indifference towards second-rate productions, and a positive disrelish for those more glaring and showy qualities which are found in works that are for a day only, and not for all

---

* *Soc.* I should say that Pericles was the most accomplished of rhetoricians. *Phædr.* What of that? *Soc.* All the higher arts require much discussion and lofty contemplation of nature; this is the source of sublimity and perfect comprehensive power. And this, as I think, was the quality which, in addition to his natural gifts, Pericles acquired from his happening to know Anaxagoras. He was imbued with the higher philosophy, and attained the knowledge of mind and matter, which was the favorite theme of Anaxagoras, and from hence he drew what was applicable to the orator's art.—Plato's Phædrus, 269–70.

time. He must have attained such an intellectual temper, such a style and tone of literary culture, as can find pleasure only in those calmer, grander, and loftier efforts which do not so much strike and startle by their brilliancy, as develop and stir the human soul by their depth, fervor, and power.

Now, the theory in question tends directly to the production of such an intellectual taste in the orator. It is a high and austere theory. It is a theory which checks extravagance, and prunes luxuriance, by subjecting the whole oratorical process to the restraints of ethics. It subordinates the beauty of poetry, and even the truth of philosophy, to the practical ends of morality. If there is any danger in the theory, it is in the direction of severity and intense truthfulness. If there is any error in the theory, it is upon the safe side. It cannot be denied that the entire influence of it is to induce such mental habits, such mental tastes, and such a mental tone, as both prepare the student for a genial appreciation of the highest models, and a free and original reproduction of them. The mind that has been developed and trained by the ethical theory of Eloquence will prefer Demosthenes to Æschines, Cicero to Hortensius, Massillon to Bossuet, Mirabeau to Lamartine, Burke and Fox to Sheridan and Phillips.

But the excellence of the influence exerted by the theory in question, in rendering the taste pure and strict, is seen more particularly in reference to current productions, and current styles and schools. The principal danger to which the rhetorician or the orator is exposed arises from the influence of contemporaneous rhetoric and contemporaneous eloquence. Dazzling and brilliant but superficial and transitory products always have their day; and during their day, minds that have not been highly trained are taken captive by them. Such minds become copyists and mannerists ; and copyists and mannerists never are, and never can be, eloquent. But a pure taste, and a genuine relish for the excellences of those great masters and models which, like the sun, are always the same in all time, is an infallible preservative against this pernicious influence of contemporaries. There is a strength and reserve in that intellectual character which has been formed by high theories, by the contemplation of grand ideals, which no storm of popular applause, no fury of fashion, can overcome or exhaust. Such a mind is self-possessed, and self-reliant. Such a mind is eagle-eyed, and critical. Such a mind calmly stands the glare of false rhetoric and false eloquence, while the weak, unarmed eye of the half-educated is dazzled and blinks. This austere judgment, this clear, calm criticism, looks by and beyond all the showy and gaudy products that are temporarily bewitching the popular taste, to those serene, grand, and absolutely beautiful forms, the *Dii majorum gentium*, in all the great literatures of the past and the present, and in them alone finds its models, and upon them alone expends its enthusiasm.

II. Having thus discussed the nature of Eloquence, we proceed to consider *the general nature of Rhetoric*, and, *its position and influence in the system of liberal education*.

In passing to the consideration of that branch of discipline whose object it is to produce and promote eloquence, we are struck in the outset with the fact that it has ever been regarded an essential part of a symmetrical system of education. If we look into the ancient world, all culture seems to have culminated in rhetoric and oratory. The whole end and aim of study, even in other and higher departments appears to have been to make the educated man a rhetorician,—using the term in its best and technical signification. The goal had in the eye, during the whole of his education, by the young Athenian, or the young Roman, was the bema or the rostrum. It was thought that unless culture enabled the mind to give expression to itself, to reveal and embody its knowledge in a form that would impress and influence other minds, it was worthless. Hence even philosophy was made subservient to oratory, as in the example of Pericles, who studied under Anaxagoras, one of the most subtle of the Greek philosophers, in order to prepare himself for the practical life of a statesman and orator. The walks of the Academy and Lyceum led directly to the Agora and the Forum.

In Grecian and Roman education, consequently, Rhetoric occupied a high position. It was not only a distinct department, but one of great influence. Genuine rhetorical power, the ability to express and impress, was regarded as the last and highest accomplishment of the educated citizen. And the same holds true, to a considerable extent, of the system of education in vogue in the modern world. If Rhetoric, within the last hundred years, has somewhat sunk down from its former "pride of place," it is mainly because of the false view that has been taken of its essential nature, and the false method in which it has been taught. During the two centuries that succeeded the revival of learning, however, its claims were never higher, or more willingly allowed. The minuteness of detail, and, we may add, the comprehensiveness on the whole of outline, exhibited by the rhetorical treatises composed two hundred years ago, are ample evidence that then, at least, there was no disposition to undervalue this branch of discipline. Indeed the over-estimate which came to be put upon it, together with the dry and mechanical method into which the somewhat formal, and yet substantially sound rhetoric of Aristotle had degenerated, contributed to that reaction which followed, and which for the last hundred years has led to an under-estimate of the whole department. Yet Rhetoric is still honored in that system of instruction by which the modern mind is being educated. Rhetoric is still one branch of human learning, one department of instruction; and whenever it is pursued in the spirit, and by the method, which its own real nature and distinguishing characteristics prescribe, it is still found to minister to the sound and vigorous development of the mind.

In discriminating the distinctive nature of Rhetoric, and in assigning it its position in the curriculum of discipline, it is necessary in the first place to direct attention to that generic classification of the sciences which so greatly assists the investigator in locating any particular one of them.

Human knowledge may be divided into two grand divisions which very exactly and conveniently distinguish the immense variety that enters into this great sum-total. Knowledge is either material or formal. A *material* department of knowledge is one in which the matter is primary, and the form is secondary. A *formal* department is one in which the form is primary, and the matter secondary. The material sciences have also been termed *real* sciences, to denote that in them the reality or substance of human knowledge is to be found. For the formal sciences are not independent, and self-sufficient. They have no positive character, no substantial contents of their own, such as the material or real sciences have. They derive all the interest and worth they possess from their connection with these latter. They exist only for these latter; because the form exists only for the substance, the manner for the matter.*

Take those portions of the general department of philosophy which go under the names of physics and ethics, as examples of branches of *material* or *real* knowledge, and consider what they contain. Here we have no hollow and empty divisions which must be filled up from other divisions in order that they may have solidity; no mere *form* of knowledge, to be filled up with knowledge itself. Natural and moral philosophy have each substantial contents of their own. The nature and operations of the human mind, and of the divine mind so far as it is cognizable by man, and the laws and principles of the material world,—these and such like are the subject matter of these two subdivisions of real science. In whatever direction the moral or natural philosopher advances, he meets with real entities and essences; he is occupied with substantial verities. Truth itself, fact itself, and thought itself, is the staple and substance of his investigations. The *form* is for him an altogether secondary thing; the *matter* is everything. He does not ask, "*how* is it?" but "*what* is it?"

But take again the department of logic, and we have a branch of *formal* knowledge. The logician establishes no one particular truth, but merely shows how any truth may

* "All rational knowledge is either *material*, and contemplates some one object, or *formal*, and is occupied merely with the forms of the understanding, and of the reason itself,—with the universal laws of thinking, generally, without regard to the objects of thought. Formal philosophy is denominated *logic;* but material philosophy, which has to do with determinate objects, and the laws and principles to which they are subjected, is twofold. For these laws are either laws of *nature* or of *spirit*. The science of the first is denominated *physics*, that of the latter is *ethics;* the former is also termed the doctrine of nature, the latter the doctrine of morals."—Kant's Practical Reason (Vorrede).

be established. He does not exhibit the actual contents of the human mind, its ideas, sentiments, and beliefs, but only those laws of mental activity in accordance with which these contents are *formed*. It is not the province of logic to exhibit thought itself, but only the process of thinking. Logic generates no fountain of living waters; it merely indicates the channel in which they must flow, if they flow at all. In investigating such departments as physics and psychology, we are occupied with the *real*,—with facts and truths that are matters of actual consciousness, or actual intuition; with the contents of our own minds. But in studying such a subject as logic, we are occupied with the *formal*—with the mere abstract notions and forms of the understanding; with the ways in which, rather than the things which, it perceives.

To see the distinction in question still more clearly, compare an entire department like fine art with an entire department like science or religion. The end and aim of art is to embody some idea in a form suited to express it. With the nature and origin of this idea it does not concern itself. It takes it as it finds it, and leaves the analysis and investigation of its interior structure to the philosopher or the theologian. The artist may, it is true, contemplate this subject matter of his art philosophically, or theologically, but only in subordination to the purposes of his profession; only in order to be able to clothe the idea in a more beautiful form. He does not, like the votary of the *real* sciences, rest in the subject matter, being satisfied with having unfolded and developed the truth in his own mind; he cannot rest until he has given expression to it in an outward embodiment. Hence we say that fine art is *formal* in its nature and character. It subordinates everything to this its ultimate and constituent end. For it, the material is secondary.

OF RHETORIC AND ELOQUENCE. 103

In reference then to this general division of the various departments of human knowledge and inquiry, Rhetoric is a formal department. It is the science of form, so far as human discourse is concerned. It is an "organic" art, as Milton * terms it; an art which furnishes the organ or instrument for communicating thought most effectively to other minds. Rhetoric, strictly speaking, is not to supply the matter, the thought itself, but is to put the material when supplied into as appropriate and fine forms as possible. The thought itself of the rhetorician must be drawn from deeper fountains than those of Rhetoric. If by thorough collegiate and professional training, he has not first filled his mind with the materials for discourse, rhetorical training and preparation will only disclose his emptiness. From the *material* departments of human knowledge, from the *real* sciences, he must have first acquired a profound and comprehensive culture, before he is qualified to become a rhetorician.†

Rhetorical discipline being thus formal in its nature presupposes on the part of the student a preparation for it. It postulates a full mind and a full heart. It takes

* Tract on Education.

† Lord Bacon remarks that it was an error in the educational course of his time, "that scholars in universities come *too soon* and *too unripe* to logic and rhetoric, arts fitter for graduates than children and novices: for these two, rightly taken, are the gravest of sciences, being the art of arts; the one for judgment, the other for ornament: and they be the rules and directions how to set forth and dispose matter; and, therefore, for minds *empty and unfraught with matter*, and which have not gathered that which Cicero calleth 'sylva' and 'supellex,' stuff and variety, to begin with those arts (as if one should learn to weigh, or to measure, or to paint the wind,) doth work but this effect, that the wisdom of those arts, which is great and universal, is almost made contemptible, and is degenerated into childish sophistry and ridiculous affectation."—Advancement of Learning, Book I.

the individual at that point in his course of education when the materials have been originated by other methods of discipline, when they are in a stir and fermentation, struggling for utterance and demanding an outflow, and teaches him *delivery*,—teaches him the method of embodying these conscious and living contents of his mind, in rounded and symmetrical forms. If, therefore, Plato had reason for writing over the door of his Academy, "let no one who is not a geometrician enter here," the rhetorician has equal reason for inscribing upon the rostrum, "let no one ascend here, who is not a scholar and a thinker."

It is of great importance here to observe the fact, that although Rhetoric is a formal department of knowledge, it must not be isolated from the real sciences, either in theory or practice. This has been the error in this department for the last century. That part of Rhetoric which is termed Invention,—that part which treats of the supply of thought,—has been greatly neglected in modern treatises, so that the whole art has been converted into a collection of rules relating to style, or Elocution,* merely. Owing partly to the intrinsic nature of Rhetoric as an art, and partly to the excessively popular character which science and scientific statements have assumed in the present age, Rhetoric has become superficial in its character and influence, so that the term "rhetorical" is the synonyme of shallow and showy. Dissevered from logic, or the necessary laws of thought, it has become dissevered from the seat of life, and has degenerated into a mere set of maxims respecting the structure of sentences, and the garnish of expression.† The rhetorician has been too

---

* The term is employed in the sense of Quintilian and Cicero.

† This is illustrated in the almost total neglect of the study of *topics* or *common places*. How very much was made of these, in the

much occupied with the externals of his subject. No grand and vital eloquence can originate on a theory which in this manner separates the form from the matter, the style from the thought. As in the natural world there is no growth and no fruit, except as the living principle and the outward form constitute a unity and identity of existence, so in the intellectual world the idea and the form in which it is manifested must inhere in each other, and interpenetrate each other, in order to real excellence of any kind. The student cannot therefore well cultivate thinking by itself, isolated from the expression of his thought; neither can he cultivate the expression of thought isolated from the process of thinking. Both processes, the philosophical and the rhetorical, must proceed *pari passu*, and simultaneously, and the result be a unity that is neither wholly formal nor wholly material in its nature. An oration considered as a rhetorical product does not consist of thought alone, any more than of expression alone. It is thought *and* expression, matter *and* form, in one common identity. Pure thought, alone and by itself, exists only in the conscious mind. Pure form, alone and by itself, exists nowhere. It is a mere notion or abstraction of the understanding, to which there is no objective correspondent. A *mere* form is a ghost, and a ghost possesses neither being nor reality.

Now, by virtue of this intercommunication of Rhetoric with all the solid material branches of knowledge, it stands midway between the pure sciences and the practical arts. It is neither wholly speculative, nor wholly practical. It is a most intimate and thorough mingling of these two qualities. Rhetoric serves, therefore, as a

ancient Rhetoric, for the purpose of opening and exhausting themes, is apparent from Aristotle's list of topics, and Cicero's compendium of them, in his *Topica*.

bond of connection between the more abstract branches, and the plain practical knowledge of common life. It is the mediator between the recondite theories of the philosopher, and the simple, spontaneous thinking of the uneducated man. What indeed is the orator, or the discourser generally, but a man who stands midway between the schools and the market-place, and interprets the one to the other; a man whose function it is to give such an expression to the lore of the learned world, as will impress and influence the unlearned world? The orator, the discourser generally, is a middle-man, who brings these two great halves, the lettered and the unlettered, together, and thus contributes to that collision of mind with mind, which is the life and soul of human literature, and of human history. For it is this *communication* of thought, which is ever going on, that keeps the world alive and stirring. Mere pure thinking, that never found an utterance of itself, by tongue or pen, even if such a thing could be, would leave the world as dull and motionless as it found it. It is the *expressed* thought, the *written* or the *vocalized* idea, that stirs and impels the general mind.

Having, in this brief manner, directed attention to the distinction between the formal and real sciences, and having assigned to Rhetoric its place among the former, at the same time also observing its vital connection with the latter, we proceed to specify some of the advantages of this method of contemplating the general subject.

1. In the first place, upon this method, the department obtains an accurate definition, and is confined to its own just limits.

There was once a time when Rhetoric was made to include vastly more than properly belongs to it; when indeed it was more like an encyclopædia of all arts and sciences, than a limited and specific branch of knowledge. Rhetoric, at one time, was almost as comprehensive a term as philosophy is at the present day. The effect of this was to distract the mind by a multiplicity of topics, and to preclude that singleness of aim, and unity of pursuit, which is the foundation of all good discourse. Such a variety and complexity as is exhibited by some of the elder treatises upon Rhetoric, is destructive of all distinctness, neatness, and elegance of form. A style formed by such an instrument must be in the highest degree loose, rambling, and unrhetorical. As matter of fact, the composition which was the fruit of such rhetorical training is generally devoid, not merely of true grace and ornament, but of the more necessary qualities of good writing, perspicuity and vivacity. Sentences are constructed in the most clumsy manner; involved, parenthetic, and incomplete to the last degree; while the general style of the whole is heavy, dragging, and dull.

The defect in these treatises is the lack of a close and clear definition in the outset, of the nature of the art itself. It was really regarded as a *material* branch of knowledge; and hence it was the duty of the rhetorician to give positive instruction upon nearly all subjects. Inasmuch as the orator needs all the knowledge he can possibly obtain; inasmuch as eloquence can successfully employ a greater amount of information than any other department, not excepting even that of history; it was supposed to be the business of Rhetoric, and of the rhetorician, to furnish it all. Hence the department, as we have remarked, became virtually an encyclopædia; not merely *a* material science, but all material science in one mass; the *omne scibile* itself. But such, we have seen, is not its nature. It is strictly, and really, a *formal* science. Its final end is simply to express, to communicate, to embody; and the more rigorously this is held to be the essential character of Rhetoric, the finer will be the forms and styles of composition that come into existence. No sharply-drawn outlines, no distinct definitions, no clean and clear developments, no round and full statements, can originate from a Rhetoric that is unlimited and undefined in its own nature. If Rhetoric includes everything, and is to furnish everything, then discourse will contain everything, and be full of everything. If, on the other hand, the term is strictly defined, and the eye of the student is kept steadily directed to the production of a pure and noble *form*, for the materials with which his mind has been stored by other sciences, and other disciplines, then there will arise "a form and combination indeed," a style and manner fit to be a model.

2. In the second place, this view of the nature and relative position of the department of Rhetoric protects it from a lifeless formality.

No branch of human knowledge is so liable to a dead formalism as Rhetoric. By its very definition, it is obliged to make the form, in distinction from the substance, the appropriate and final end of its investigations and instructions. It is not surprising, consequently, that this formal and formalizing tendency should become too strong in the course of time, and that Rhetoric should become a feeble and artificial department, instead of a vigorous and creative one. Human nature is hypocritical. Its tendency is to the form rather than to the substance; to the show rather than to the reality. This characteristic is not confined to the moral side of man's nature. It enters very largely into his intellectual being. Indeed, the effects of the apostasy are as plainly to be seen in the human intellect, as in the human heart. What is this formality, this lack of sincerity and genuineness, in our mental processes, but the effect of a corruption that has vitiated the mind, as well as the heart? If we closely examine ourselves, we shall find an absence of veracity, of integrity, of godly simplicity and sincerity, to be as marked and evident in our intellectual, as in our moral condition. The whole *head* is sick.

Now, when a department of human knowledge, by its very intrinsic nature, and vocation, falls in with this corrupt tendency of man's nature, it is no wonder that its history should be marked by degeneracy; that it should constantly grow more and more formal, and ungenuine, in its own nature and influence. When the theoretic definition harmonizes with the practical bent, when high abstract science is in unison with an actual tendency of man's nature, it is not surprising that the development, unchecked and unmodified by other agencies, should be in the highest degree false and fatal. If the blind lead the blind, both fall into the ditch.

The history of Rhetoric, and we may add of the whole department of fine art, proves and illustrates the truth of this remark. We find in every nation which had an eloquence, and an art, one period of fresh powerful talent and activity in these departments, and then long periods of feeble, formal, and lifeless efforts. The form constantly encroached upon the idea, until it crowded it out. The distinction between formal and real science become a division, and a separation, so that each was pursued alone by itself, to the great injury of the former, and to the death and destruction of the latter. Compare, e. g., the eloquence of Demosthenes with the oratory of the Sophists. The former proceeds from thought, from truth, as the principle of all eloquence, form and style being moulded and determined by it. The latter starts from form and style itself, which is continually subjected to a repetition of touches and retouches, without any inward moulding, any living formation.

> Like shadows on a stream, the forms of art
> Impress their character on the smooth surface,
> ....but no soul
> Warmeth the inner frame.*

But the view that has been presented of the nature of Rhetoric, and of its relation to the whole field of human knowledge and inquiry, is preclusive of this besetting bad tendency in the department. While recognizing the essentially formal character of Rhetoric, and thus giving it a distinct place in the circle of the sciences, and thereby confining it within its own limits, it, at the same time, directs attention to the deeper soil into which its roots must strike, and from which it must derive its nourishment and vigor. The rhetorical training of the student, on this method, is concurrent with all his other training, and becomes the medium of its communication to other minds. His general culture is benefited by his discipline in this direction, for the whole body of it is set in motion, and action, by every effort to give form and expression to it.

The whole tendency of such a theory of Rhetoric is to produce, in practice, masculine and vital discourse. The student is headed right by it, if we may use the term, and is taught to apply his best power to the evolution of truth, and the production of thought in his own mind, not surely to the neglect of the form in which it is to be expressed, but in order to the highest and most perfect elaboration of the form. Commencing with the matter, he proceeds to the form, which is to take shape and character, and all its qualities, from that primitive material for

---

* Schiller altered.

whose sake alone it has any existence at all. For, says Chaucer,

> Well may men knowen, but it be a fool,
> That every part deriveth from his hool.
> For Nature hath not taken his beginning
> Of no partie ne cantel of a thing,
> But of a thing that parfit is and stable
> Descending so, til it be corrumpable.*

The rhetorician is taught to be severe with himself, to forget himself in the theme, that he may exhibit it with that boldness and freedom of manner, that daring strength and grandeur of treatment, which is absolutely beyond the reach of him who is anxious respecting the impression he may make; who, in short, is tormented by too much consciousness of self, at a time when he should be absorbingly conscious of the theme.

According to the theory here presented, the oration, meaning by this every rounded and complete discourse, is the evolution of an idea that is the germ and principle of the whole composition. But nothing can be of greater benefit to the student, than, in the very beginning of his intellectual life, to be habituated to compose in the light, and by the guidance, and under the impulse, of ideas; than to be enabled to discover those germinal truths which are pregnant with life, and which, when embodied with freedom and power in a discourse, constitute the groundwork of the finest creations of the human mind. And apart from the benefit which is to be derived from this habit and ability, for the practical purposes of Rhetoric, what a benefit is derived from it in respect to the private contemplations and enjoyment of the scholar! Supposing he does not need this ability, because he is never called upon to speak or write to his fellow-men, (a supposition

* Chaucer: Knight's Tale.

that is hardly to the credit of an educated man in this peculiar age,*) does he not need it, in order that his own mind may reach essential truth, and may, in its own reflections, follow the method and order of reason? In what a serene and constant illumination does that mind dwell, which is able in its meditations to find the fontal truth as it were by instinct, and to unfold it by its own light, and in accordance with its own structure!

By such a theory the student is introduced into the world of ideas, laws and principles, and is taught to begin with these, and from them to work out towards detail, elaboration, and ornament. It is a mysterious world, it is true, and it must be, from the very fact that it is the source and origin. But it is the very office-work of thinking to convert these ideas into clear conceptions; to put these vast unlimited truths into definite and intelligible discourse; in fine, in the strict meaning of the term, to *develop* truth. He is the mystical and obscure discourser who leaves truth just as he finds it; who does not, by the aid of close thinking and a rigorous remorseless logic, compel the dark pregnant idea to yield up its secret; who does not force the contents out of the all-comprehending law or principle. And he is the clear and intelligible discourser, in the only high sense of the term; clear while solid, intelligible while weighty; who, not starting in light to make things light, starts in darkness and works his way out into high noon. In both the Pagan and Christian cosmogonies, creation emerged from old night.

Most certainly, the influence of such a theory of Rhetoric is enlivening to the mind. Setting aside the fact,

---

* " Ob eamque causam eloqui copiose, modo prudenter, melius est, quam vel acutissime sine eloquentia cogitare : quod cogitatio in se ipsa vertitur, eloquentia complectitur eos, quibus cum communitate juncti sumus."—Cicero, De Officiis, Lib. I. cap. 44.

that it is the only one by the aid of which eloquence can come into existence, it is the only *working* theory, it is most certainly a great point gained, if an art, so often supposed to be at furthest remove from earnestness and vividness, which is regarded too commonly as the art by which the ornaments are furnished when the solid and real work has been done, is shown to have its native seat and source in both logic and ethics. The expression of thought by this theory becomes a sincere act, and the mind, while giving utterance to its reflections, is really contributing to the moral culture and development of the man. The productions of such a Rhetoric are marked by that grave and conscientious character which is the natural fruit of simplicity and genuineness in the mental processes. The effect of the theory is seen even in the language employed. It is no longer stiff, stilted, and aloof from the thought, but pliant, vital, and consubstantial with it.

3. It is obvious in the third place, that the view under consideration imparts an interest to the department of Rhetoric which it is entirely destitute of, upon any other theory.

For, as we have already remarked, no strictly formal department of knowledge is independent and self-subsistent. If we confine ourselves to a mere art, without respect to the more profound principles that lie under it, our minds soon become weary and spiritless. Such is the affinity between the human intellect and fundamental truth, such is the hungering after *substantial* knowledge and *real* science, that it cannot be permanently interested in any branch of inquiry, or of activity, that does not ultimately lead it down into these depths. Essential truth is the element, and the aliment, of a rational mind, and nothing short of this form of truth can long satisfy its wants. Unless, therefore, rhetorical discipline conducts the mind ultimately to these perennial fountains of stimulation and nourishment, it will soon become irksome in its nature, and wearisome in its influence. All this training in the art of composition will only serve to drink up the vigorous juices, and kill out the life of the mind.

If, on the contrary, rhetorical study and practice be grafted into the vigorous stock of a preëxisting culture, if the student come to it with a well-trained and fully informed mind, the result of industry and fidelity in the academical, collegiate, and professional courses of instruction through which he has passed; then this part of his labor as an educated man will be the most interesting and congenial of all. We have, perhaps, experienced the exquisite pleasure which the intellect feels in the hour of vigorous creative production; the high swelling enthusiasm of the mind, as it careers over a field of noble and lofty thought. We have, perhaps, experienced that enlargement and elevation of soul, which accompanies the distinct intuition of principles, and a firm masterly grasp of them. "The highest joy," says Schiller, "is the freedom of the mind, in the living play of all its powers;" and there is no sphere in which this play of the intellect is so full and so free, as that of authorship, as that of composition. None of the other processes in the course of education can compare with it, for depth and heartiness of interest. The processes of memorizing, of comparing, of judging, of analyzing, of combining, and of close attention,—the processes that occur in the classical, mathematical, historical, and philosophical disciplines,— are each and all of them inferior in fresh living interest, to the process of original production. In these former instances, the mind is somewhat passive, and but a portion of its power is in exercise. But in the act and process of original authorship, the mind becomes a unit and unity, all its powers are concentrated into one, and the productive process is a most original and vital union of all the knowledge, all the feeling, all the imagination, and all the moral force of the man. The historian Niebuhr, speaking of the historian's vocation, remarks that he who calls past ages into being enjoys a bliss analogous to that of creating.* With equal truth, may we say of that mind which is able, in the conscious awakening of all its powers, to give full and satisfactory utterance to its thick-coming thoughts, that it enjoys the joy of a creator. If there is one bright particular hour in the life of the educated man, in the career of the scholar, it is that hour for which all other hours of student life were made, —that hour in which he gives original and full *expression* to what has slowly been gendering within him. Now, what this bright hour is to the general life of the educated man, rhetorical discipline and practice is to the sum-total of education. If pursued in the right method, and after the proper preparatory work has been done, it imparts an interest to general study and general culture, such as can-

* "I have found," he says in one of his letters, "my former experience irresistibly confirmed, that with me the body depends entirely on the mind, and that my indisposition almost always arises from some impediment to the free action of my mind, which seems to introduce disorder into all the functions of the bodily machine. When my mind is exerting itself freely and energetically upon a great subject, and I advance successfully from one point to another, displaying their mutual connection as I proceed, I either feel no physical inconveniences, or if they show themselves, they disappear again very quickly. No man can have a more vivid perception, that *creating* is the true essence of life, than I have derived from my internal experience. But if I am altogether restricted to a passive state of mind, the whole machine comes to a stop, and my inward discomfort brings on an unhealthy condition of body, of which I have an unmistakable outward sign, in the contrast between the free and strong circulation of the blood in the former state, and its irregularity in the latter."—Life and Letters, p. 179.

not exist without it. How dull and stupid is the life of a book-worm; of a mind which passes through all the stages of education, except that last and crowning one, by means of which it is put into *communication* with the great world of scholars and letters. Such a mind is always destitute of that most interesting and infallible sign of genuine culture, enthusiasm. It has done nothing for long years but *absorb*. Knowledge has had the same effect upon its inner fabric and structure, which the sweet rains of heaven have upon the rootless fallen pine. The noble shaft becomes struck with the sap-rot.

The history of literature furnishes many examples of men whose knowledge only increased their sorrow, because it never found an efflux from their own minds into the world. Knowledge uncommunicated is something like remorse unconfessed. The mind not being allowed to go out of itself, and to direct its energies towards an object and end greater and worthier than itself, turns back upon itself, and becomes morbidly self-reflecting and self-conscious. A studious and reflecting man of this class is characterized by an excessive fastidiousness, which makes him dissatisfied with all that he does himself, or sees done by others; which represses, and finally suppresses, all the buoyant and spirited activity of the intellect, leaving it sluggish as "the dull weed that rots by Lethe's wharf." The poet Gray is an example in point. In the instance of this in many respects highly interesting literary man, the acquisition of culture far outran the expression and communication of it. The scholar overlaid the author. Even the comparatively few attempts which this mind made to embody its thoughts were hampered by its excessive introspection. Had Gray thrown himself out with freedom and boldness upon the stream of original production, which might have been made to flow from his richly-endowed and richly-informed mind, he would have been stronger, greater, and happier as a literary man. Neither would his productions have lost that perfection of symmetry, and elaborate hard finish which they exhibit; while at the same time they would have had breathed into them that warm breath of life, which they do not now possess, and for the lack of which no mere art can ever compensate. Certain it is that a closer, warmer contact with the mind of his age, through a more daring and exuberant authorship on his part, would have imparted a spring and buoyancy to the literary character of Gray that would have rendered it a more influential and interesting one than it now is.

As an example of the freshening and invigorating influence of the constant and free communication of thought upon the intellect, take Sir Walter Scott. His mind was one of the healthiest, and most robust, that we meet with in the history of literature. It was also one of the happiest, the most free from morbid exercises and activities. Something was undoubtedly due to its native structure, but very much was owing to those habits of authorship which it early acquired, and long kept up. Suppose that Scott had immured himself in his library, had given free play to his acquisitive and antiquarian tendencies, without developing and using his originating and productive talent, can we suppose that his intellect would have been that warm, breezy, sunny spot that it always was? It is true that he finally broke his powers down, by attempting the Herculean task of rescuing the great publishing house with which he had become connected from bankruptcy; but this *dead lift* of the mental powers is not what we are speaking of. It is the moderate, and uniform, yet free and bold expression of the thoughts of an educated mind, in distinction from the dull, lethargic, uniform suppression of them, of which we are speaking, and for which we are pleading.

In this way, the ethical theory of Rhetoric, while resulting in a practical and energetic Eloquence, exerts a vivifying influence upon the entire culture of the student. It gives *employment* to the sum total of his acquisitions, instead of permitting it to remain idle in his mind. It *elaborates* and *uses*, for the purposes of popular instruction and impression, all the material with which the mind is filled, instead of allowing it to remain a lifeless mass, a *caput mortuum*, by itself. Mathematical, classical, historical, philosophical, and theological knowledge, instead of being held in the memory from a mere feeling of vanity, is set to work from a sense of duty. The Rhetoric of the man has affinities with the scholarship of the man. It is homogeneous with it. It moulds it, and embodies it. For the rhetorician, upon this theory, and under this training, is not one in whom two distinct disciplines exist side by side, with no interpenetration. He is not at one time a dull sluggish recipient of knowledge, and at another a dull formal communicator of knowledge; discharging two functions which in him have no connection with each other. He is at all times a genial and vital receiver, and a genial vital communicator. It was once said of a famous jurist, that his knowledge had passed out of his memory into his judgment. We may say of the genuine rhetorician, that his knowledge is continually passing out of his passive into his active nature. It enters into the circulation of the soul, and becomes vitalized by its living currents. The scholar and the orator are not separated from each other, but constitute one living personality.

But what an energy is imparted to culture, by a training that thus tasks to the utmost for acquisitions, and then vivifies those acquisitions to the utmost in order to popular oratorical impression ! It is safe to say that the literature of a nation is vigorous and alive, only in proportion as it has oratorical elements in it; and that the very height of its living energy appears in its eloquence and oratory. What other portion of Greek literature throbs with such intense life as the speeches of Demosthenes? If there be any of the *vis vivida vitae* in Roman literature, that literature which, unlike all others, was born old, and never exhibits any of the morn and liquid dew of youth,—if there be any fresh vital force in Roman letters, is it not to be found in the orations of Cicero? And where, in the modern world, do the most vehement and passionate energies of the human intellect expatiate and career, if not in the vastly widened arena of political and sacred eloquence,—if not on that theatre where the active, practical interests of man for time and for eternity come up for discussion and decision?

The importance of a high and philosophic theory of eloquence and oratory, when considered in its bearings upon the education of the American mind, is plain and great. The American is sensitive to eloquence, and is inclined to be influenced by the rhetorician and orator more than by the poet or the philosopher. We are in our youth as a nation; in that forming period which in Grecian, in Roman, and in English history, is marked by the ballad and romance literature. Unlike our predecessors we have not been much influenced by these lighter and imaginative species, but even in our infancy and youth have sought a "manlier diet." We affect eloquence and oratory, rather than the ballad and the romance. If we compare the literature of America with that of Europe, for the last hundred years, we find that our success has been altogether greatest in this department. During this period we have produced no poetry equal to that of England, no philosophy equal to that of Germany, and no science equal to that of France. But the most unwilling admirer must acknowledge that we have produced a body of eloquence and oratory which, taken as a whole, is equal to contemporaneous English or Continental eloquence. The eloquence called out in the debates upon the adoption of the Constitution, and all along down from that time to the present, in expounding and defending it; the panegyrical eloquence of the country elicited by the commemoration of great events, or of patriotic men; nay even the ruder and less elaborate efforts incident to the political contests that occur so often: all these have resulted, within the period of the last hundred years in the republican States of America, in a body of oratorical literature with which nothing could so well compare, as that which was called forth (but which has not been handed down), in the democracies of Greece, from the time when the Olympian Pericles thundered in the Agora, to the time when Demosthenes sucked the poisoned quill.

The American mind ought therefore to be under the influence of a high theory, and a strict taste, in order that this tendency may receive its very best education; and in order that American eloquence may continue to be characterized by solid and sterling qualities. The national mind has been too seriously occupied with great interests, to become meretricious in its rhetoric and eloquence. The Revolution that established liberty and the government, and the national crises that have occurred since, were no time for an inflated and bombastic display. Energy and thoughtfulness characterize our favorite and model orators. But peace, and prosperity, and perfect security, relax the mind and its theories. There is now danger that the form outrun the substance; that congressional debates, that judicial, panegyrical, and sacred eloquence, all of them become less truthful and forceful in their character, while they become more florid and dazzling.

What better corrective, then, can there be, than a good educational theory, upon the whole subject, in both the individual and the public mind; in both the auditor and the orator? If audiences are intolerant of a rhetoric that separates the form from the matter, the style from the thought, the public speaker will know it, and act accordingly. If the auditor insists that eloquence have a soul of truth, and of thought, within it, the orator will yield, and become a more thoughtful man, that he may minister to the public want. The result will be a rhetoric and an oratory that first patiently accumulates knowledge, and then thoroughly elaborates it, for the purposes of popular instruction and impression,—an eloquence

"not like those rills from a height
Which sparkle and foam, and in vapor are o'er;
But a current that works out its way into light
Through the filtering recesses of thought and of lore."

THE CHARACTERISTICS AND IMPORTANCE OF A NATURAL RHETORIC.*

THERE is no greater or more striking contrast, than exists between a thing that is alive, and a thing that is dead; between a product of nature, and a product of mechanism; between a thing that has a principle within it, and a "thing of shreds and patches." The human mind notices this contrast between the various objects that come before it, the quicker and the more sharply, because it is itself a living thing, and because its own operations are unifying, organizing, and vivifying, in their nature. We sometimes speak of the mechanism of the human understanding, and of a mechanizing process as going on within it. But this language is metaphorical, and employed to denote the uniformity and certainty of intellectual processes, rather than their real nature. Man is a living soul, and there is no action anywhere, or in anything, that is more truly and purely vital, more entirely diverse from and hostile to the mechanical and the dead, than the genuine action of the human mind. Hence it is that the mind notices this contrary quality and characteristic in an object with the

* An inaugural discourse at Auburn, June 16, 1852.

rapidity of instinct, and starts back from it with a sort of organic recoil. Life detects death, and shrinks from death, instantaneously. Nature abhors art and artifice, as decidedly as, according to the old philosophy, it abhors a vacuum.

This distinction between the natural and the artificial, furnishes a clue to the difference which runs through all the productions of man, and reveals the secret of their excellence or their defects. How often and how spontaneously do we sum up our whole admiration of a work by saying, "it is natural," and our whole dislike by the words, "it is artificial?" The naturalness and life-likeness in the one case, are the spring of all that has pleased us; the formality and artifice in the other, are the source of all that has repelled or disgusted us. Even when we go no further in our criticism, this general statement of conformity or oppugnancy to nature, seems to be a sufficient criticism. And with good reason. For, if a production has nature, has life in it, it has real and permanent excellence. It has the germ and root of all excellences. And if it has not nature or life in it; if it is a mechanical, or an artificial, or a formal thing; it has the elements of all defects and all faults in it.

It will be noticed here, that we have used the term Art in its more common and bad sense, of contrariety to Nature, and not in that technical and best signification of the word, which implies the oneness and unison of the two. For, true Art, Fine Art, has Nature in it, and the genuine artist, be he painter, or poet, or orator, is one who paints, or sings, or speaks, with a natural freedom and freshness. Hence it is, that we are impressed by the great productions of Fine Art, in the same way that we are by the works of Nature. A painting, warm from the easel of Claude Lorraine, appeals to what is alive in us, in the same genial way that a vernal landscape does. — An oration from a clear brain, a beating heart, and a glowing lip, produces effects analogous to those of light, and fire, and the electric currents. In this way, a mysterious union is found to exist between outward nature, and that inward nature in the soul of man which we call genius; and in this way we see that there is no essential difference between Nature and Art.*

But in the other and more common sense of the term Art; and the sense in which we shall employ it at this time; there is no such mystic union and unison between it and Nature. It is its very contrary; so much so, that the one kills and expels the other; so much so, that, as we have said, the one affords a universal test of the faultiness, and the other of the excellence, of the productions of the human mind, in all departments of effort. For the Natural is the true, while the Artificial is the false. *Truth* is the inmost essence of that principle by which a production of the human mind is so organized and vitalized, as to make a fresh and powerful impression. — Whenever in any department of effort, the human mind has reached verity, and is able to give a simple and sincere expression to it, we find the product full of nature, full of life, full of freshness, full of impression. This,

---

* Nature's own work it seemed, (nature taught art.)
            Paradise Regained, ii. 295.
All nature is but art unknown to thee.   Pope.
Nature is the art of God.   Sir Thomas Browne.
 There is a nature in all artificial things, and again, an artifice in all compounded natural things.   Cudworth.
 The art of seeing nature is in reality the great object of the studies of the artist.   Sir Joshua Reynolds.
 Art may, in truth, be called the *human world*.   Allston.
 For a philosophic statement of this theory see Kant's Urtheilskraft §§ 45, 46, and Schelling's discourse upon the relation of Art to Nature.

and this ultimately, is the plain secret of the charm in every work of genius and of power. In every instance, the influence which sways the observer, or the hearer, or the reader, is the influence of the veritable reality, of the real and the simple truth. The Artificial, on the contrary, is the false. Examine any formal production whatever, and we shall be brought back in the end to a pretence, to a falsehood. The mind of the author is not filled with the truth, and yet he pretends to an utterance of the truth. Its working is not genial and spontaneous like that of nature, and yet he must give out that it is. From the beginning to the end of the process, therefore, an artificial production is essentially untrue, unreal, and hence unnatural.

We have thus briefly directed attention to this very common distinction between the Natural and the Artificial, and to the ground of it, for the purpose of introducing the general topic upon which we propose to speak on this occasion: viz.

The Characteristics and importance of a Natural Rhetoric, with special reference to the work of the Preacher.

There is no branch of knowledge so liable to an artificial method, as that of Rhetoric. Strictly defined, it is, indeed, as Milton calls it, an instrumental art, and hence, from its very nature, its appropriate subject-matter is the *form* of a discourse. While Philosophy, and History, and Theology, are properly occupied with the substance of human composition; with truth itself and thought itself; to Rhetoric is left the humbler task of putting this material into a form suited to it. Hence, it is evident, that by the very nature and definition of Rhetoric, this department of knowledge and of discipline is liable to formalism and artificiality. While the mind is carried by the solid, material, branches of education, further and further into the very substance of truth itself; while History, and Philosophy, and Theology, by their very structure and contents, tend to deepen and strengthen the mental processes; Rhetoric, in common with the whole department of Fine Art, seems to induce superficiality and formality. And when a bad tendency seems to receive aid from a legitimate department of human knowledge, it is no wonder that it should gain ground until it convert the whole department into its own nature. Hence, as matter of fact, there is no branch of knowledge, no part of a general system of education, so much infected, in all ages, with the merely formal, the merely hollow, the merely artificial, and the totally lifeless, as Rhetoric. The epigram which Ausonius wrote under the portrait of the Rhetorician Rufus, might, with too much truth, be applied to the Rhetorician generally:

Ipse rhetor, est imago imaginis.*

The need, therefore, of a Rhetoric that educates like nature, and not artificially; a Rhetoric that organizes and vitalizes the material that is made over to it for purposes of form; is apparent at first glance. Without such a method of expression, the influence of the solid branches of education themselves is neutralized. However full of fresh and original thought the mind may be, if it has been trained up to a mode of presenting it, that is in its own nature artificial and destructive of life, the freshness and originality will all disappear in the process of imparting it to another mind. A Rhetoric that is conformed to nature and to truth, is needed, therefore, in order that the department itself may be co-ordinate with those higher departments of knowledge in which the foundation of

---

* Ausonii Epig. LI.

mental education is laid. Without such a concurrence with the material branches of education, such a merely formal and instrumental branch as that of Rhetoric, is useless, and worse than useless. For it only diverts the mind from the thought to the expression, without any gain to the latter, and to the positive detriment of the former.

1. Rhetoric, therefore, can be a truly educating and influential department, only in proportion as it is *organizing* in its fundamental character. In order to this, it must be grounded first of all in logic, or the laws of thinking, and so become not a mere collection of rules for the structure and decoration of single sentences, but a habit and process of the human mind. The Rhetorician must make his first sacrifice to the stern deities. In an emblematic series by one of the early Florentine engravers, Rhetoric is represented by a female figure of dignified and commanding deportment with a helmet surmounted by a regal crown on her head, and a naked sword in her right hand. And so it should be. Softness, and grace, and beauty, must be supported by strength and prowess; the golden and jewelled crown must be defended by the iron helmet, and the steel sword. A rhetorical mind, therefore, in the best and proper sense of the term, is at bottom a constructive mind; a mind capable of methodizing and organizing its acquisitions and reflections into forms of symmetry, and strength, and in a greater or less degree of beauty. It is a mind which, in the effort to express itself, begins from within and works outward, and whose product is, for this reason, characterized by the unity and thorough compactness of a product of Nature. Such, for example, was the mind of Demosthenes, and such a product is the Oration for the Crown. The oratorical power of this great master is

primarily a constructive talent; an ability to methodize and combine. Take away this deeply-running and rigorous force by which the various parts of the discourse, the whole *materiel* of the plan and division, are compelled and compacted together, and this orator falls into the same class with the Gorgiases and the false Rhetoricians of all ages. Take away the *organization* of the Oration for the Crown, and a style and diction a hundred fold more brilliant and gorgeous than that which now clothes it, would not save it from the fate of the false Rhetoric of all ages.

Such again, for example, was the mind of the Apostle Paul, and such was the character of his Rhetoric. Those short epistles, which like godliness are profitable for all things, and ought to be as closely studied by the sermonizer as they are by the theologian, are as jointed and linked in their parts as the human frame itself, and as continuous in the flow of their trains of thought as the current of a river. The mind of this great first preacher to the Gentiles, this great first sermonizer to cultivated and sceptical Paganism, was also an organizing mind. How naturally does Christian doctrine, as it comes forth from this intellect whose native characteristics were not destroyed, but only heightened and purified, by inspiration — how naturally and inevitably does Christian truth take on forms that are fitly joined together, and compacted by that which every joint supplieth; statements that are at once logic and rhetoric, and satisfy both the reason and the feelings. For does not the profoundest theologian study the Epistle to the Romans to find ultimate and absolute statements in sacred science, and does not the most unlettered Christian read and pray over this same epistle, that his devotions may be kindled and his heart made better? Does not, to use the illustration of the Christian Father, does not the lamb find a fording place and the elephant a swimming place in this mighty unremitting stream?

This thoroughness in the elaboration of the principal ideas of a discourse, and this closeness in compacting them into the unity of a plan, is, therefore, a prime quality in eloquence, and it is that which connects Rhetoric with all the other departments of human knowledge, or rather makes it the organ by and through which these find a full and noble expression. For, contemplated from this point of view, what is the orator but a man of culture who is able to *tell* in round and full tones what he knows; and what is oratory but the art whereby the acquisitions and reflections of the general human mind are *communicated* to the present and the future. We cannot, therefore, taking this view of the nature of Rhetoric as essentially organizing in its character, separate it from the higher departments of History, or Philosophy, or Theology, but must regard it as co-ordinate and concurrent with them. The rhetorical process is to go on in education, along with these other processes of acquisition and information and reflection, so that the final result shall be a mind not only disciplined inwardly but manifested outwardly to other minds; so that there shall be not only an intellect full of thought, and a heart beating with feeling, and an imagination glowing with imagery, but a living expression of them all, in forms of unity and simplicity and beauty and grandeur. In this way Rhetoric really becomes, what it was once claimed to be, the very crown and completion of all culture, and the rhetorical discipline, the last accomplishment in the process of education, when the man becomes prepared to take the stand on the orator's bema before his fellow men, and dares to attempt a transfer of his consciousness into them.

2. The second characteristic of a natural Rhetoric is the *amplifying* power. If Rhetoric should stop with the mere organizing of thought, it might be difficult to distinguish it from logic. But this constructive talent in the Rhetorician, is accompanied by another ability which is more purely oratorical. We mean the ability to dwell amply upon an idea until it has unfolded all its folds, and lays off richly in broad full view. We mean the ability to melt the hard solid ore with so thorough and glowing a heat, that it will run and spread like water. We mean the ability to enlarge and illustrate upon a condensed and cubic idea, until its contents spread out into a wide expanse for the career of the imagination and the play of the feelings.

This union of an organizing with an amplifying power, may be said to be the whole of Rhetoric. He who should combine both in perfect proportions, would be the ideal orator of Cicero. For while the former power presents truth in its clear and connected form for the understanding, the latter transmutes it into its imaginative and impassioned forms, and the product of these two powers, when they are blended in one living energy, is Eloquence. For Eloquence, according to the best definition that has yet been given, is the union of Philosophy and Poetry in order to a practical end.* When, therefore, the logical organization is clothed upon with the imaginative and impassioned amplification, there arises " a combination and a form indeed ; " a mental product adapted more than all others to move and influence the human mind.

* Theremin's Rhetoric, Book i. Chapters iii., iv.

But we shall see still more clearly into the essential characteristics of a Natural Rhetoric, by passing, as we now do, after this brief analysis, to the second part of our discourse, which proposes to treat of the worth and importance of such a Rhetoric to the preacher.

1. And in the first place, a natural as distinguished from an artificial Rhetoric, is of the highest worth to the preacher because it is *fruitful.*

The preacher is one who, from the nature of his calling, is obliged to originate a certain amount of thought within a limited period of time, which is constantly and uniformly recurring. One day in every seven, as regularly as the motion of the globe brings it around, he is compelled to address his fellow men upon the very highest themes, in a manner and to an extent that will secure their attention and interest. No profession, consequently, makes such a steady and unintermittent draught upon the resources of the mind as the clerical, and no man so much needs the aid of a fertile and fruitful method of discoursing as the Christian preacher. Besides this great amount of thinking and composition that is required of him, he is moreover shut up to a comparatively small number of topics, and cannot derive that assistance from variety of subjects, and novelty in circumstances, which the secular orator avails himself of so readily. The truths of Christianity are few and simple, and though they are richer and more inexhaustible than all others, they furnish little that is novel or striking. The power that is in them to interest and move men, must be educed from their simple and solid substance, and not from their great number or variety. The preacher may, it is true, be able to maintain a sort of interest in his hearers by the biographical, or geographical, or archaeological, or historical, or literary, accompaniments of the Scriptures but his permanent influence and power over them as a preacher must come from his ability to develop clearly, profoundly, and freshly, a few simple and unadorned doctrines. Far be it from me to undervalue the importance of that training and study, by which we are introduced into that elder and oriental world in which the Bible had its origin, and with whose scenery, manners and customs, and modes of living and thinking, it will be connected to the end of time. No student of the Scriptures, and especially no sacred orator, can make himself too much at home in the gorgeous East; too familiar with that Hebrew spirit which colors like blood the whole Bible, New Testament as well as Old Testament. But at the same time he should remember that all this knowledge is only a means to an end; that he cannot as a preacher of the Word, rely upon this as the last source whence he is to derive subject matter for his thinking and discourse year after year, but must by it all be carried down to deeper and more perennial fountains, to the few infinite facts and the few infinite truths of Christianity.

The need, therefore, of a Rhetorical method that is in its own nature fertile and fruitful, is plain. And what other ability can succeed but that organizing and amplifying power, which we have seen to be the substance of the Rhetoric of Nature as the contrary of Art. Through the former of these, the preacher's mind is led into the inmost structure and fabric of the individual doctrine, and so of the whole Christian system; and through the latter he is enabled to unroll and display the endless richness of the contents. It is safe to say, that a mind which has once acquired this natural method of developing and presenting Christian truth, cannot be exhausted. No matter how much drain may be made upon it, no matter how often it may be called upon to preach the "things new and old," it cannot be made dry. The more it is drawn from, the more salient and bulging is the fulness with which it wells up and pours over. For this *organic* method is the key and the clue. He who is master of it, he with whom it has become a mental habit and process, will find the treasures of wisdom and knowledge in the Scriptures opening readily and richly to him. He will find his mind habitually in the vein.

2. And this brings us to a second characteristic of a Natural Rhetoric, whereby it is of the greatest worth to the preacher, viz., that it is a *genial* and *invigorating* method. All the discipline of the human mind ought to minister to its enjoyment and its strength. That is a false method of discipline, by which the human mind is made to work by an ungenial effort, much more by spasms and convulsively. It was made to work like nature itself, calmly, continuously, strongly, and happily. When, therefore, we find a system of training, resulting in a labored, anxious, intermittent, and irksome, activity, we may be sure that something is wrong in it. The fruits of all modes of discipline that conform to the nature of the human mind and the nature of truth, are freedom, boldness, continuity, and pleasure, of execution. In this connection weakness and tedium are faults; sickness is sin.

But the mental method for which we are pleading, while making the most severe and constant draft upon the mental faculties, at the same time braces them and inspires them with power. The mind of the orator, in this slow organization and continuous amplification of the materials with which it is laboring, is itself affected by a reflex action. That truth, that divine truth, which the preacher is endeavoring to throw out, that it may renovate and edify the soul of a fellow being, at the same time strikes in, and invigorates his own mind, and swells his own heart with joy.

This feature, this genial vigor, in what we have styled a Natural Rhetoric, acquires additional importance when we recur to the fact that has already been mentioned, viz., that inasmuch as Rhetoric is a formal or instrumental department, its influence is liable to become, and too often has become, debilitating to the human mind. When this branch of discipline becomes artificial and mechanical in its character, by being severed too much from those profounder, and more solid, departments of human knowledge from whose root and fatness it must derive all its nourishment and circulating juices; when Rhetoric degenerates into a mere collection of rules for the structure of sentences and the finish of diction; no studies or training will do more to diminish the resources of the mind, and to benumb and kill the vitality of the soul, than the Rhetorical. The eye is kept upon the form merely, and no mind, individual or national, was ever made strong or fertile by the contemplation of mere form. The mind under such a tutorage works by rote, instead of from an inward influence and an organic law. In reality, its action is a surface-action, which only irritates and tires out its powers. Perhaps the strongest objections that have been advanced against a Rhetorical course of instruction, find their support and force here. Men complain of the dryness, and the want of geniality, of a professed Rhetorician. The common mind is not satisfied with his studious artifice, and his measured movements, but craves something more; it craves a robust and hearty utterance, a hale and lifesome method. Notice that it is not positively displeased with this precision and finish of the Rhetorician, but only with the lack of a genial impulse under it. It is its sins of omission that have brought Rhetoric into disrepute.

But when the training, under consideration, results in a genial and invigorating process, by which the profoundest thinking and the best feeling of the soul are discharged to the utmost, and yet the mind feels the more buoyant for it, and the stronger for it, all such objections vanish. There is, we are confident, there is a method of disciplining the mind in the direction of Rhetoric, and for the purposes of form and style, that does not in the least diminish the vigor and the healthiness of its natural processes. If there is not, then the department should be annihilated. If there can be no Rhetorical training in the schools, but such as is destructive of the freshness, and originality, and geniality, of native impulses and native utterances, then it were far better to leave the mind to its unpruned and tangled luxuriance; to let it wander at its own sweet will, and bear with its tedious windings and its endless eddies. Here and there, at least, there would be an onward movement, and the inspiration of a forward motion. But it is not so. For, says Shakspeare:

> There is an Art which . . . shares
> With great creating Nature.

There is a close and elaborate discipline which is in harmony with the poetry, and the feeling, and the eloquence, of the human soul, and which, therefore, may be employed to evoke and express it. There is a Rhetoric which, when it has been wrought into the mind, and has become a spontaneous method and an instinctive habit with it, does not in the least impair the elasticity and vigor of nature, because in the phrase of the same great poet and master of form from whom we have just quoted, " It is an Art that Nature makes, or rather an Art which itself is Nature." Such a Rhetoric may, indeed, be defined to be an Art, or discipline, which enables man to be natural; an Art that simply develops the genuine and hearty qualities of the man himself, of the mind itself. — For the purpose of all discipline in this direction, is not to impose upon the mind a style of thought and expression unnatural and alien to it, but simply to aid the mind to be itself, and to show itself out in the most genuine and sincere manner. The Rhetorical Art is to join on upon the nature and constitution of the individual man, so that what is given by creation, and what is acquired by culture, shall be homogeneous, mutually aiding and aided, reciprocally influencing and influenced. And let not this mental veracity, this truthfulness to a man's individuality and mental structure, be thought to be an easy acquisition. It is really the last and highest accomplishment. It is a very difficult thing for a discourser to be *himself*, genuinely and without affectation. It is a still more difficult thing for an orator, a man who has come out before a listening and criticising auditory, to be himself; genuinely, fearlessly and without mannerism, communicating himself to his auditors precisely as he really is. A simple and natural style, says Pascal, always strikes us with a sort of surprise; for while we are on the lookout for an *author*, we find a *man*, while we are expecting a formal *art*, we find a throbbing *heart*. This is really the highest grade of culture, and the point toward which it should always aim, viz: to bring Nature out by means of art; and Rhetorical discipline, instead of leaving the pupil ten-fold more formal and artificial than it found him, ought to send him out among men, the most artless, the most hearty, and the most genuine, man of them all.

Now of what untold worth is such a mental method and habit to the preacher of the Word! On this method, literally and without a metaphor, the more he works the stronger he becomes, the more he toils the happier he is. He finds the invention and composition of discourse a means of self-culture and of self-enjoyment. He finds that that labor to which he has devoted his life, and to which, perhaps, in the outset, he went with something of a hireling's feeling, is no irksome task, but the source of the noblest and most buoyant happiness. That steady unintermittent drain upon his thought and his feeling which he feared would soon exsiccate his brain and leave his heart dry as powder, he finds is only an outlet for the ever accumulating waters!

This invigorating and genial influence of the Rhetorical method now under consideration, furthermore, is of special worth in the present state of the world. There never was a time when the general mind was so impatient of dulness as now. He who addresses audiences at the present day must be vigorous and invigorating, or he is nothing. Hence the temptation, which is too often yielded to by the sacred orator, to leave the legitimate field of Christian discourse and to range in that border land which skirts it, or perhaps to pass into a region of thought that is really profane and secular. The preacher feels the need of saying something fresh, vigorous, and genial, and not being able to discourse in this style upon the old and standing themes of the Bible, he endeavors to christianize those secular and temporal themes with which the general mind is already too intensely occupied, that he may find in them subjects for entertaining, and, as he thinks, original discourse But this course on the part of the Christian minister, must always end in the decline of spiritual religion, both in his own heart and in that of the Church. Nothing, in the long run, is truly edifying to the Christian man or the Christian Church, that is not really religious. Nothing can renovate and sanctify the earthly mind, but that which is in its own nature spiritual and supernatural. Not that which resembles Christian truth, or which may be modified or affected by Christian truth, can convict of sin and convert to God, but only the substantial and real Christian truth itself. Nothing but material fire can be relied upon as a central sun, as a radiating centre.

The Christian preacher is thus shut up to the old and uniform system of Christianity in an age when, more than in any other, men are seeking for some new thing; when they are seeking and demanding stimulation, invigoration, animation, and impression. His only true course, therefore, is to find the new in the old; to become so penetrated with the spirit of Christianity, that he shall breathe it out from his own mind and heart, upon his congregation, in as fresh and fiery a tongue of flame as that which rested upon the disciples on the day of Pentecost; to enter so thoroughly into the genius and spirit of the Christian system, that it shall exhibit itself, through him, with an originality and newness kindred to that of its first inspired preachers, and precisely like that which characterizes the sermonizing of the Augustines and the Bernards, the Luthers and the Calvins, the Leightons, the Howes, and the Edwardses, of the Church. What renders the sermons of these men so vivific and so invigorating to those who study them, and to the audiences who heard them? Not the variety or striking character of the topics, but the thoroughness with which the truth was conceived and elaborated in their minds. Not an artificial Rhetoric, polishing and garnishing the outside of a subject in which the mind has no interest, and into the interior of which it has not penetrated; but an organizing Rhetoric, whereby the sermon shot up out of the great Christian system, like a bud out of the side of a great trunk or a great limb, part and particle of the great whole; an amplifying Rhetoric whereby the sermon was the mere evolution of an involution, the swelling, bursting, leafing out, blossoming, and fructuation, of this bud.

3. And this brings us, in the third place, to the worth of this Rhetorical method to the preacher, because it is *closely connected with his theological training and discipline.*

It is plain, from what has been said, that eloquent preaching cannot originate without profound theological knowledge. The eloquent preacher is simply the thorough theologian who has now gone out of his study, and up into the pulpit. In other words, eloquence in this as well as in every other instance is founded in knowledge. Cicero says that Socrates was wont to say that all men are eloquent enough on subjects whereon they have knowledge;[*] a saying which re-appears in the common and homely rule for eloquence, "*Have* something to say, and then say it."

Hence a Rhetorical training which does not sustain intimate relations to the general culture and discipline of the pupil, is worthless. At no point does an artificial Rhetoric betray itself so quickly and so certainly as here. We feel that it has no intercommunication with the character and acquisitions of the individual. It is a foreign method, which he has adopted by a volition, and

---

[*] De Oratore, i. 14.

not a spontaneous one which has sprung up out of his character and culture, and is in perfect sympathy with it. But the Rhetoric of nature has all the theological training of the preacher back of it as its support, beneath it as its soil and nutriment. All that he has become by long years of study and reflection, goes to maintain him as a Rhetorician, so that his oratory is really the full and powerful display of what he is and has become by vigorous professional study. The Rhetoric is the man himself.

In this way, a showy and tawdry manner is inevitably avoided, as it always should be, by the preacher. It cannot be said of him, as it can be of too many, " He is a *mere* Rhetorician." For this professional study, this lofty and calm theological discipline, this solemn care of human souls, this sacred professional character, will all show themselves in his general style and manner, and preclude every thing ostentatious or gaudy, much more every thing scenic or theatrical. The form will correspond to the matter. The matter being the most solemn and most weighty truth of God, the form will be the most chastened, the most symmetrical, and the most commanding, manner of man.

And in this way, again, the rhetorical training of the preacher will exert a reflex influence upon his theological training. A true sacred Rhetoric is a sort of practical theology, and is so styled in some nomenclatures. It is a practical expansion and exhibition of a scientific system for the purpose of influencing the popular mind. When, therefore, it is well conceived and well handled, it exerts a reflex influence upon theological science itself, that is beneficial in the highest degree. It cannot, it is true, change the nature and substance of the truth, but it can bring it out into distinct consciousness The effort to popularize scientific knowledge, the endeavor to put logic into the form of rhetoric, imparts a clearness to conceptions, and a determination to opinions, that cannot be attained in the closet of the mere speculatist. Not until a man has endeavored to transfer his conceptions; not until he has pushed his way through the confusion and misunderstandings of another man's mind, and has tried to lodge his views in it; does he know the full significance and scope of even his own knowledge.

But especially is this action and re-action between theology and sacred Rhetoric of the highest worth to the preacher, because it results in a due mingling of the theoretic and the practical in his preaching. The desideratum in a sermon is such an exact proportion between doctrine and practice, such thorough fusion of these two elements, that the discourse at once instructs and impels; and he who supplies this desideratum in his sermonizing, is a powerful, influential, and eloquent, preacher. He may lack many other minor things, but he has the main thing; and in time these other minor things shall all be added unto him. In employing a Rhetoric that is at once organizing and amplifying in its nature and influence, the theological discipline and culture of the preacher are kept constantly growing and vigorous. Every sermon that is composed on this method, sets the whole body of his acquisitions into motion, and, like a bucket continually plunged down into a well and continually drawn up full and dripping, aerates a mass that would otherwise grow stagnant and putrid.

4. Fourthly and finally, the worth of a natural, as distinguished from an artificial, Rhetoric, is seen in the fact that it is connected, most intimately, *with the vital religion of the man and the preacher*. For no Rhetoric can

be organizing and vivifying, that is not itself organic and alive. Only that which has in itself a living principle, can communicate life. Only that which is itself vigorous, can invigorate. The inmost essential principle, therefore, of a Rhetoric that is to be employed in the service of religion, must be this very religion itself: deep, vital, piety in the soul of the sacred orator. Even the pagan Cato, and the pagan Quinctilian after him, made goodness, integrity and uprightness of character, the foundation of eloquence in a secular sphere, and for secular purposes. The orator, they said, is an upright man, first of all an *upright man,* who understands speaking. How much more true then is it, that Christian character is the font and origin of all Christian eloquence; that the sacred orator is a holy man, first of all a *holy man,* who understands speaking.

We shall not, surely, be suspected of wishing to undervalue or disparage a department to which we propose to consecrate our whole time and attention, and, therefore, we may with the more boldness say, that we have always cherished a proper respect for that theory which has been more in vogue in some other denominations than in our own, that the preacher is to speak as the spirit moves him. There is a great and solid truth at the bottom of it, and though the theory unquestionably does not need to be held up very particularly before an uneducated ministry, we think there is comparatively little danger in reminding the educated man, the man who has been trained by the rules and maxims of a formal and systematic discipline, that the spring of all his power, as a Christian preacher, is a *living spring.* It is well for the sacred orator, who has passed through a long collegiate and professional training, and has been taught sermonizing as an art, to be reminded that the living principle, which is to render all this culture of use for purposes of practical impression, is vital godliness; that he will be able to assimilate all this material of Christian eloquence, only in proportion as he is a devout and holy man. Without this interior religious life in his soul, all his resources of intellect, of memory, and of imagination, will be unimpressive and ineffectual; the mere iron shields and gold ornaments that crush the powerless Tarpeia.

For the first and indispensable thing in every instance is *power*. Given an inward and living power, and a basis for motion, action, and impression, is given. In every instance we come back to this ultimate point. There is a theory among philosophers, that this hard, material world, over which we stumble, and against which we strike, is at bottom two forces or powers, held in equilibrium; that when we get back to the reality of the hard and dull clod, upon which " the swain treads with clouted shoon," we find it to be just as immaterial, just as mobile, just as nimble, and just as much a living energy, as the soul of man itself. Whether this be truth or not within the sphere of matter, one thing is certain, that within the sphere of mind we are brought back to forces, to fresh and living energies, in every instance in which the human soul makes an eloquent impression, or receives one. Examine an oration, secular or sacred, that actually moved the minds of men, a speech that obtained votes, or a sermon that, as we say, saved souls, and you find the ultimate cause of this eloquence, so far as man is concerned, to be a *vital* power in the orator. The same amount of instruction might have been imparted, the same general style and diction might have been employed in both cases, but if that eloquent *power* in the man had been wanting, there would have been no actuation of the hearer, and consequently no eloquence.

It is, therefore a great and crowning excellence of the Rhetorical method which we have been describing, that its lowest and longest roots strike down into the Christian character itself. It does not propose or expect to render the preacher eloquent without personal religion. It tells him on the contrary, that although God is the creator and sovereign of the human soul, and can therefore render the truth preached by an unregenerate man and in the most unfeeling irreligious manner, effectual to salvation, yet that *the preacher* must expect to see men moved by his discourses, only in proportion as he is himself a spiritually-minded, solemn, and devout man. Here is the *power*, and here is its hiding place, so far as the finite agent is concerned. In that holy love of God and of the human soul, which Christianity enjoins and produces; in that religious affection of the soul which takes its origin in the soul's regeneration; the preacher is to find the source of all his eloquence and impression as an orator, just as much as of his usefulness and happiness as a man and a Christian. Back to this last centre of all, do we trace all that is genuine, and powerful, and influential, in Pulpit Eloquence.

But by this is not meant merely that the preacher must be a man of zealous and fervid emotions. There is a species of eloquence, which springs out of easily excited sensibilities, and which oftentimes produces a great sensation in audiences of peculiar characteristics, and in some particular moods. But this eloquence of the flesh and the blood, without the brain; this eloquence of the animal, without the intellectual spirits; is very different from that deep-toned, that solemn, that commanding eloquence, which springs from the life of God in the soul of man We feel the difference, all men feel the difference, between the impression made by an ardent but superficial emotion, and that made by a deep feeling; by the sustained, equable, and strong, pulsation of religious affections, as distinguished from religious sensibilities. When a man of the latter stamp feels, we know that he feels upon good grounds and in reality; that this stir and movement of the affections is central and all-pervading in him; that the eternal truth has taken hold of his emotive nature, moving the *whole* of it, as the trees of the wood are moved with the wind. It is this moral earnestness of a man who habitually feels that religion is the chief concern for mortals here below; it is this profound consciousness of the perfections of God and of the worth of the human soul; which is the inmost principle of sacred eloquence, the *vis vivida vitæ* of the sacred orator.

I have thus, as briefly as possible, exhibited the principal features of what is conceived to be a true method in rhetorical instruction and discipline; not because they are new, or different from the views of the best Rhetoricians of all ages, but merely to indicate the general spirit in which I would hope, by the blessing of God, to conduct the department of instruction committed to my care by the guardians of this Seminary. The department of Sacred Rhetoric and Pastoral Theology is one that, from the nature of the case, is not called upon to impart very much positive information. Its function is rather to induce an intellectual method, to form a mental habit, to communicate a general spirit to the future clergyman. It is, therefore, a department of growing importance in this country, and in the present state of society and the Church. Perhaps the general tone and temper of the clerical profession was never a matter of more importance than now. The world, and this country especially, is guided more and more by the general tendencies of particular classes and professions. In politics, a party or class, that really *has* a tendency, and maintains it persistently for a length of time, is sure in the end to draw large masses after it. In reforms, a class that is pervaded by a distinctive spirit, which it sedulously preserves and maintains, is sure of a wide influence, finally. In literature, or philosophy, or theology, a school that has a marked and determined character of its own, and keeps faith with it, will in the course of time be rewarded for its self-consistency by an increase in numbers and in power. In all these cases, and in all other cases, the steady, continuous stream of a general tendency sucks into its own volume all the float and drift, and carries it along with it. And the eye of the reflecting observer, as it ranges over the ocean of American society, can see these currents and tendencies, as plainly as the eye of the mariner sees the Gulf-stream.

How important, then, is any position which makes the occupant to contribute to the formation of a general spirit and temper, in so influential a class of men as the clerical! Well may such an one say, Who is sufficient for this thing? For myself, I should shrink altogether from this toil, and this responsibility, did I not dare to hope that the providence of that Being, who is the sovereign controller of all tendencies and all movements in the universe, has led me hither. In his strength would I labor, and to Him would I reverently commend myself and this institution.

THE RELATION OF LANGUAGE, AND STYLE, TO THOUGHT.*

"It is a truth," (says Hartung in beginning his subtle and profound work on the Greek Particles,) "as simple as it is fruitful, that language is no arbitrary, artificial, and gradual invention of the reflective understanding, but a necessary and organic product of human nature, appearing contemporaneously with the activity of thought. Speech is the correlate of thought; both require and condition each other like body and soul, and are developed at the same time and in the same degree, both in the case of the individual and the nation. Words are the coinage of conceptions freeing themselves from the dark chaos of intimations and feelings, and gaining shape and clearness. In so far as a man uses and is master of language, has he also attained clearness of thought; the developed and spoken language of a people is its expressed intelligence."† Consonant with this, William Humboldt remarks that "speech must be regarded as naturally inherent in man, for it is altogether inexplicable as a work of his inventive understanding. We are none the better for allowing thousands of years for its invention.

---
* Reprinted from the Bibliotheca Sacra; Nov. 1848, and July 1851.
† Partikeln Lehre, Bd. I. §§ 1, 2.

There could be no invention of language unless its type already existed in the human mind. Man is man only by means of speech; but in order to invent speech he must be already man."

In these extracts it is asserted that language is an *organic* product of which thought is the organizing and vitalizing principle. Writers upon language have generally acknowledged a connection of some sort between thought and language, but they have not been unanimous with respect to the nature of the connection. The common assertions that language is the "dress" of thought — is the "vehicle" of thought — point to an outward and mechanical connection between the two: while the fine remark of Wordsworth that "language is not so much the dress of thought as its incarnation," and the frequent comparison of the relation which they bear to each other, with that which exists between the body and the soul, indicate that a *vital* connection is believed to exist between language and thought.

The correctness of this latter doctrine becomes apparent when it is considered that everything growing out of human nature, in the process of its development and meeting its felt wants, is of necessity *living* in its essence, and cannot be regarded as a dead mechanical contrivance. That language has such a natural and spontaneous origin is evident from the fact, that history gives no account of any language which was the direct invention of any one man, or set of men, to supply the wants of a nation utterly destitute of the ability to *express* its thought. Individuals have bestowed an alphabet, a written code of laws, useful mechanical inventions, upon their countrymen, but no individual ever bestowed a language. This has its origin in human nature, or rather in that constitutional necessity, under which hu man nature in common with all creation is placed by Him who sees the end from the beginning, which compels the invisible to become visible, the formless to take form, the intelligible to corporealize itself. That thought is invisible and spiritual in essence, is granted by all systems of philosophy excépt the coarsest and most unphilosophic materialism. It is therefore subject to the universal law, and *must* become sensuous — must be *communicated.*

In the case of the primitive language, spoken by the first human pair, we must conceive of it as a *gift* from the Creator, perfectly correspondent, like all their other endowments, to the wants of a *living soul.* As in this first instance the bodily form reached its height of being and of beauty, not through the ordinary processes of generation, birth, and growth, but as an instantaneous creation; so too the form of thought, language, passed through no stages of development (as some teach) from the inarticulate cry of the brute, to the articulate and intelligent tones of cultivated man, but came into full and finished existence simultaneously with the fiat that called the full-formed soul and body into being. It would not have been a perfect creation, had the first man stood *mute* in mature manhood, and that too in his unfallen state and amidst the beauty and glory of Eden. As the posterity of the first man come into existence by a process, and as both soul and body in their case undergo development before reaching the points of bloom and maturity, language also in their case is a slow and gradual formation. It begins with the dawn of reflective consciousness, and unfolds itself as this becomes deeper and clearer. In the infancy of a nation it is exquisitely fitted for the lyrical expression of those thoughts and feelings which rise simple and sincere in the national mind and heart, before philosophical reflection has rendered them complex, or advancing civilization has dried up their freshness. As the period of fancy and feeling passes by and that of reason and reflection comes in, language becomes more rigid and precise in its structure, conforms itself to the expression of profound thought, and history and philosophy take the place of the ballad and the chronicle.

Now the point to be observed here is, that this whole process is spontaneous and natural; is a growth and not a manufacture. Thought embodies itself, even as the merely animal life becomes sensuous and sensible through its own tendency and activity. When investigating language, therefore, we are really within the sphere of life and living organization, and to attempt its comprehension by means of mechanical principles would be as absurd as to attempt to apprehend the phenomena of the animal kingdom by the principles that regulate the investigation of inorganic nature. It is only by the application of dynamical principles, of the doctrine of life, that we can get a true view of language or be enabled to use it with power.

It is assumed then that thought is the life of language; and this too in no figurative sense of the word, but in its strict scientific signification as denoting the principle that organizes and vivifies the form in which it makes its appearance. It is assumed that thought is as really the living principle of language as the soul is the life of the body, and the assumption verifies itself by the clearness which it introduces into the investigation of the subject, and by the light which it flares into its darker and more mysterious parts. That *fusion*, for instance, of the thoughts with the words, which renders the discourse of the poet glowing and tremulous with feeling and life can be explained upon no other supposition than that the immaterial entity born of beauty in the poet's mind actually materializes itself, and thus enlivens the otherwise lifeless syllables. Nothing but a *vital* connection with the thoughts that breathe, can account for the words that burn.

We are not therefore to look upon language as having intrinsic existence, separate from the thought which it conveys, but as being *external* thought, *expressed* thought. Words were not first invented, and then assigned to conceptions as their arbitrary, and intrinsically meaningless signs; mere indices, having no more inward connection with the things indicated, than the algebraic marks, + and —, have with the notions of increase and diminution. In the order of nature, language follows rather than precedes thought, and is subject to all its modifications from its first rise in the consciousness of the individual and the nation, up to that of the philosopher and the philosophic age in a nation's history. Language in essence is thought, is thought in an outward form, and consequently cannot exist, or be the object of reflection dissevered from the vital principle which substantiates it. The words of the most thoughtless man do nevertheless contain some meaning, and words have effect upon us only in proportion as they are filled with thought.

And this fulness must not be conceived of as flowing into empty moulds already prepared. It is a statement of one of the most profound investigators of physical life, that the living power merely *added* to the dead organ is not life;* i. e. that no intensity whatever of physical life

* Carus' Physiologie, Bd. 1. Vorrede. He denies the correctness of the following formula upon which, he affirms, the mechanical school of physiologists proceeds: todtes Organ + Kraft = Leben.

streamed upon and through a *dead* hand lying upon a dissecting table can produce life in the form of the living member. The living member cannot come into existence except as growing out of a living body, and the living body cannot come into existence unless life, the immaterial and invisible, harden into the materiality and burst into the visibility of a minute seminal point which teems and swells with the whole future organism; a point or dot of life from which as a centre, the radiation, the organization, and the circulation may commence. In like manner it is impossible, if it were conceivable, to produce human language by the superinduction of thought upon, or by the assignation of meaning to, a mass of unmeaning sounds already in existence. When a conception comes into the consciousness of one mind, and seeks expression that it may enter the consciousness of another mind, it must be conceived of as uttering itself in a word which is not taken at hap-hazard, and which might have been any other arbitrary sound, but which is *prompted* and *formed* by the creative thought struggling out of the world of mind, and making use of the vocal organs in order to enter the world of sense.

We cannot, it is true, verify all this by reference to all the words we are in the habit of using every day, because we are too far off from the period of their origin, and because they are oftentimes combinations of simple sounds that were originally formed by vocal organs differing from our own by marked peculiarities, yet the simplicity and naturalness of the Greek of Homer, or the English of Chaucer, which is no other than the affinity of the language with the thought, the sympathy of the sound with the sense, cause us to *feel* what in the present state of philology most certainly cannot be proved in the case of every single word, that primarily, in the root and heart, language is self-embodied thought. Yet though it is impossible at present in the case of every single word to verify the assumption upon which we have gone, it is not difficult to do this in the case of that portion of the language in which there is emphasis and intensity of meaning. The verb, by which action and suffering (which in the animal world is but a calmer and more intense activity) are expressed, is a word often and evidently suited to the thought. Those nouns which are names not of things but of acts and energies, are likewise exceedingly significant of the things signified. The motions of the mouth, the position of the organs, and the tension of the muscles of speech, in the utterance of such words as *shock, smite, writhe, slake, quench,* are produced by the force and energy and character of the conceptions which these words communicate, just as the prolonged relaxation of the organs and muscles in the pronunciation of *soothe, breathe, dream, calm,* and the like, results naturally from the nature of the thought of which they are the vocal embodiment.

And this leads us to notice that this view of the origin and nature of language acquires additional support from considering that the vocal sound is the product of physical organs which are started into action and directed in their motion by the soul itself.* Even the tones of the animal are suited to the inward feeling by the particular play of muscles and organs of utterance. The feeling of pleasure *could* not, so long as nature is herself, twist these muscles and organs into the emission of the sharp scream of physical agony, any more than it could light up the eye with the glare and flash of rage.

Now if this is true in the low sphere of animal exist-

* See on this point Wallis's English Grammar, and Hearne's Langtoft's Chronicle, Vol. I. Preface.

ence, it is still more true in the sphere of intellectual and moral existence. If life is true to itself in the lower, it is true to itself in the higher realm of its manifestation. When full of earnest thought and feeling the mind *uses* the body at will, and the latter naturally and spontaneously subserves the former. As thought becomes more and more earnest, and feeling more and more glowing, the body bends and yields with increasing pliancy, down to its minutest fibres and most delicate tissues, to the working of the engaged mind; the organs of speech become one with the soul, and are swayed and wielded by it. The word is, as it were, *put into the mouth*, by the vehement and excited spirit.

>When the mind is quickened, out of doubt,
>The organs, though defunct and dead before,
>Break up their drowsy grave and newly move
>With casted slough and fresh legerity.*

As well might it be said that there is no vital and natural connection between the feeling and the blush in which it mantles, or the tear in which it finds vent, as that the word—the "*winged word*"—has only an arbitrary and dead relation to the thought.

Again, it is generally conceded that there is an inherent fitness of gesture, attitude and look, to the thought or feeling conveyed by them; but do attitude, gesture, and look, sustain a more intimate relation to thought and feeling than language does; language, at once the most universal as well as most particular in its application, the most exhaustive and perfect, of all the media of communication between mind and mind, between heart and heart? The truth is, that *all* the media through which thought becomes sensuous and communi-

* Henry IV. Act IV. Sc. 1.

cable are in greater or less degree, yet in *some* degree, *nomogeneous and con-natural with thought itself*. In other words they all, in a greater or less degree, possess manifest propriety.

It is to be borne in mind here, that the question is not whether thought could not have embodied itself in other forms than it has, whether other languages could not have arisen, but whether the existing forms possess adaptedness to the thought they convey. Life is not compelled to manifest itself in one only form, or in one particular set of forms, in any of the kingdoms, but it *is* compelled to make the form in which it does appear, vital like itself. The forms, for aught that we know, may be infinite in number, in which the invisible principle may become sensible, but the *corpse* is no one of them.

Thought as the substance of discourse is logical, necessary, and immutable, in its nature, while language as the form is variable. The language of a people is continually undergoing a change, so that those who speak it in its later periods, (it very often happens,) would be unintelligible to those who spoke it in its earlier ages. Chaucer cannot be read by Englishmen of the present day without a glossary.* Again, the languages of different nations differ from each other. There is great variety in the changes of the verb to express the passive form. The subject is sometimes included in the verb, sometimes is prefixed, and sometimes is suffixed to it. The Malay language assumes the plural instead of the

---

* Yet even in this case, as Wordsworth truly remarks, " the *affecting* parts are almost always expressed in language pure, and universally intelligible even to this day."—*Preface to Lyrical Ballads*. The more *intense* and *vital* the thought, the nearer the form approaches the essence, the more universal does it become.

singular as the basis of number, all nouns primarily denoting the plural. Some use the dual and some do not; some give gender and number to adjectives, and others do not; some have the article and some have not. And yet all these different languages are equally embodiments of thought, and of the same thought substantially. For the human mind is everywhere, and at all times, subject to the invariable laws of its own constitution, and that logical, immutable, truth which stands over against it as its correlative object, is developed in much the same way among all nations in whom the intellect obtains a development. The vital principle—logical, immutable, truth in the form of human thought—is here seen embodying itself in manifold forms, with freedom and originality, and with an expressive suitableness in every instance.

That a foreign language does not seem expressive to the stranger is no argument against the fundamental hypothesis. It is expressive to the native-born, and become so to the stranger in proportion as he acquires (not a mere mechanical and book knowledge, but) a vital and vernacular knowledge of it. And this expressiveness is not the result of custom. Apart from the instinctive association of a certain word with a certain conception, there is an instinctive sense of its intrinsic fitness to communicate the thought intended—of its expressiveness. For why should some words be *more* expressive than others, if they all equally depend upon the law of association for their significance? And why is a certain portion of every language more positive, emphatic, and intense, than the remaining portions? There is in every language a class of words which are its life and life-blood, a class to which the mind, in its fervor and glow, *instinctively* betakes itself in order to free itself of its thoughts in the most effective and satisfactory manner. But this is irreconcilable with the hypothesis that all words are but lifeless signs, acquiring their signification and *apparent* suitableness from use and custom, and all consequently being upon the same dead level with respect to expressiveness.

Still another proof that the connection between language and thought is organic, is found in the fact that the relation between the two is evidently that of action and reaction.

We have seen that language is the produce of thought but this is not to be understood as though language were a mere *effect*, of which thought is the mere *cause*. The mere effect cannot *react* upon the pure cause. It is thrown off and away from its cause (as the cannon ball is from the cannon), so that it stands insulated and independent with respect to its origin.

This is not the case with language. Originated by thought, and undergoing modifications as thought is developed, it, in turn, exerts a reflex influence upon its originating cause. In proportion as language is an exact and sincere expression, does thought itself become exact and sincere. The more appropriate and expressive the language, the more correct will be the thought, and the more expressive and powerful will be the direction which thought takes.

But if language were a mechanical invention, no such reaction as this could take place upon the inventor. While connected with thought only by an arbitrary compact on the part of those who made use of it, it would be *separated* from thought by origin and by nature. Not being a living and organic product, it could sustain to thought only the external and lifeless relation of cause and effect, and consequently would remain one and the same amid all the life, motion, and modification, which the immaterial principle might undergo.

Of course if such were the relation between the two, it would be impossible to account for all that unconscious but real *change* ever going on in a spoken language, which we call *growth* and *progress*. Language upon such an hypothesis would remain stationary in substance, and at best could be altered only by aggregation from without. New words might be invented and added to the number already in existence, but no change could occur in the spirit of the language, if it may be allowed to speak of spirit in such a connection.

Furthermore, if there is no vital relation between language and thought, it would be absurd to speak of the beneficial influence upon mental development (which is but the development of thought) of the study of philology. If in strict literality the relation of language to thought is that of the invention to the mind of the inventor, then the study of this outward, and in itself lifeless instrument, would be of no worth in developing an essence so intensely vital, so full of motion, and with such an irrepressible tendency to development, as the human mind.

It is however a truth and a fact that the study of a well organized language is one of the very best means of mental education. It brings the mind of the student into communication with the whole mind of a nation, and infuses into his culture its good and bad elements —the whole genius and spirit of the people of whose mind it is the evolution. In no way can the mind of the individual be made to feel the power and influence of the mind of the race, and thereby receive the greatest possible enlargement and liberalizing, so well as by the philosophic study of language A rational method of education makes use of this study as an indispensable discipline, and selects for this purpose two languages distinguished for the intimate relation which they sustain to the particular forms of thought they respectively express. For the Greek language is so fused and one with Grecian thought, that it is living to this day, and has been the source of life to literature ever since its revival in the fifteenth century; and the rigid but majestic Latin is the exact embodiment of the organizing and imperial ideas of Rome.

These languages exhibit the changes of thought in the Greek and Roman mind. They take their form and derive their spirit from the peculiarities of these nations. Hence the strong and original influence which they exert upon the modern mind. If these languages really contained no tincture of the intellect that made them and made use of them, if they communicated none of the spirit of antiquity, they would indeed be "dead" languages for all purposes of mental enlivening and development.

But it is not so. The Greek and Roman mind with all that passed through it, whether it were thought or feeling, whether it were individual or national, instead of remaining in the sphere of consciousness merely, and thus being kept from the ken of all after ages, projected itself, as it were, into these fine languages, into these noble forms, and not only became a κτῆμα ἐς ἀεί for mankind, but also a possession with whose characteristics the possessor is in sympathy, and from which he derives intellectual nourishment and strength.

A further proof that language has a living connection with thought, is found in the fact that feeling and passion suggest language.

Feeling and passion are the most vital of all the activities of the human soul, flowing as they do from the heart, and that which is prompted by them may safely be affirmed to have life. That words the most expressive and powerful fly from the lips of the impassioned thinker is notorious. The man who is naturally of few words, becomes both fluent and appropriate in the use of language, when his mind glows with his subject and feeling is awakened.

But the use of language is the same in kind and character with its origin. The processes through which language passes from the beginning to the end of its existence are all of the same nature. As in the wide sphere of the universe, preservation is a constant creation, and the things that are, are sustained and perpetuated on principles in accordance with the character impressed upon them by the creative fiat, so in all the narrower spheres of the finite, the use and development are coincident and harmonious with the origin and nature. We may therefore argue back from the use and development to the origin and nature; and when we find that in all periods of its history human language is suggested, and that too in its most expressive form, by feeling and passion, we may infer that these had to do in its origin, and have left something of themselves in its nature. For how could there be a point and surface of communication between words and feeling, so that the latter should start out the former in all the freshness of a new creation, if there were no *interior* connection between them. For language as it falls from the lips of passion is tremulous with life—with the life of the soul — and imparts the life of the soul to all who hear it.

If, then, in the actual every-day use of language, we find it to be suggested by passion, and to be undergoing changes both in form and signification, without the intervention of a formal compact on the part of men, it is just to infer that no such compact called it into existence. If, upon watching the progress and growth of a language, we find it in continual flux and reflux, and detect everywhere in it, change and motion, without any consciously directed effort to this end on the part of those who speak it, it is safe to infer that the same unconscious spontaneousness characterized it in its beginning. Moreover, if in every-day life we unconsciously, yet really, use language not as a lifeless sign of our thought, but believe that in employing it we are really expressing our mind, and furthermore, if we never in any way agreed to use the tongue which we drank in with our mother's milk, but were born into it and grew up into its use, even as we were born into and grew up under the intellectual and moral constitution imposed upon human nature by its Creator, we may safely conclude that language, too, is a provision on the part of the author of our being, and consequently is organic and alive.

Indeed, necessity of speech, like necessity of religion and government and social existence, is laid upon man by his constitution, and as in these latter instances whatever secondary arrangements may be made by circumstances, the primary basis and central form is fixed in human nature, so in the case of language, whatever may be the secondary modifications growing out of national differences and peculiarities of vocal organs, the deep ground and source of language is the human constitution itself.

Frederick Schlegel, after quoting Schiller's lines:

> Thy knowledge, thou sharest with superior spirits;
> Art, oh man! thou hast alone,

calls language "the general, all-embracing *art* of man." This is truth. For language is embodiment—the embodiment not indeed of one particular idea in a material form, but of thought at large, in an immaterial yet sensible form. And the fact that the material used is sound—the most ethereal of media—imparts to this "all embracing art" a spirituality of character that raises it above many of the fine arts, strictly so called. It is an embodiment of the spiritual, yet not in the coarse elements of matter. When the spiritual passes from the intelligible to the sensible world by means of art, there is a coming down from the pure ether and element of *incorporeal* beauty into the lower sphere of the defined and sensuous. The pure abstract idea necessarily loses something of its purity and abstractedness by becoming embodied. By coming into appearance for the sense it ceases to be in its ineffable, original, highest state for the reason—for the pure intelligence. Art, therefore, is degradation—a stooping to the limitations and imperfections of the material world of sense, and the feeling awakened by the form, however full it may be of the idea, is not equal in purity, depth, and elevation, to the direct beholding of the idea itself in spirit and in truth.*

We may, therefore, add to the assertion of Schlegel, and say, that language is also the highest art of man.—With the exceptions of poetry and oratory, all the fine arts are hampered in the full, free, expression of the idea by the uncomplying material. Poetry and oratory, in

---

* It is interesting in this connection to notice that the Puritan, though generally charged with a barbarian ignorance of the worth of art, nevertheless in practice took the only strictly philosophic view of it. That stripping flaying hatred of form, *per se*, which he manifested, grew out of a (practically) intensely philosophic mind which clearly saw the true relation of the form to the idea—of the sensible to the spiritual.

common with language, by employing the most ethereal of media, approach as near as is possible for embodiments to the nature of that which they embody; but the latter is infinitely superior to the two former, by virtue of its infinitely greater range, and power of exhaustive expression. Poetry and eloquence are confined to the particular and individual, while language seeks to embody thought in all its relations and transitions, and feeling in all its manifoldness and depth. The sphere in which it moves, and of which it seeks to give an outward manifestation is the whole human consciousness, from its rise in the individual, on through all its modifications in the race. It seeks to give expression to an inward experience, that is " co-infinite with human life itself."

Viewed in this aspect, human language ceases to be the insignificant and uninteresting phenomenon it is so often represented to be, and appears in all its real meaning and mystery. It is an *organization*, as wonderful as any in the realm of creation, built up by a necessary tendency of human nature seeking to provide for its wants, and constructed too, upon the principles of that universal nature, which Sir Thomas Brown truly affirms to be "the art of God." * Contemplate, for a moment, the Greek language as the product of this tendency, and necessity, to express his thought imposed upon man by creation. This wonderful structure could not have been put together by the cunning contrivance, and adopted by the formal consent, of the nation, and it certainly was not preserved and improved in this manner. Its pliancy and copiousness and precision and vitality and harmony,

---

* Die philosophische Bildung der Sprachen, die vorzuglich noch an der ursprünglichen sichtbar wird, ist ein wahrhaftes durch den Mechanismus des menschlichen Geistes gewirktes Wunder. — Schelling's vom Ich. u. s. w. § 3.

whereby it is capable of expressing all forms of thought, from the simplicity of Herodotus to the depth of Plato, are qualities which the unaided and mechanizing understanding of man could not have produced. They grew spontaneously, and gradually, out of the fundamental characteristics of the Grecian mind, and are the natural and pure expression of Grecian thought. Contemplate, again, our own mother tongue as the product of this same foundation for speech laid in human nature by its constitution. Its native strength and energy and vividness, and its acquired copiousness and harmony, as exhibited in the simple artlessness of Chaucer, and " the stately and regal argument" of Milton, are what might be expected to characterize the Latinized Saxon.

A creative power, deeper and more truly artistic than the inventive understanding, produced these languages. It was that plastic power, by which man creates form for the formless, and which, whether it show itself universally in the production of a living language, or particularly in the works of the poet or painter, is the crowning power of humanity. In view of the wonderful harmonies and symmetrical gradations of these languages, may we not apply the language of Wordsworth:

> Point not these mysteries to an art
> Lodged above the starry pole,
> Pure *modulations* flowing from the heart
> Of Divine love, where wisdom, beauty, truth,
> With order dwell, in endless youth. *

We should not, however, have a complete view of the relation of language to thought, if we failed to notice that in its best estate it is an imperfect expression. — Philosophy ever labors under the difficulty of finding

---

* Power of Sound.

terms by which to communicate its subtle and profound discoveries, and there are feelings that are absolutely unutterable. Especially is this true of religious thought and feeling. There is a limit within this profound domain beyond which human speech cannot go, and the hushed and breathless spirit must remain absorbed in the awful intuition. Here, as throughout the whole world of life, the principle obtains but an imperfect embodiment. There is ever something more perfect and more glorious beyond what appears. The intelligible world cannot be entirely exhausted, and therefore it is the never-failing source of substantial principle and creative life. In the case before us, truth is entirely exhausted by no language whatever. There are depths not yet penetrated by consciousness, and who will say that even the consciousness of such a thinker as Plato can have had a complete expression, even through such a wonderful medium as the Greek tongue? The human mind is connected with the Divine mind, and thereby with the whole abyss of truth; and hence the impossibility of completely sounding even the human mind, or of giving complete utterance to it; and hence the possibility and the basis of an unending development for the mind and an unending growth for language.

We are aware that the charge of obscurity may be brought against the theory here presented, by an advocate of the other theory of the origin and nature of language. We have no disposition to deny the truth of the charge, only adding that the obscurity, so far as it pertains to the theory (in distinction from the presentation of the theory, for which the individual is responsible,) is such as grows out of the very nature and depth and absolute truth of the theory itself. We have gone upon the supposition that human language, as a form, is neither hollow nor lifeless — that it has a living principle, and that this principle is thought. Now life is and must be mysterious; and at no point more so than when it begins to organize itself into a body. Furthermore, the spontaneous, and to a great extent, *unconscious* processes of life, are and must be mysterious. The method of genius — one of the highest forms of life — in the production of a Hamlet, or Paradise Lost, or the Transfiguration, has not yet been *explained*, and the method of human nature, by which it constructs for itself its wonderful medium of communication — by which it externalizes the whole inner world of thought and feeling — cannot be rendered plain like the working of a well poised and smoothly running machine throwing off its manufactures.

Simply asking then of him who would render all things clear by rendering all things shallow, *by whom*, *when*, *where*, and *how*, the Greek language, for example, was invented, and by what historical compact it came to be the language of the nation, we would turn away to that nobler, more exciting, and more rational theory, which regards language to be " a necessary and organic product of human nature, appearing contemporaneously and parallel with the activity of thought." This theory of the origin of language throws light over all departments of the great subject of philology, finds its gradual and unceasing verification as philological science advances under a spur and impulse derived from this very theory, and ends in that philosophical insight into language, which, after all, is but the clear and full intuition of its mystery — of its life.

Having thus specified the general relation of language to thought, we naturally turn to the uses and applications of the theory itself. Its truth, value, and fruitfulness, are nowhere more apparent than in the department of Rhetoric and Criticism. For this department takes special cognizance of the more living and animated forms of speech — of the glow of the poet, and the fire of the orator. It also investigates all those peculiarities of construction, and form, in human composition that spring out of individual characteristics. It is, therefore, natural to suppose that a theory of language which recognizes a power in human thought to organize and vivify and modify the forms in which it appears, will afford the best light in which to examine those forms; just as it is natural to suppose that the commonly received theory of physical life, will furnish a better light in which to examine vegetable and animal productions, than a theory like that of Descartes, e. g. which maintains that the forms and functions in the animal kingdom are the result of a mechanical principle. Life itself is the best light in which to contemplate living things.

We propose therefore in the remainder of this essay to follow the same general method already pursued, and examine the nature of style, by pointing out its relation to thought.

Style is the particular manner in which thought flows out, in the case of the individual mind, and upon a particular subject. When, therefore, it has, as it always should have, a free and spontaneous origin, it partakes of the peculiarity both of the individual and of the topic upon which he thinks. A genuine style, therefore, is the free and pure expression of the individuality of the thinker and the speciality of the subject of thought.— Uniformity of style is consequently found in the productions of the same general cast of mind, applied to the same general class of subjects, so that there is no distinguishable period in the history of a nation's literature, but what exhibits a style of its own. The spirit of the age appears in the general style of its literary composition, and the spirit of the individual — the tone of his mind — nowhere comes out more clearly than in his manner of handling a subject. The grave, lofty, and calm, style of the Elizabethan age is an exact representation of the spirit of its thinking men. The intellectual temperament of the age of Queen Anne flows out in the clear, but diffuse and nerveless, style of the essayists.

From this it is easy to see that style, like language, has a spontaneous and natural origin, and a living connection with thought. It is not a manner of composing, arbitrarily or even designedly chosen, but rises of its own accord, and in its own way, in the general process of mental development. The more unconscious its origin, and the more strongly it partakes of the individuality of the mind, the more genuine is style. Only let it be carefully observed in this connection, that a *pure* and *sincere* expression of the individual peculiarity is intended. Affectation of originality and studied effort after peculiarity produce *mannerism*, in distinction from that manner of pure nature, which alone merits the name of style.

If this be true, it is evident that the union of all styles, or of a portion of them, would not constitute a perfect style. On the contrary, the excellence of style consists in its having a bold and determined character of its own — in its bearing the genuine image and superscription of an individual mind at work upon a particular subject. In a union of many different styles, there would be nothing simple, bold, and individual. The union would be a mixture, rather than a union, in which each ingredient would be neutralized by all, and all by each, leaving a residuum characterless, spiritless, and lifeless.

Style, in proportion as it is genuine and excellent, is

sincere and artless. It is the free and unconscious emanation of the individual nature. It alters as the individual alters. In early life it is ardent and adorned; in mature life it is calm and grave. In youth it is flushed with fancy and feeling; in manhood it is sobered by reason and reflection. But in both periods it is the genuine expression of the man. The gay manner of L'Allegro and Comus is as truly natural and spontaneous, as the grave and stately style of Paradise Regained and Samson Agonistes. The individuality of a man like Milton passes through great varieties of culture and of mood, and there is seen a corresponding variety in the ways in which it communicates itself; yet through this variety there runs the unity of nature; each sort of style is the sincere and pure manner of the same individual taken in a particular stage of his development.

No one style, therefore, can be said to be the best of all absolutely, but only relatively. That is the best style relatively to the individual, in which his particular cast of thought best utters itself, and in which the peculiarity of the individual has the fullest and freest play. That may be called a good style generally, in which every word *tells* — in which the language is full of thought, and alive with thought, and so fresh and vigorous as to seem to have been just created — while at the same time the characteristics of the mind that is pouring out in this particular manner, are all in every part, as the constructing and vivifying principle.

The truth of this view of style is both confirmed and illustrated by considering the unity in variety exhibited by the human mind itself. The mind of man is one and the same in its constitution and necessary laws, so that the human race may be said to be possessed of one universal intelligence. In the language of one of the most elegant and philosophic of English critics,* " It is no unpleasing speculation to see how the *same reason*, has at all times prevailed: how there is *one truth*, like one sun, that has enlightened human intelligence through every age, and saved it from the darkness of sophistry and error." Upon this sameness of intelligence rest all absolute statements, and all universal appeals. Over against this universal human mind, as its corresponding object and counterpart, stands truth, universal in its nature and one and the same in its essence.

But besides this unity of the universal, there is the variety of the individual, mind. Truth, consequently, coming into consciousness in the form of thought in an individual mind, undergoes modifications. It is now contemplated not as universal and abstract, but as concrete and in its practical relations. It is, moreover, seen, not as an unity, but in its parts, and one side at a time. Philosophical truth in Plato differs from philosophical truth in Aristotle, by a very marked modification. Poetical truth is one thing in Homer and another in Virgil. Religious truth assumes a strikingly different form in Paul and Luther, from that which it wears in John and Melanchthon. And yet poetry, philosophy, and religion, have each their universal principles — their one abstract nature. Each, however, *appears* in the form imposed upon it by the individual mind; each wears that tinge of the mind through which it has passed, which is denominated style.

No man has yet appeared whose individuality was so comprehensive and universal, and who was such a master of form, that he exhausted the whole material of poetry, or philosophy, or religion, and exhibited it in a style

---

* Harris. Preface to Hermes.

and form absolutely universal and final. Enough is ever left of truth, even after the most comprehensive presentation, for another individuality to show it in still a new and original form. For there is no limit to the manner of contemplating infinite and universal truth. Provided only there be a peculiarity — a particular type of the human mind — there will be a peculiarity of intuition, and consequently of exhibition.

The most comprehensive and universal individual mind was that of Shakspeare, and hence his productions have less of style, of peculiar manner, than all other literary productions. Who can describe the style of Shakspeare? Who is aware of his style? The style of Milton is apparent in every line, for he was one of the most *sui-generic* of men. But the form which truth takes in Shakspeare, is as comprehensive and universal as the drama, as all mankind. This is owing to that Protean power by which, for the purposes of dramatic art, he converts himself into other men, takes their consciousness, and thereby temporarily loses his own limited individuality. But that Shakspeare was an individual, that a peculiar type of humanity formed the basis of his personal being, and that he had a style of thought of his own, it would be absurd to doubt. And had he attempted other species of composition than the drama, (which by its very nature requires that the individuality of the author be sunk and lost entirely in the various characters,) had he taken, like Milton, a particular theme as the "great argument" for his poetic power, doubtless the *man*, the *individual*, would have come into sight.*

---

* In corroboration of this, it may be remarked that we have far more sense of the *individuality* of Shakspeare, while perusing his poems and sonnets, than while studying his dramas.

Style of expression thus springing out of the style of thought, is therefore immediately connected with the structure and character of the individual mind. It consequently has an unconscious origin. On the basis laid in the individual's characteristics, and by and through the individual's mental growth, his manner of expression is formed. There is a certain style which fits the individual — which, and no other, is *his* style. It is that manner of presenting thought, into which he naturally falls, when his mind is deeply absorbed in a subject, and when he gives no heed to the form into which his thought is running.

It is not to be inferred from this, that style has no connection with culture. It has a most immediate and vital connection with the individual's education. Not only all that he is by nature, but all that he becomes by culture, tends to form his style of thought and expression; but, be it observed, *unconsciously* to him. For an incessant aim, a conscious, anxious effort to form a given style, is the destruction of style. Under such an inspection and oversight, Nature cannot work, even if the mind under such circumstances, could absorb itself in the theme of reflection. There must be no consciousness during the time and process of composing, but of the subject. The subject being all in all, for the thinker, the form into which his thought runs, with all the modification and coloring which it really, though *unconsciously* to him, receives from his individualism, and from the whole past of his education, is his *style* — his genuine and true manner.

The point to be observed here is, that style is the *consequent*, so far as it is related to culture. For, the culture itself takes its direction and character from the original tendency of the individual, (for every one in the end obtains a mental development coincident with his mental bias,) and style is but the unconscious manifestation of this culture. Style — genuine style — can never be the conscious antecedent of culture. It cannot be first selected, and then the whole individuality of the mind, and the whole course of education, be forced to contribute to its realization. One cannot antecedently choose the style of Burke, e. g. as that which he would have for his own, and then deliberately realize his choice. It is true that a mind similar to that of Burke in its structure, and in sympathy with him through a similarly fruitful and opulent culture, would spontaneously form its style upon, and with, his. But the process, in this case, would not be a deliberate and conscious imitation, but an unconscious and genial reproduction. It would be the consequent of nature and of culture, and not the antecedent. The individual would not distinctly know that his was the style of Burke, until it became apparent to others that it actually was.

Here, too, as in every sphere in which the *living* soul of man works, do we find the genuine and beautiful product originating freely, spontaneously, and unconsciously. Freely, for it might have been a false and deformed product, yet spontaneously and unconsciously, for it cannot be the subject of reflection and matter of distinct knowledge until *after* it has come into existence. By the thronging stress and tendency of the human soul, which is so created as to contain within itself the principle and direction of its own movement, is the product originated, which then, and not till then, is the possible and legitimate subject of consciousness, analysis, and criticism. The style of a thinking mind is no exception to this universal law. It is formed, when formed according to nature — when formed as it was destined to be, by that creative idea which prescribes the whole never-ending development of the creature — it is formed out of what is laid in the individual constitution, and through what is brought in by the individual culture, unconsciously to the subject of the process, and yet freely, so far as his nature and constitution are concerned.

If the view that has been taken of style, be correct, it is evident, that in the formation of style, no attempt should be made to change the fundamental character imposed upon it by the individual constitution. The type is fixed by nature, and no one should strive, by forcing nature, to obtain a manner essentially alien and foreign to him. The sort of style which belongs to the individual by his intellectual constitution is to be taken as given. The direction which all culture in this relation takes, should proceed from this as a point of departure, and all discipline and effort should end in an acquisition that is homogeneous with this *substantial ground* of style. Or still more accurately, the individuality itself is to be deepened and made more capacious and distinct, by culture, and is then to be poured forth in that *hearty unconscious* purity of manner which is its proper and genuine style.

And this leads us to consider the true method of forming and cultivating style.

If the general view that has been presented of the nature both of language and style be correct, it is plain that the mind itself, rather than the style itself, should receive the formation and the cultivation. Both language and style are but *forms* in which the human mind embodies its thought, and therefore the *mind*, considered as the originating power — as that which is to find an utterance and expression — should be the chief object of culture, even in relation to style. A cultivated mind con tains within itself resources sufficient for all its purposes. The direct cultivation of the mind, is the indirect cultivation of all that stands connected with it.

And this is eminently true of the formal, in distinction from the material departments of knowledge — of those "organic (or instrumental) arts," as Milton calls them, "which enable men to discourse and write perspicuously, elegantly, and according to the fitted style of lofty, mean or lowly." For inasmuch as these formal departments of knowledge are not self-sufficient, but derive their substance from the material departments, it is plain that they can be cultivated with power and success only through the cultivation of these latter. Rhetoric, in order to be anything more than an idle play with words and figures of speech — in order to a substantial existence, and an energetic power — must spring out of logic; and logic again, in order to be something more than a dry and useless permutation of the members of syllogisms, must be grounded in the necessary laws of thought, and so become but the inevitable and the living movement of reason. Thus are we led in from the external to the internal as the solid ground of action and origination, and are made to see that the culture must begin here, in every instance, and work out. All these arts and sciences are the architecture of the rational and thinking mind of man, and all changes in them, either in the way of growth or decline, proceed from a change that has first taken place in their originating ground. They are in reality the index of the human mind, and show with most delicate sensibility all that is passing, in this ever-moving principle. What are the languages literatures, laws, governments, and (with one exception) religions of the globe but the history of the human mind — the outstanding monument of what it has *thought!*

It may be said with perfect truth, therefore, that the formation and cultivation of the mind, is the true method of forming and cultivating style. And there are two qualities in mental culture which exert such a direct and powerful influence upon style as to merit in this connection a particular and close examination. They are depth and clearness.

By depth of culture is meant that development of the mind *from its centre*, which enables it to exert its very best power, and to accomplish the utmost of which it is capable. The individual mind differs in respect to innate capacity. Some men are created with a richer and more powerful intellectual constitution than others. But all are capable of a *profound* culture; of a development that shall bring out the entire contents and capacity, be they more or less. By going to the centre of the mind— by setting into play those profounder faculties which though differing in degree, are yet the same in kind, in every man—a culture is attained that exerts a most powerful and excellent influence upon style. Such mental education gives *body* to style. It furnishes the material which is to *fill* the language and *solidify* the discourse. The form in which a profoundly cultivated mind expresses itself is never hollow; the language which it employs not being alone—mere words—is never dead. It may, perhaps, be silent at times, for such a mind is not necessarily fluent, but when it *does* speak, the product has a marked character. The thought and its expression form an identity; are coined at one stroke.

For a deeply educated mind spontaneously seeks to know truth in its reality, and to express it in its simplicity. Unconsciously, because it is its nature to do so, it penetrates to the heart of a subject, and discourses upon it with a simplicity and directness which precludes any separation between the thought and the words in which it is conveyed. The mind which has but a superficial knowledge of the subject-matter of its discourse cannot render the language it employs *consubstantial* with its thought. We feel that the words have been *hunted up* by a vacant mind, instead of *prompted* by a full one. Thought and language stand apart, because thought has not reached that degree of profundity, and that point of clear intuition, and that height of energy, in consciousness, at which it utters itself in language that is truly one with itself, and alive with itself. Whenever a profoundly cultivated mind directs itself to an object of contemplation it becomes identical with it, while in the act of contemplation. The distinction between the contemplating subject, and the contemplated object, vanishes for the time being; the mind, as we say popularly, and yet with strict philosophic truth, is *lost* in the theme, and the theme during this temporary process, becomes but a particular state of the mind. The object of contemplation, which at first was *before* the mind is now *in* the mind; that to which the mind came up as to a thing objective and extant, has now been transmuted into the very consciousness of the mind itself, and is therefore the mind itself, *taken and held in this temporary process.** It fol-

* The doctrine of the identity of subject and object in the act of consciousness is a true and safe one, it seems to us, only when stated with the limitation above; only when the identity is regarded as merely *relative*—as existing only *in, and during the act of consciousness.* If, however, the identity is regarded as *absolute* and *essential*—if it be asserted that, apart from consciousness and back of consciousness, the subject and object, the mind and the truth, are absolutely but one essence—then we see no difference between the doctrine and that of the "substantia una et unica" of Spinoza. The identity in this case, notwithstanding the disclaimer of Schelling, is *sameness* of substance, and there is but one substance in the universe. The truth is, that sub-

lows, consequently, that the *style* in which this fusion of truth with intellect flows out, must be as near the perfection of form as it can be. The style of such a mind is similar to the style of the Infinite mind, as it is seen in nature. It is characterized by the simplicity and freedom of nature itself. Nor let this be regarded either as irreverent or extravagant. We are confessedly within the sphere of the finite and the created, and therefore are at an infinite remove from Him "who is wonderful in working," and yet there is something strongly resembling the workings of creative power, in the operations of a mind deeply absorbed in truth and full of the idea. As the Divine idea becomes a phenomenon—manifests itself in external nature—by its own movement and guidance, it necessarily assumes the very perfection of manner.—The great attributes of nature, the sublimity and beauty of creation, arise from the oneness of the form with the idea —the transfusion of mind into matter. In like manner, though in an infinitely lower sphere and degree, the human idea, profound, full, and clear in consciousness, throws itself out into language, in a style, free, simple, beautiful, and, it may be, sublime like nature itself. And all this arises because thought does its own perfect work— because truth arrived at in the consciousness of the profound thinker is simply suffered to exercise its own vitality, and to organize itself into existence. It is not so much because the individual makes an effort to embody the results of his meditation, as because these results have their own way, and take their own form, that the style of their appearance is so grand. It has been asserted above,

ject and object are not, absolutely, one essence, but two ; but *become* one temporarily, in the act of consciousness, by virtue of a *homogeneity* rather than an absolute identity, of essence.

that style, in its most abstract definition, is the universal appearing in the particular. In other words, it is the particular and peculiar manner in which the individual mind conceives and expresses truth, which is universal. Now it is only by and through *depth* of mental cultivation, that truth, in its absolute reality and in its vital energy, is reached at all. A superficial education never reaches the heart of a subject—never brings the mind into contact and fusion with the real substance of the topic of discourse. Of course, a mind thus superficially educated in reality has nothing to express. It has not reached that depth of apprehension, that central point where the solid and real truth lies, at which, and only at which, it is qualified to discourse. It may, it is true, speak *about* the given topic, but before it can speak it *out*, in a grand, impressive style, and in discourse which, while it is weighty and solid, also dilates and thrills and glows with the living verity, it must, by deep thought, have effected that *mental union* with it of which we have spoken.

A mind, on the contrary, that has received a central development, and whose power of contemplation is strong, instead of working at the surface, and about the accidents, strikes down into the heart and essence, and obtains an actual view of truth; and under the impulse imparted by it, and by the light radiated from it at all points, simply represents it. In all this there is no effort at expression— no endeavor at style—on the part of the individual. He is but the medium of communication, now that, by his own voluntary thought, the union between his mind and truth has been brought about.—All that he needs to do is, to absorb himself still more profoundly in the great theme, and to let it use him as its organ. It will flow through his individualism, and take form and hue from it, as inevitably as the formless and colorless light, acquires both form and color by coming into the beautiful arch of the sky.

By clearness, as an element in culture, is meant such an education of the mind, as arms it with a penetrating and clear vision, so that it beholds objects in distinct outline. When united with depth of culture, this element is of great worth, and diffuses through the productions of the mind some of the most desirable qualities. Depth, without clearness of intuition, is obscurity. Though there may be substantial thinking, and real truth may be reached by the mind, yet like the ὕλη out of which the material universe was formed, according to the ancient philosophy, it needs to be irradiated by light, before it becomes a defined, distinct, and beautiful form. Indeed, without clearness of intuition, truth must remain in the depths of the mind, and cannot be really expressed. The mind, without close and clear thinking, is but a dark chaos of ideas, intimations, and feelings. It is true, that in these is the substance of truth, for the human mind is, by its constitution, full of truth; yet these its contents need to be *elaborated*. These undefined ideas need to become clear conceptions; these dark and pregnant intimations need to be converted into substantial verities; and these swelling but vague feelings must acquire definition and shape; not merely that the consciousness of one mind may be conveyed over into that of another, but also in order to the mind's full understanding of itself.

And such culture manifests itself in the purity and perspicuity of the style in which it conveys its thoughts. Having a distinctly clear apprehension of truth, the mind utters its conceptions with all that simplicity and pertinence of language which characterizes the narrative of an honest eye-witness. Nothing intervenes between thought and expression. The clear, direct view, *instan-*

taneously becomes the clear, direct statement. And when the clear conception is thus united with the profound intuition, thought assumes its most perfect form. The form in which it appears, is full and round with solid truth, and yet distinct and transparent. The immaterial principle is embodied in just the right amount of matter; the former does not overflow, nor does the latter overlay. The discourse exhibits the same opposite and counterbalancing excellences which we see in the forms of nature—the simplicity and the richness, the negligence and the niceness, the solid opacity and the aërial transparence.*

* Shakspeare affords innumerable exemplifications of the characteristic here spoken of. In the following passages notice the *purity* and *cleanliness* of the style in which he exhibits his thought. As in a perfect embodiment in nature, there is nothing ragged, or to be sloughed off:

  * * * Chaste as the icicle
That's curded by the frost from purest snow,
And hangs on Dian's temple.
Coriolanus, V. 3.

* * * * * This hand
As soft as dove's down, and as white as it;
Or Ethiopian's tooth, or the fann'd snow,
That's bolted by the northern blasts twice o'er.
Winter's Tale, IV. 3.

Or if that surly spirit, melancholy,
Had baked thy blood, and made it heavy, thick;
Which else runs tickling up and down the veins.
King John, III. 3.

And I, of ladies most deject and wretched,
That sucked the honey of his music vows,
Now see that noble and most sovereign reason,
Like sweet bells jangled, out of tune, and harsh.
Hamlet, III. 1.

It is rare to find such a union of the two main elements of culture, and consequently rare to find them in style. A profoundly contemplative mind is often mystic and vague in its discourse, because it has not come to a clear, as well as profound, consciousness—because distinctness has not gone along with depth of apprehension. The discourse of such a mind is thoughtful and suggestive, it may be, but is lacking in that scientific, logical, power which penetrates and illumines. It has warmth and glow, it may be, but it is the warmth of the stove (to use the comparison of another)—warmth without light.

On the other hand, it often happens that the culture of the mind is clear but shallow. In this case nothing but the merest and most obvious commonplace is uttered, in a manner intelligible and plain enough, to be sure, but without force or weight, or even genuine fire, of style. Shallow waters show a very clear bottom, and but little intensity of light is needed in order to display the pebbles and clean sand. That must be a "purest ray serene"—a pencil of strongest light—which discloses the black, rich, wreck-strown depths. For the clearness of depth is very different from the clearness of shallowness. The former is a positive quality. It is the positive and powerful irradiation of that which is solid and dark, by that which is ethereal and light. The latter is a negative quality. It is the mere absence of darkness, because there is no substance to be dark—no *body* in which (if we may be allowed the expression) darkness can inhere. Nothing is more luminous than solid fire; nothing is more flashy than an ignited void.

These two fundamental characteristics of mental culture lie at the foundation of style. Even if the secondary qualities of style could exist without the weightiness and clearness of manner which spring from the union of profound with distinct apprehension, they would exist in vain. The ornament is worthless, if there is nothing to sustain it. The bas-relief is valueless, without the slab to support it. But these secondary qualities of style—the beauty, and the elegance, and the harmony—derive all their charm and power from springing out of the primary qualities, and in this way, ultimately, out of the deep and clear culture of the mind itself—from being the white flower of the black root.

Style, when having this mental and natural origin, is to be put into the first class of fine forms. It is the form of thought; and, as a piece of art, is as worthy of study and admiration, as those glorious material forms which embody the ideas of Phidias, Michael Angelo, and Raphael. It is the form in which the human mind manifests its freest, purest, and most mysterious activity—its thinking. There is nothing mechanical in its origin, or stale in its nature. It is plastic and fresh as the immortal energy, of which it is the air and bearing.

SCIENTIFIC AND POPULAR EDUCATION.*

THE general and growing interest in the subject of Education is one of the most hopeful features of the present age. Throughout the country, the public mind is becoming increasingly awake to the importance of knowledge, and the nation as a body is coming to regard Education as one of the great national interests. Already is it provided for and protected, as commerce, and manufactures, and agriculture are provided for; and the number is already large who clearly see and feel that it is of more importance, and exerts a far greater influence upon the perpetuity of the Republic, than any or all of the economical interests united.

There is, however, one characteristic attending this general interest upon the subject of Education which cannot but strike the eye of a thoughtful observer. It is a characteristic which, as history shows, invariably attends all action of the popular mind in proportion as this becomes more extensive and far-reaching, and a characteristic that is injurious in its influence if it does not find its counterpart and corrective. We refer to the tendency to *popularize* knowledge in an excessive degree. By this is not meant the disposition to diffuse knowledge among the greatest number possible, but the disposition to render

* Reprinted from the Bibliotheca Sacra, January, 1850.

all knowledge superficial, and *in this form* to diffuse it through society. If we mistake not, there are signs of a disposition to destroy the distinction between popular and scientific knowledge, and while engaged in the laudable effort to spread information as widely as possible among all classes, to do it at the expense of that profound and scientific culture which must exist *somewhere*, in *some* portion of the community at least, in order to the perpetuity and vitality of even the common information of society.

There is no better way of correcting this and kindred errors, than by establishing profound and comprehensive views respecting the whole subject, and the subject as a whole. It is a defective view of knowledge as a *whole*, an incomplete view of the *system* of education which lies at the bottom of the error in question. It is forgotten that the body of knowledge which is sought to be diffused is an organism with central and superficial parts, and that the complete system of instruction which proposes to impart this knowledge is an organized system, of which no better definition can be given than that all its parts are vitally connected, and are reciprocally means and ends. Popular knowledge, therefore, cannot be diffused separated from scientific knowledge, and this latter again requires to pass through the tests of popularization, in order that it may be proved to have a real and not imaginary existence; in order that it may be seen to be one with truth and real being, and not the mere figment of the brain. It will be our object, accordingly, to mark distinctly the difference between scientific and popular knowledge, and to show the necessity and worth of those institutions whose office it is to impart scientific in distinction from popular education.

Knowledge traced to its ultimate is in the form of fundamental truths. These fundamental truths, or first principles, as applied to particular cases, or run out to meet the ordinary wants of mankind, lose their scientific and profound appearance, become popular in their character, useful in their results, and go to constitute the common every-day knowledge of society. The gold originally in the form of heavy bullion has become light coin, and a useful circulating medium.

There is, for example, an amount of information diffused through society which is sufficient for the practical purposes of commerce, manufactures and agriculture; and, by virtue of the common intelligence in these departments, the ship sails swiftly, the machine works well, and the earth brings forth abundantly. But it is not expected, and under the present arrangements of society it is not rational to expect, that all who work in these spheres should possess a thorough knowledge of those principles of physics —those first truths of astronomy, and chemistry, and mechanics, and mathematics—which lie under all this action of man. And yet this body of principles, the physical *science* which is beneath this practice and practical application, is essential knowledge; sustaining the same relation to all the arts, manufactures, and improvements, all the comforts and elegancies of civilization, that the flowers and fruit of the tree sustain to the black root underground. And upon the preservation and further development of these fundamental truths, depend the permanence of the present civilization, and its progressive improvement.

Again, there is in the midst of the people an amount of information respecting legal and civil affairs, sufficient to make them careful of their personal rights, and watchful over the acts and intentions of government. No people on the face of the globe are so well informed in all that pertains to judicial and civil matters, as the people of the United States. An appeal to reason and law always goes home to the mind of the mass, and produces a deep and great movement, as it could not, if we were an uninformed and barbarous population. Still, it will not do to say that this knowledge, though adequate for all the wants of common life, is equal in degree and depth to that which is implied in a thorough understanding of the *sciences* of law and government. It will not do to say, that the great body of us are possessed of such a clear and deep insight into the first principles of legal and political philosophy as characterized the framers of the Constitution of the United States. And we do tacitly, but in a free and manly way, acknowledge this, when, in order to form or revise a code of laws or a constitution, we meet and choose the wisest and most thoughtful of our number to do this important work—a work that requires a more than ordinary and popular acquaintance with law and legislation.

Again, in this Christian land there is an amount of knowledge concerning God and the eternal world, the soul of man and its obligations, which is enough to constitute every man responsible before his Judge, and enough, if rightly improved, to bring about right relations between man and God. But, besides this common knowledge upon moral and religious subjects, there is a *science* of morals and religion, for the study and exposition of which, we are willing to sustain a particular class of men in the midst of us. It is because we desire to have our ordinary knowledge upon these highest of subjects made still more clear, and vivid, and efficacious, that we listen every Sabbath to one whose business it is to investigate and expound the *principles* of the word of God.

Thus it is apparent that when we go below the surface, and get at knowledge in its solidity and substance, we find it in the form of principles—we find it science. Below all the manifold *uses* and *applications* of knowledge, as they appear in the ordinary life of men, there lies the great deposit of primary truth, inexhaustible in itself, and ever yielding new treasures to the educated and thoughtful mind. *Now, with this lower stratum of truth mankind must have communication, or their course is backward in all respects.* New inventions in the arts soon become old and pass out of use; what at first were striking facts soon lose their novelty; the old modes of presenting those truths which from their very nature are the same yesterday, to-day, and forever, become wearisome—in fine, the floating information of a community is soon worn out, and becomes powerless, unless, from the region of principles, there is constantly coming off upon it an invigorating influence; unless the ingenious mind of a Watt or a Fulton, now and then, startles society and forms a new era in its civilization, by a wonderful application of an old but buried principle of natural philosophy; unless the thoughtful mind of a Newton pours through old science the light and life of a new principle, which to the end of time is to influence this domain of knowledge with as steady and extensive power as that of gravitation itself; unless the mighty and passionate spirit of a Luther awakens the religious consciousness of all Europe to the recognition of that great primal doctrine of Christianity, on which man's eternal life hangs.

Having said thus much upon knowledge in its scientific and in its practical form, and of the right relation of the latter to the former, we proceed to speak of *colleges* as the institutions for keeping up this right relation; as the instrumentality whereby science and practice are kept connected, and made to interpenetrate each other, to their mutual benefit, and to the growth of mankind in knowledge.

I. One way whereby colleges do this is by not suffering the distinction between scientific and practical knowledge to be lost sight of, and by keeping in existence an education that is founded upon the study of first principles.

It is the aim of the higher institutions of learning, to give what is called a "liberal" education: that is, one which is distinguished from that given in common schools, by being both more extensive and more profound. The lower institutions of learning take the mind in the earlier period of its existence, when it is best fitted for the acquisition of all that part of knowledge which is gained by the memory, while the college receives it at the beginning of that period when its powers commence their maturity, and it is prepared to get that knowledge of principles, of which we have spoken, which comes from reflection. In the theory of education adopted by our wise forefathers, and, as history shows, by all wise founders of commonwealths, the future citizen is to be surrendered to the primary school during the years of boyhood, when the imagination and memory are active, that he may learn to read and write, and may acquire all that knowledge of geography and arithmetic and history which is fitted for his years, and which will be useful in the transaction of the ordinary business of after life. When the higher faculties begin to dawn, and the years of reflection are coming in, he is then to be transferred to an institution which will guide him into the paths of science, and introduce him into that world of principles from which he is to derive, if he ever does, high moral and intellectual power, and make himself a strong man among men. Colleges and Common Schools are therefore not to be opposed to each other. Each has its own proper work to do. The one cannot do the work of the other, and even if it could, yet boyhood cannot receive the instruction of opening manhood, and calm and reflective manhood craves a more profound learning than that which satisfies inquisitive and acquisitive boyhood. The two are not independent of each other like two different machines, but are living members of the same body, and therefore the one cannot say to the other, "I have no need of thee," nor can the other say to the one, "I have no need of thee."

Colleges are thus a standing evidence of the validity of the distinction between scientific and practical knowledge. Their aim is to give an education which will develop the *mind itself*, irrespective, for the time being, of the uses that may be made of learning; knowing that if there only be produced within the youth the *power* to work, the occasions and the incitements to exercise it will not be wanting in a world that is full of work. And they do this not so much by imparting an amount of separate facts of which immediate use may be made, as by awakening the intellect of the young man to the recognition of first truths in the various departments of learning. It cannot be too carefully remembered, that a collegiate, or liberal education, differs from what is called a common education, by its having more than the latter can the *faculties* of the individual, the very mind itself, in its eye. Its object is not mainly to furnish the mind with enough to meet daily wants, but to fill it with power, and to ground it in principles, as a reserved fund upon which to draw at any time and during all time. It is a mistake to suppose that that only is useful knowledge, of which an immediate and palpable use can be made, in the acquisition of wealth, or in providing for the daily wants of the body. This is indeed useful, but it is not enough for all the exigencies of this life even, and it surely is not enough for those of the life to come. When revolutions in human affairs break out, when states are to be founded, when institutions that are to affect the progress of the race are to be established, when laws are to be made—when, in short, the primary and foundation-work, depending upon primary and fundamental truths, is to be done—then the liberal education shows itself to be the useful education. In these trying times, the reserved fund of mental power and clear intuition of principles may be drawn upon, and its untold worth be seen in the origination of a great instrument like the American Constitution, or in the start of a great idea like that of popular liberty which is to work through masses of men with superhuman power.*

We say, then, that if the distinction between the knowledge of principles and the knowledge of facts is an important one, the preservation of the distinction, and the foundation of a particular sort of education upon it, are still more important. Moreover, unless the current information of society is kept moving and alive, by the presence and the power of a system of liberal education, and by those who are yearly coming out fresh from the contact with science and principles, it speedily diminishes in amount, and loses the vitality it once possessed, and society sinks down into barbarism. The reign of barbarism began in Greece, when the liberal education of its young men fell into the hands of the sophists, who substituted the denial and disputation of first principles, for that clear and profound enunciation of them which characterized an elder day. When this class of public teachers appeared, there was a great amount of useful knowledge current in

* For some excellent thoughts upon the relation of scientific to popular knowledge, see an article upon theology, by Ullmann, in the Studien und Kritiken for 1849. The truly fruitful effort for the people and popular life, he says, is not merely the direct and immediate effort, but the thorough cultivation, also, of all those departments of knowledge whose results cannot pass over into common life, except at second hand, and by radiation.

Grecian society, but it soon betrayed the lack of that vigor which arises from the diffusion of correct principles in politics and morals, and which had kept it fresh and healthy, and not many years elapsed before this whole mass of current and common information was found to be utterly powerless towards the preservation and glory of the state when threatened by Philip, and crumbled away like some noble shaft that has been struck with the sap-rot.

Neither let it be supposed, that by making and preserving the distinction between a common and a liberal education, any injury is done to useful and practical knowledge. It is only by the maintenance and widest possible diffusion of scientific learning, that this common every-day knowledge arises and is current; for the common information of society is nothing more or less than the fine and diffusive radiance of a more substantial and profound culture. This light, spreading and penetrating in all directions, is an effluence from a ball of solid fire. All this general and practical information which distinguishes an enlightened from a savage, or though civilized yet ignorant state of society—which distinguishes England and the United States from Africa and South America—did not grow up spontaneously from the earth; is not the effect of a colder climate or a harder soil. It has been exhaling for centuries from colleges and universities; it has been distilling for ages from the alembic of the scholar's brain.

The condition of society at any one given time, must be looked upon as the total result of past institutions. It is false, and absurd, to assume that the present form of things started into being in a twinkling, and is totally unconnected with what has gone before. This is true of all that enters into the idea of social existence, but it is emphatically true of the general state of information. And if we would know why there is at this present moment such a great amount of intelligence among the descendants of English colonists, and such an entire absence of intelligence among the descendants of Spanish colonists on this western continent, we have only to remember that the English brought over books, and built churches and founded colleges simultaneously, while the Spaniards did no such thing, but attempted to found and perpetuate state governments, and to rear up society, upon the current maxims of worldly and selfish policy. If, when Hernando Cortez subjugated Mexico to the Spanish crown, and provided for the colonization of that region, he had laid such foundations for national existence and growth as were laid by the Puritans, and that population for three centuries had been feeling the vigor of just principles, in social intercourse, in legal arrangements, in government and religion, it would not be the ignorant and powerless mass it is. If he had provided for the investigation of the principles of knowledge, and for raising up a body of thoughtful and wise men, leading and powerful spirits, like those who planned and acted in the great emergency in our history, would not have been wanting in her hour of national trial.

II. And this leads us to notice a second way whereby the higher institutions of learning keep scientific and popular knowledge in connection, and thus elevate and improve the whole body of the people in a commonwealth. And this is, by constantly sending out into society *professional* men.

Most of the members of the three professions are college graduates, and the few who have raised themselves to posts of honor and usefulness by their own resolute and private study are no testimony against the fact, that professional influence is founded upon scientific knowledge. These few instances only go to show that if there is a fixed determination, a man may overcome all obstacles, and may become an eminent physician, jurist, or divine, not because of the want of direct aid from the higher institutions of learning, but in spite of that want. And even these do not acquire their knowledge entirely independent of universities. Even these must have access to a library of old books, which, one with some degree of truth has asserted to be the true university, and which, at any rate, is the expression of the thought and research of universities.

It may be said, therefore, without fear of contradiction, that professional life and influence grows out of collegiate education, and can grow from no other root. And if we would estimate the effect upon society of the decline and fall of the higher literary institutions, we must first estimate the effect of the entire removal from among us of the physician, the lawyer, and the clergyman, and of the entire destruction of the three great sciences of medicine, law, and theology. It is a forcible saying of Cicero, that the Athenian state could no more have been sustained and regulated without that grave and venerable court, the Areopagus, than the world could be sustained and regulated without the providence of God. With greater truth and force, it may be affirmed that modern society might as easily be kept in prosperous existence without the providence of God, as without the presence and pervading power of those professions whose province it is to investigate and expound natural, civil, judicial, and religious truth; for they are themselves one of the most benignant of Divine providences.

But we shall, perhaps, be able to form a more correct estimate of the worth of professional men, and consequently of those institutions which train them up, by an examination of the business and influence of each class separately.

1. It is the business of the physician to study the nature and laws of life, especially of animal life, and still more especially of human life, that he may understand the causes of disease and death. It is also his business to study material nature, that he may know the various elements that enter into it, and their relation to the chief practical purposes of his profession, viz. the preservation of health, and the cure of disease. Setting aside, therefore, the palpable and immediate benefit which the individual derives from the medical man as he stands by his bed-side, there is an amount of information put in currency by him, which ministers much to that general cheerfulness and absence of anxious apprehensions, which, like fresh breezes and bright sunshine, contributes much to the physical well-being of society. The investigations and influence of the medical profession rid community of that superstitious dread respecting the strange processes of nature, and the wonderful functions of animal life, which, indeed, in its highest intensity is to be found only in savage society, but which, in its milder but nevertheless most fearful form, marks the history of ages highly educated in other branches of knowledge, but ignorant of this, because its cultivation had not kept pace with that of the other. For example, whole communities in Europe, during the middle ages, were often set in a tremor by natural phenomena that would not startle the child of the present day, because the ignorant imagination of the time filled the mysterious, it is true, yet beautiful and harmless world of vegetable and animal life, with malignant powers and horrible spirits. And had there been as much general information respecting the science of medicine, as there was respecting those of law and theology,

among the early inhabitants of New England, that most strange and awful chapter in its history which records the story of the Salem witchcraft would be wanting. The gloom and horror—a gloom and horror which could not have been thicker and deeper, if the world of evil spirits had really been let loose upon men—that hung over that community like a black cloud, could not possibly be made to throw its shadow across the present generation, not surely because it is morally better or wiser than its holy fathers, but because the strange marvels of animal organization, and nervous excitement, have been traced to causes originating in that " God who is light, and in whom there is no darkness at all."

2. It is the business of the jurist to study the principles of law, the science of justice. This science stands beside that of religion, and has very profound and close affinities with it. So very nearly are these two sciences connected, that history shows that where clear and correct views of the one have prevailed, clear and correct views of the other have also prevailed. In proportion as a community is possessed of a deep sense of the sacred nature of justice, it is possessed of a correspondingly profound sense of the solemn nature of religion.

The cause of this lies in the fact that justice, which is the substance and staple of law, is the most fundamental of all fundamentals, whether the being of the Creator or of creation is contemplated. Justice is the deepest of all the "deep things of God," underlying the whole Godhead, and constituting the equilibrium of the Divine character. Even mercy, an attribute which is sometimes supposed to be the very contrary of justice, and in necessary incompatibility with it, derives from it its very essential nature —its mercifulness. Mercy shows its distinguishing quality, its real peculiarity, only in the light and flame of law;

for no man has ever known and felt the mercy of God, until he has first known and felt what God might in *justice* do unto him. Again, the idea of justice is a constituent of man's being, and if, owing to his fall and corruption, the positive sense of justice is often slumbering, the negative side of the idea, the sense of injustice, of being wronged, is one of the quickest and keenest of which he is conscious.

For these reasons, the science of law is no trivial or superficial science, but strikes its roots down into that solemn world of holiness and righteousness, with which every man by creation is connected, either for weal or woe, according to the relation which his spirit shall be found to sustain to it in the day of judgment. If, therefore, the spirit of law and the sense of justice are deep and pervading in society, the truths of religion will be more fully apprehended, and its duties will be more likely to be esteemed paramount, than would be the case, if a lawless and unjust spirit were abroad. By being reverential towards civil law, man, in so far, becomes reverential towards Divine law; for it is a power ordained of God, and the feeling towards that which is ordained transfers itself to Him who ordains. The doctrines of religion make their way far more easily through a law-revering and law-abiding people, than through a disorganized and disorganizing mass, held together by no right sentiment of any sort, by no just tie, civil or political.

Such being the fact, it is evident that the legal profession, if deeply penetrated and pervaded by the spirit of law and justice, is a most important instrument in the arrangements of Providence, for working out the well-being of the state and the improvement of mankind at large. By means of the study of the principles of justice, and the performance of legal business, law is constantly kept before the public mind, and its spirit is more or less permeating society. The mind of the people is made solemn in the process, and better prepared to receive the truths and principles of the Christian religion, to which great remedial and saving system of truth, all other systems should be subservient and preparatory.

3. And this brings us to the third of the three professions whose foundation is laid by collegiate education— the clerical. The worth of this profession cannot be overestimated, if we take into account the importance of the science upon which it rests, the opportunity it has of getting the popular ear, and the perfecting influence which it is capable of exerting upon society.

The science which is the subject-matter of the clergyman's investigation and exposition is that of religion. It must, necessarily, be matter of consciousness, because its principles are practical as well as theoretic, and, therefore, in order to their thorough apprehension, require entrance as much into the practical heart as into the speculative head. The principles of this science are addressed to the highest faculties of the human soul and provide for its well-being during the infinite portion of its existence. They therefore run deep and reach out wide, and both directly and indirectly affect the whole individual, the whole state, the whole race. Religion, either as a power of salvation or condemnation, seizes every rational being with a grasp never to be shaken off, and having made an entrance to his joy or anguish, is never to be expelled. If his whole being is brought into sweet harmony with its laws and truths, he dwells in heaven; if his whole being is alienate from its purity and holiness, it still remains, because it must, since he is rational, and he dwells in hell.

Religion, as its etymology denotes, is the great bond

which is to hold the rational creation together and to God. There is no other bond of such strength and extent. All the other ties that bind finite spirits together derive their permanent power from this great vinculum, and if its Author should suffer it to be broken, the primitive material chaos would be but a faint emblem of the disorder and ruin that would reign in the intelligent universe. And especially would man be the sufferer, in such a tremendous catastrophe; for, cut loose from all the restraints which natural and more especially revealed religion impose, the unchecked depravity of a fallen race would bring it into awful dissension and collision with itself.

Religious principles are therefore the most important of all. In the Divine idea and plan, all other knowledge is to derive its vigor and life from them, and they are intended to run through all the individuals and all the institutions of the human race. Through the arts and through the sciences, through the laws and the legislation, through the manners and the customs, through the thoughts and the opinions, through the individual life, the domestic and social life, the political life—in fine, through all the immense material embraced in the whole being and action of mankind, this pure and mighty power is intended to stream.

But not only is the clerical profession important because of the magnitude of the science upon which it is founded, it is also important because of the opportunity given to it for getting the attention of man. By Divine appointment, every seventh day of human life is given to this profession, that it may have a hearing. Wherever the Christian religion goes, be it into civilized or savage nations, the herald of Christianity has a set time to proclaim its doctrines, which is as regular in its coming as the rising of the sun.

This dedication of a seventh part of human life to the hearing of Christian truth is one of those many permanent arrangements of Divine Providence that exert mighty influences without observation. We may say what we will of the power of the press, and the rapidity of communication, and all the other engines of modern times for influencing and improving mankind, there is no instrumentality which, for the kind and degree of its influence upon society, is to be compared with the stated preaching of the Sabbath day. Think of the nature of the truths preached and of the magnitude and solemnity of the consequences connected with their reception or rejection, and then remember that through the length and breadth of this land, and of all Protestant lands, in thousands of churches, millions are listening to the preacher; that the principles of religion, even when they do not effect a saving lodgment in the heart, yet give vigor and clearness to the intellect; that from these churches and congregations, a strong and restraining influence is continually going off and diffusing itself through that portion of society which does not place itself within hearing of Divine truth; and moreover remember that this does not occur once every year, but once every week, and estimate, if possible, the amount of influence exerted by the clerical profession upon the permanence and progression of society.

We have thus briefly considered the business and influence of the three professions, and it must be evident to every reflecting mind, as we turn back to their connection with scientific in distinction from practical education, and their origin in the higher literary institutions, that such education is invaluable, and such institutions are indispensable. The decay and destruction of the higher literary institutions involves the decay and destruction of scientific knowledge, and of professional life, instruction, and influence. It must be apparent even to the most superficial observer, that the removal and want of a physician, a lawyer, and a clergyman, in a particular town, would work disastrously upon both its temporal and external interests. Cut off from all connection with professional life and influence, disease and the still more dreadful fear of disease would ravage it; not having the fear and reverence of law before their eyes, because they have not its expounder and representative in the midst of them, a cruel injustice would rule in the breasts of the physically strongest, as unlimited as the selfishness of the human heart; and with no one to preach the truths and offer the consolations of the Christian religion, the population would become more brutal than the brutes, because the wants of *man* would be unsupplied. If all this is apparent to a superficial glance, what will he see who glances wide and deep, over and through a whole commonwealth destitute not only of the system of liberal learning, but of those institutions and classes of men whose business it is to perpetuate, improve, and diffuse it?

The result then to which we arrive is, that only by the maintenance and improvement of scientific education can even the popular intelligence of the present age be preserved. This has its root and life in that more profound wisdom which is slowly evolved, from age to age, by the scientific, the liberally educated mind; which in the phrase of Milton, is "the result of all his considerate diligence, all his midnight watchings, and expense of palladian oil." And those institutions whose proper office it is to impart this education are not an accidental and unnecessary, but an organic part of state institutions, and should no more be torn off alive and bleeding from the body politic, than any other members should be. The whole population has an interest in their preservation, because they have an interest in the preservation of courts of justice, of legislative assemblies, of the pulpit and church of God. The solid well-being of a commonwealth depends on them. Their first founders on this continent were the Puritans, and they were among the earliest of the rock-foundations laid by those wise men. The whole sound growth, the whole healthy development of New England, has been directly connected with their existence and influence. Our benevolent and learned physicians, our judicious and calm-eyed jurists, our serious and thoughtful clergy, have been trained up in them. And, finally, they have ever been great defences against the downward tendencies of human nature when left to itself, by cherishing in the public mind that conservative veneration for law and order, and intelligence, and morality, which is the best of all preparations for the reception of the saving doctrines of the Christian religion.

INTELLECTUAL TEMPERANCE.*

Gentlemen:

You have invited me to address you upon a subject which, in its widest extension, is closely connected with the true cultivation of man. *Temperance*, in the ancient and full meaning of this word, must enter as a pervading element into the whole of human development, if it is to be right, fair, and harmonious. I am conscious, therefore, of the greatness of the theme; and, while I distrust my ability to handle it, I feel confidence when I remember that if in any way it should happen to come before your minds in the clearness of its own light, and in the fulness of its own power, it would exert an influence which you could not resist. I am encouraged, when I remember that I may be the means of rousing *your* minds, and of impelling *you* to the contemplation of a subject which, if seen in all its relations, and felt in all its force, would have a great effect upon the course of your discipline.

There are two Greek words that are translated by the one word, temperance. The one signifies a right mixture; a due combination and mingling of elements. The other signifies to be strong; to have control. The corresponding Latin word, which has been transferred to our language, has primary reference to time, and thus to

* A discourse at the University of Vermont, April 30, 1844.

limitation and restraint within appointed bounds. These different words indicate that the Greek and the Roman mind had one and the same general conception, which it would express by them. The idea of *self-control* underlies each of them, and according as this attribute is seen in a different phase, a different word is employed to denote it. Did the ancient mind behold self-control resulting in a right commingling of all the elements of the being; a fusion into a precious amalgam of elements which, if separated from each other, or blended together in wrong proportions, would be worthless; it called this self-control, εὐκρασία. Again, if it viewed self-control as resulting in inward strength, and in endowing the being with a power over the low and mean part of him, it denominated the cause, ἐγκράτεια. Again, if it looked at self-control as setting metes and bounds beyond which the appetites and passions must not go, and as appointing the times and seasons when the several powers of man might and might not be operative, it called self-control *temperantia*.

Temperance in its essence, then, is self-control. In its widest sense; in its application to all the parts of the human constitution, and to all the departments of human life and action; it is evidently a word full of meaning. As denoting a principle that may, and ought to run through all the powers of man, intellectual as well as sensuous, making them its bearer, imparting health and vigor to them, freeing them from passionate impulses, causing them to work orderly and harmoniously, and thus securing that beautiful and perfect result which should come from the development of a creature made in the image of the First Perfect and the First Fair—as denoting such a principle as this, temperance is one of those words, the knowledge of which, in the language of Coleridge, is of more value than to know the history of a campaign.

The entrance of this principle of self-control into the material part of man, and its efficiency in the subjection of the appetites of the body, have been almost exclusively dwelt upon, especially in our own time. And this fact shows that even in his efforts at self-improvement, man unconsciously reveals his moral ignorance and degradation. The very fact that men have so generally contented themselves with the subjection of the appetites and passions of the body, and have not striven to control the more refined and more dangerous passions of the mind and heart, evinces that man is not naturally inclined to aim at the ideal, and to reach after absolute perfection. Not that what has been done should have been left undone, but that which has been left undone should have been done. Man ought not to be subject to his eating and drinking, and he ought not to be a slave to his pride and ambition. He ought not to rest content until he has control of himself in all the spheres of his life; until every power of his being is under the sway of law.

Since temperance, in its extended signification, opens such a boundless field of inquiry and thought; since the principle of rational self-control so connects itself with all that man is, and can become; the thorough study of it, and the complete apprehension of it, must be the work and result of a life, of an immortal life. We shall find enough to occupy our meditations for the present hour, if we confine ourselves to one aspect of the subject. And I invite your attention to: *The influence of temperance, or self-control, upon intellectual development.*

The soul of man is a kingdom by itself. It is under a constitution and laws, like a state. The Republic of Plato, and the Town of Man-Soul of Bunyan,—the two of the race who, in many respects, have attained the deepest insight into man,—are proofs that the closest analogy exists between the state and the mind; that what is true of one may be transferred to the other. The representations of the Apocalypse; the plan, the architecture and adornment of the City of God; are likewise evidence that the finite spirit has its polity like the state; that the purity, stability, and harmony of the soul are best symbolized by the purity, stability, and harmony of a realm. And the study of the soul itself discloses that the same qualities must enter into man's growth as an individual, that enter into his growth as a nation, or a race. That which contributes to the true well-being of man individually, promotes the true well-being of man collectively. The genuine culture of every man as a part, is the genuine culture of humanity as a whole.

A profound writer upon the state mentions permanence and progression, as the two fundamental elements in its well-being.* By the harmonious balance of these two counterpoising interests, the state is to exist and grow. The genuine growth of the individual mind, in like manner, depends upon the presence of these two elements. That intellectual culture which is not at once permanent and progressive is ungenuine.

The mind requires conservatism and permanence in culture, that its progress may be steady and permanent. There is no real conflict between conservatism and progress, though such is a common opinion. No mind can move forward, except as it moves forward from a preceding position. It conserves in order to progress. The child learns to walk, only after it has learned to stand. Men must hold on upon all the old attainments, in order to make new ones. That discipline alone is progressive which never loses anything; which, selecting only good materials, takes

---

* Coleridge: Church and State.

them up and incorporates them permanently with the substance of the understanding. Tried by this test, how often does intellectual culture prove to be defective. When the student looks back upon the whole of his education, he finds that not all of it has been stable; that not all of it is with him. He sees, as he looks at the studies of certain periods of his life, that they did not contribute to his permanent growth; that certain states of his intellect, certain prepossessions for certain authors, certain moods of his mind towards certain systems of truth or falsehood, were not elements of culture adapted to the deepest and highest needs of the soul. The student, when he has become well acquainted with his past course of study, is compelled to acknowledge, with sorrow, that too much of the food with which he has striven to satisfy the cravings of the intellect, did not become organic, did not turn into flesh and blood, did not prove to be a means of vitalization, but was rejected by the mind, when it had recovered itself from its momentary intoxication, as not nourishing the principle of its life. That is a happy scholar, too, who, as he looks into his mind, finds that by its innate vigor it has entirely purged out the poison, and has rid itself wholly of the bad effects of such a process. That student should be a grateful being, who can say that no one of the periods of student-life has left a deleterious influence behind it; a deleterious influence that is "felt in the blood and felt along the heart."

Every scholar should aim to cultivate the intellect in such a manner that the culture shall be right, and therefore shall stay with him. No element of knowledge ought to be appropriated by the mind that ought not to become a part of the mind; an immortal part of an immortal mind. The characteristics of the discipline should be such as to permit of its going along with the person, through the whole of his endless existence as a rational being. Is that to be called culture which does not last? which, like the dry bark of the tree, is to be thrown off periodically? Does a mood of the intellect, a prejudice of the mind, which is shallow because it has been awakened by an unworthy object, which endures but for a brief time, and gives place to another as shallow as itself, contribute anything to permanent and genuine education? Does that mental application which affords no food for profound thought, and rouses none of the original and fundamental powers of the man, deserve the name of study? Do the fleeting and shifting notions and opinions that come and go and go and come, in some periods of our life, deserve the name of discipline? Do they awaken that which is deepest in the mind? Do they make an entrance into "that place of understanding which is hid from the eyes of all living, and kept close from the fowls of the air"? These vaporous clouds which brush across the sky do not stir the blue depths of the ether; they have no influence in purifying the "ancient heavens," that they may "be fresh and strong."

Progression is self-evidently a necessary element in intellectual discipline. By progression is not meant the mere accumulation of facts, the mere aggregation of information, but the steady increase of intellectual power, the constant evolution of that energy which is latent in every human mind. The life-power by which the mind is to progress is within it, and he who most industriously and boldly draws upon it, while he nourishes it with all good learning, will make the farthest advance. Intellectual progress is the gradual unfolding of all the mental faculties; the development of the vitality of the mind. Hence, those who have made the greatest advance in mental discipline, and have contributed most to the progress of the race, have been distinguished for their ability to draw upon the native force of their own intellects.

True progression in mental discipline is, therefore, intimately united with permanency of cultivation. The one cannot be without the other; the one nourishes the other. When, on the one hand, the mind is acquiring a culture that has its abiding seat in its most fundamental powers, it is advancing the development of these powers; and this, we have seen, is the definition of mental progress. And when, on the other hand, the mind appropriates only those elements which by nature are adapted to its growth, and, like a tree, carefully rejects all those which do not permit of a solid and vital assimilation, its culture is permanent.

And here, again, I appeal to the student's consciousness upon this point. As he looks into his intellect, to see whether it has made true progress in all its career, he is mournfully conscious that the fulness of its inherent power has by no means been brought out by culture. The consciousness of weakness, and the distrust of his own mind, are most generally caused by the sense of unfaithfulness, and the lack of thoroughness in self-training. It is indeed true, that they are sometimes the result of a praiseworthy humility, especially when the mind stands in front of the immense problems of human life and destiny; yet even in this case, the scholar can say: "When I am weak, then am I strong; though I distrust myself, I have, nevertheless, a calm confidence." Happy is that scholar, who, as he looks within, can say: "I am all that I could possibly be, at this stage of my intellectual growth; my powers, at this period of my existence, could not have been more fully unfolded than they are; I am conscious of an inward energy that has its root and ground in a cultivation that has always been permanent and progressive."

Blessed is that student, who, at any and every stage of his life can say: "I have always nurtured my mind with its proper food; I have never weakened its force, for a moment even, by food not convenient for it; I have never stopped the spring of its living impulse; it has constantly had a free and pure play."

Having thus seen that permanence and progression are essential elements in true intellectual discipline, and having briefly noticed their characteristics and relations to each other, it will be easy to see that their existence is impossible, unless the mind is under the sway of the principle of self-control; unless the scholar obey the injunction of the apostle: "Giving all diligence, add to your knowledge temperance."

Any one who attentively watches the workings of his mind soon becomes aware that it has tendencies to wayward, fitful, and passionate movements. Its energy does not always go forth in an even flow, and its powers do not always work in a manner proportioned to their relative worth. The fancy often rules the reason; the power of irregular and lawless association often overcomes the power of methodical and orderly thought; and hours that ought to have brought up a mass of solid and pure truth, from the deep mines of the spirit, construct nothing but daydreams and air-castles. There is, indeed, no agent so wayward, and yet so mighty in the use of its power, as the human mind. When its energy has ceased to be under the influence of that self-government which a man is obligated to exercise over his entire being, it works with an absolute intensity. There is, for the thoughtful observer, no sight more terrific than the vision of an intellect expending the fulness of its immortal vigor upon wrong objects, and putting forth its supernatural power lawlessly.

This waywardness and lawlessness of mind, this intellectual intemperance, is utterly incompatible with genuine discipline. There can be neither permanence nor progression in a culture of this kind. Such workings of the intellect rack and wear it. This convulsive and unnatural use of mental power has ruined the noblest minds; minds strong and stable in their natures; minds which it took a lifetime to ruin. But when the human intellect is under this principle of self-control, and when it meekly, and constantly, and wholly surrenders itself to its actuation, it is developed rightly and grows beautifully. For, this self-government, this temperate restraint, if traced to the fountain, will be found to flow "fast by the oracle of God." It is a principle alive with the breath of Law, and instinct with that Reason which is the parent of order, harmony, and beauty, both in the realm of nature and the realm of spirit. The scholar who submits to it will be freed from those wayward impulses, and passionate movements, to which we have seen the mind has a natural tendency. Like the great power of gravitation in nature, this power, if all in every part of the soul, will bespeak its presence. It will reveal itself by harmony, by symmetry, by regularity of mental action; in a word, by all the characteristics of genuine cultivation.

There are several results of this intellectual temperance, which still further enforce, and illustrate, what has been said respecting the permanent and progressive discipline of the mind.

The scholar who has control over his intellect possesses the power of *methodical thought*. By this is meant the ability to surrender the mind to the guidance and actuation of its highest law. When we examine the laws of mental action that are within us, we find that some are immethodical and irregular in their operation, and that if we yield our minds to their impulse they produce no solid and abiding thought. The fancy and the law of association include, perhaps, the substance of these lower laws of mental action, and every one knows that he who habitually surrenders himself to the guidance of his fancy, and who floats along supinely upon the current of the vain images, the obscure feelings, and the dreamy sensations that are called forth by the power of involuntary association, is an inefficient day-dreamer, and incapable of manly thought.

There is a higher law than these, which is the true regent of the mind. There is a part of us which demands truth, and not unsubstantial fancies; which yearns after eternal verities, and not airy nothings; which strives to stop the flow of immethodical and fanciful association, and to cause the true Hippocrene, the inexhaustible fountain of methodical thought, to gush forth. There is a part of us which checks the wanderings of the intellect, and seeks to lead it into the path of reason and law—that "path which no fowl knoweth, and which the vulture's eye hath not seen." There is a law of mental action which, if obeyed, introduces logic, clearness, profundity, and truth into the mental operations.

The power of methodical thinking, as I have remarked, is the ability to surrender the mind entirely and continuously to the actuation of this its higher law. It is an ability which no scholar, who knows the meaning of it, dares say that he possesses in absolute perfection. It is an ability which, by the mass of professed students even, is possessed in a very imperfect degree. It is an ability which, when it exists in a high degree, imparts a force to the intellect that is almost superhuman, and to the workings of which no limits can be set. If the power of methodical, scientific, concatenated thought once becomes deeply seated, and a fixed habit in a mind, an eternal culture and an eternal progress have begun in it. All the fine intellectual power of the race has come from this power; all the reason and truth which the human mind has evolved in past ages own it as their parent. The musical truth of Plato, the solid truth of Bacon, the sober truth of Hooker, and the lofty truth of Howe, all own it as their father.

But that discipline which enables the mind to keep upon the track of pure truth, and, in the phrase of Bacon, to "hound" the nature of it, of necessity cultivates it in a genuine manner. Truth is the aliment and the element of the mind, and if, by any process, the mind is enabled to live by it and in it, it will grow. Think how your intellect would have unfolded, if the whole past course of your study had been a train of deep, methodical contemplation; if you had never allowed your mind to expend its energies in a desultory, involuntary way; if all its activity had been deliberate, voluntary, and ever referring to the true end of the scholar's being—the attainment of absolute verity! Think of the results that would have come from such a discipline. How completely master you would be over your intellect; how easily and yet how mightily you could control its power; what a grasp you would have upon the legitimate objects of human knowledge!

Germany, the land of scientific thought, affords an astonishing instance of the might, I had almost said the omnipotence, arising from the subjection of the intellect to the law of method. Whatever judgment may be passed upon the various systems of German philosophy, no one can deny that they exhibit a depth, a height, a breadth, and a rounded completeness of system that betoken a marvellous power of consecutive thought, and more, perhaps, than any other phenomena in literary history, manifest the boundless energy inhering even in the finite mind. Look, for example, at that system in which the speculative intellect of the race seems to have reached its culmination—the system of Hegel. See how wonderfully the power of systematic thought works, and what a mighty power of construction it possesses. See how, by its supernatural magic, the system rises like St. Peter's cathedral, with a

> "Vastness which grows, but grows to harmonize;
> All musical in its immensities."

Now, this power of concatenated thinking results from the temperate restraint which the mind has acquired over itself. It has gained the ability to subject those fitful and desultory movements of which I have spoken, to the law of method; to make all the intellectual powers move on harmoniously towards the attainment of a prescribed end. Although it is true that mere system-building, of itself, contributes little more to the right discipline of man than mere castle-building (for the products of the speculative understanding contribute no more to the practical life of the spirit than the products of the fancy), yet when we consider the influence and tendency of this scientific habit of the mind, we find that it has worth, and, in the end, promotes a permanent and progressive culture.

And this naturally suggests a second result of intellectual temperance. The scholar who can control his mind, so that it can think in a long, uninterrupted train, will have it brought into *contact with noble and ennobling objects*. No man can follow the leading of a contemplative and methodical intellect, without coming into great and sublime regions, where there are grand and lofty objects of vision. The reason of this lies in the fact that truth is infinite, and has a living connection existing between all its parts. The mind that has touched the borders, if truly progressive, must go to the centre of the land. One truth is connected with all truth. The methodical mind, therefore—the mind which will not and cannot be diverted by trifling and alien objects—will be led on and on in an endless progression. One truth seen points to the next; one relation of truth to other truths suggests another and still another relation to other and still other truths, and the mind thus launches further and further into the infinite ocean of thought. And as it "goes sounding on its dim and perilous way," it will see sublime and animating scenes. It will come into new hemispheres with new constellations; it will sail amid the dazzling glitter and the thundering crash of the icy ocean; it will plough up the phosphoric light of the tropic seas. And even when the student is led on by a merely speculative interest; even when he does not seek truth that he may *become* better by it, but solely that he may *know;* he derives some genuine cultivation unconsciously. He learns, at least, to hold his mind to one subject, and to think in trains. To resume our comparison, as the intellect is passing through the many worlds of truth into which concatenated thinking brings it, and is skirting their borders, influences from them will come off to it.

>"As when to them who sail
>Beyond the Cape of Hope, and now are passed
>Mozambic, off at sea northeast winds blow
>Sabæan odors from the spicy shore
>Of Araby the bless'd."

Even the merely speculative thinker feels some of the influence which the great objects of practical thought, and practical faith, exert upon the spirit. Hence, such thinkers as Spinoza and Hegel, though utterly erroneous in their pantheistic premise and their pantheistic conclusions, do nevertheless exhibit a loftiness of scholastic character, and a sedateness of mental habitude, that cannot exist in a man who leads an unthinking and frivolous life. They seem to have acquired from the mere atmosphere of the temple some of the solemnity of the true worshipper.

This tendency of methodical thought to bring the intellect into contact with noble objects is most certainly a source of good culture. The mind takes its tone and character from the themes of its contemplation, and if these are noble and lofty, the mind will become so likewise. Even those high scientific problems which are abstract and cold for the heart, and cannot furnish all the cultivation which an immortal being needs, are infinitely worthier than those low and trivial subjects upon which the mind, unless restrained, will naturally expend its force. If the scholar is marked by intellectual temperance; if he has acquired the power of orderly thought, and the ability to keep his intellect in one train of reflection, he will, as a matter of course, be conversant with great subjects. It is only a fanciful and lawless application of the mind, which can be content with the vanities of literature. That intellect which is self-controlled, and master of itself, will feel a degradation in an immethodical and desultory use of its power, and will not be at home except among high truths and themes.

I turn, now, to notice briefly two other qualities which are at once signs and results of genuine mental culture, and are also intimately connected with intellectual self-control. I mean *freedom* and *enthusiasm*. These terms are often misunderstood. They are often associated with lawlessness and disorder. Of course if this be their nature, they cannot be signs and results of self-control. This is not their nature. Freedom, in its true meaning, is self-subjection to law; and hence holiness is the only true freedom, and the Holy Spirit is the only "free spirit."* Enthusiasm is defined, by an eminent thinker, to be the enlargement and elevation of soul that arise from the intuition of ultimate principles.† If these are the correct definitions of freedom and enthusiasm, it is evident that they can exist in an intellect only when it is self-governed, and that they will exist necessarily, if it is self-governed. That scholar who rules his mind, and thus checks its waywardness, is a free scholar. As that man is possessed of a bold, courageous, physical freedom, who has self-possession, and can at all times keep in check the timid instincts of the physical nature, so that scholar is free in the higher sense, who has habitual control over the instincts of the intellect. For self-control is for the mind, what self-possession is for the body. And the student who is under law is also full of enthusiasm. The deepest and most joyful enthusiasm issues from the calm intensity of that contemplation which is the result of discipline. All lofty feeling in the soul springs from moods that are deep; that are fed by great principles and profound meditation; even as the deepest green of the leaf, and the stateliest growth of the trunk, shoot up from roots that strike far down into a strong black mould. Genuine enthusiasm in the scholar is the infallible sign of genuine and thorough discipline.

I cannot but direct your earnest thought to these two attributes of the disciplined scholar. Freedom and enthusiasm are the bloom and flower of the scholar's life

* Psalm li. 12.
† Coleridge: Statesman's Manual, Works. I., 433. Harpers' Edition.

There is no vision so gladdening to the heart of the lover of letters as the vision of an intellect under self-control, rejoicing in the consciousness of power and freedom, and rushing onward with a subdued yet deep enthusiasm through the infinite realm of truth. There is enjoyment, likewise, in the possession of these intellectual qualities. Schiller has asserted that the highest enjoyment is the freedom of the mind, in the living play of all its powers. This is not the highest enjoyment, for there is a higher joy than that of the intellect; but it is the highest enjoyment of the intellect. And it is joy, to feel the gush and play of intellectual power; to be conscious of the living currents of a mind healthy and free, under the principle of self-control. But these qualities, contributing so greatly to the progress and happiness of the scholar, must be earned by a thorough discipline. Like all things great and good, they are the fruit of struggle, and of self-surrendry to law.

Thus have we seen that intellectual temperance, the rational self-control of the intellect, secures a permanent and progressive culture that manifests itself in the power of methodical thought, in an habitual intercourse with noble and ennobling objects of reflection, and in intellectual freedom and enthusiasm.

The principles which have been advanced can be substantiated by an appeal to literary history. And I invite you to look at the glorious ages of English literature, for a proof that intellectual self-control secures genuine intellectual discipline. Go back into the sixteenth and seventeenth centuries, and consider the Bacons, the Hookers, the Raleighs, the Miltons—those masculine births of the masculine ages of England. The scholar, as he goes back to these men and their times, feels himself to be in a sedate age, an age of reason, and law, and intellectual self-government. These were men of thorough self-restraint, and, therefore, men of methodical thought, of calm, rational insight into philosophy, statesmanship, and divinity. If we happen to name these great names in the same breath with the Byrons and Rousseaus of modern days, we feel that there is a difference in kind. The sobriety of intellect, the mental abstinence, and the solidity of culture in the former, are of no kith or kin with that waywardness of intellect, that fitfulness of mental action, that entire absence of stable discipline, and that utter incapability of lofty thought, which characterize the latter. The great men whom I have named did "give all diligence to add to their knowledge temperance." Their knowledge was permeated by temperance. Temperate in their principles, and temperate in their application of them; temperate in their opinions, and temperate in their enunciation of them; temperate in their feelings, and temperate in their exhibition of them; all ages will ever resort to them for wise, prudent, and profound thought. All ages will ever go to them for their own thorough discipline, and will look upon their minds as the most remarkable examples of solid, sober, mental cultivation. The greatness of their strength is not owing to their natural superiority over all men since their day. Great men have been among us, as great by nature as they. But it is owing to the calm temperate control which they possessed over their minds; to the patient, methodical habit of their intellects. Their whole long lives were a permanent and progressive discipline. Their growth was slow, pure, and solid, like that of the British oak. In the phrase of Bacon, they are " the Herculeses and not the Adonises of literature." And they were also free and enthusiastic intellects. Nowhere do we find more bold and unshackled thought than in the age from Elizabeth to Charles the Second, and yet no age has developed more of absolute truth in the higher domains of knowledge. These men were animated by the freedom and lofty enthusiasm of truth and reason, and hence they moved, even among the deepest and most solemn themes, "as with the steps of the gods."

I have thus, Gentlemen, directed your attention to the relation of temperance, the ancient εὐκρασία and ἐγκράτεια, to mental discipline. I have selected this particular aspect of its influence, because it addresses itself to the sympathies and aspirations of true scholars. I know that if the lofty purpose and the high resolve of the genuine student are in your breasts, your thoughts will gather around the great subject of self-control, and you will have an earnest longing that your intellects may be under its actuation. I know that the mere interests of the intellect are sufficient to awaken a desire, that this faculty may develop itself under the influence of a principle that will secure to it a permanent and progressive culture, and will swell it with a free enthusiasm. I have also dwelt upon this part of the great subject, because it presents what should be the high and worthy aim of the scholar, and because, if by any means you may be prevailed upon to reach after it, the low and grovelling propensities of the animal part will be more likely to slumber. Not that high intellectual discipline necessarily and infallibly secures temperance of body. The past history of literary men shows that it does not. But the *tendency* of such self-control over the intellect is to produce self-control over the sense. I have, therefore, felt that every aspiration after true intellectual discipline, that may be roused in you, has some influence to draw you away from the intoxicating bowl. I feel that if you are able to soar in the high regions of pure intellectual cultivation, and of serene thought, you will find it harder, in the hour of temptation, to descend and grovel. I know that if you are capable of the clear pure joy arising from the intuition of great truths, you will have less and less inclination for the delirious and mad joy that steams up from the wine-cup and the revel.

But in all that I have said, I have remembered that the intellect is but a part, and an inferior part, of man; and that its actuation by the principle of self-control is no more the *chief* end of man, than is the subjection of the passions of the body. There is a part of us higher than the intellect; a part whereby we are capable of aspirations and feelings far purer and loftier than those of the intellect—the reverence, the love, and the adoration of the Eternal God; a part whereby we are capable of a discipline more deep, more boundless, and more sublime than that of the mind—the discipline of the cherubim and seraphim. And I have also remembered, that upon the cherishing of these higher aspirations, and the progression of this higher discipline, depends your success in completely controlling both the intellect and the sense. All power comes from above, and goes downward. It never comes from beneath and goes upward. The organic controls the inorganic; the vital force subdues the chemical; the voluntary governs and uses the animal. It is in vain, in any of the kingdoms, to attempt to bring up power from below. Beneficent and really controlling force, descends from something that is higher, to something that is lower. In order, therefore, that your mind and body may be subjected perfectly to self-control, your *heart* must first vitalize the principle, and send it down to them warm, plastic, and vivifying. You must not suppose that you can attain an absolute self-government over even the lower part of you, unless the higher part is also controlled by the law and Spirit of God. In this nobler portion of your being, the radical discipline must begin. From this point alone, can rational self-control radiate into your entire constitution. If it goes out from this centre, you will become a thoroughly-disciplined, a *holy* being; for the principle of self-control will then show itself to be no other than the principle of religion, and temperance will be the surrendering of the human spirit to the Holy Spirit, of the human will to the Infinite Will.

I know, therefore, that if any scholarly aspirations are ever awakened in you, and the wish ever rises within to attain genuine mental discipline, you will infallibly fail to realize them in a *perfect* manner, unless you seek aid from the Most High. I know that your wish will never become your strong and abiding *will;* that you will never become even what, as scholars merely, you in your more hopeful and aspiring moments long to become; without the new birth of the soul. Ours is a fallen spirit, and we shall never acquire perfect sway over any or all of its powers, unless we go through the great process of regeneration. I might refer you, if you needed proof of this, to those great men whom I have already named. They were religious men. Even those of them who mingled much with the world, and were much absorbed in the distracting cares of the state, preserved a religious temper and tone. They felt that the power of the Invisible must actuate them, if they were to keep their robes white; if they were to succeed in attaining a complete self-government. Hear the "Student's Prayer," of Lord Bacon: "This also we humbly and earnestly beg, that human things may not prejudice such as are divine; neither that from the unlocking of the gates of sense, and the kindling of a greater natural light, anything of incredulity or intellectual night may arise in our minds, towards divine mysteries. But rather, that, by our mind thoroughly cleansed and purged from fancy and vanities, and yet subject and perfectly given up to the divine oracles, there may be given unto faith the things that are faith's." Hear Milton speak of his great work, as one "not to be raised from the heat of youth, or vapors of wine, like that which flows at waste from the pen of some vulgar amourist, or the trencher fury of a rhyming parasite ; nor to be obtained from the invocation of dame Memory and her syren daughters; but by devout prayer to the Eternal Spirit who can enrich with all utterance and knowledge, and sends out his seraphim with the hallowed fire of his altar, to touch and purify whom he pleases." *

I would, then, that this subject might lead you, in the end, to the Fountain of law and righteous self-control. I would that you might not aim merely at temperance of body, or temperance of mind, but might seek the highest and most difficult of all attainments, a temperate *will;* one that is at one with the law of God. If this be in you and abound, it will be easy to overcome the blandishments of the sense, and the waywardness of the intellect. The will is the main part of you ; and if you knew the meaning of this power ; if you apprehended the fulness of its life, the inexhaustibleness of its fountains and reservoirs, and felt that all heaven with its harmony, or all hell with its lawlessness, will come out of it, according as it is actuated by the Spirit of God, or by the spirit of Self, you would earnestly seek its renewal in the Divine Image.

If all your powers become pervaded by Holy Will, and it invigorates and actuates them, you will become a calm, a self-controlled, and a harmonious being. The passions of the body, and the more subtle passions of the intellect

---

* Milton : Reason of Church Government, Book II.

and heart will gradually disappear. You will gradually acquire stability, profundity, purity, and loftiness of cultivation, and your soul will exhibit that most beautiful of all growths—the development of immortal energy under Law.

> "So build we up the being that we are;
> Thus deeply drinking in the soul of things
> We shall be wise perforce; and while inspired
> By choice, and conscious that the will is free,
> Shall move unswerving, even as if impelled
> By strict necessity, along the path
> Of order and of good. Whate'er we see,
> Whate'er we feel, shall tend to feed and nurse,
> By agency direct or indirect,
> Our faculties; shall fix in calmer seats
> Of moral strength, and raise to loftier heights
> Of divine love, our intellectual soul."

THE PURITAN CHARACTER.*

The seed, or principle, of a man's character is in existence before him. He is born with it. This proves its transmission from progenitors, and this proves its priority to birth. In order, therefore, to a full comprehension of individual character, we must go back to the species of which the individual is a part. A man's sinful character, for example, cannot be understood, unless it is referred to the apostasy of man*kind*. This was a free act. The individual, consequently, though deriving his character, is responsible for it. The two conceptions of inheritance and guilt, by this explanation, are not incompatible; and while insisting upon personal accountability, not only for particular actions, but for the general disposition from which they proceed, we need not deny the connection of this latter with what has gone before—with the sin of the race.

These remarks are true, measurably, of the character of a nation. Every national character is, in an important sense, the result of what has preceded it. It is not the result in such a sense that the nation is irresponsible in possessing it; but in the sense that former ages and nations exerted a great, though not a necessitating influence upon its origin and growth. All nations are united together; equally receiving influence from the past, and equally transmitting it to the future. Does a nation

* Reprinted from the Christian Observatory, March, 1847.

form a settled national character, entirely independent of the past? A new star sometimes appears in the sky, shining with its own light, differing from all other stars in glory, and seemingly independent of all the rest of the host of heaven. But not so with national character. It does not emerge into existence suddenly and independently; but is a slow formation, in great measure shaped and tinged by former ages, institutions, and characters.

These remarks are true of the Puritan character; and, before proceeding to describe its prominent trait, let us consider it in its origin, and its relation to what preceded it.

The main elements of the Puritan character are *Old-English*. They came down from the early periods of England's national existence. The great Alfred was essentially a Puritan. That trait which led him to devote one-third of his time to religion, and the remainder of it to a severe and strict discharge of the duties devolving upon him in the course of a reign strewed all through with dangers, obstacles, and discouragements, is intimately allied to that which made the Pilgrims so deeply religious and so strictly dutiful men. This character continued, but underwent some modifications, through the influence of the Norman invasion, and far more through the influence of advancing civilization. The primitive English character, thus modified, continued through the times of Elizabeth, producing great men in divinity, philosophy, statesmanship, and poetry. After this period it began to be withdrawn from the mass of the nation into a narrower circle. The nation, as a body, ceased to be animated by the vigorous and pure life of their fathers; and the result was growing superstition and unspirituality in religion, and increasing despotism in government. But there did remain an inner circle, in which the old spirit dwelt and reigned. Driven from the extremities, the life retreated to the heart; and in the age of the first Charles, the old English character, of which Alfred was the type, existed, in a most pure and dense form, in a small and despised portion of the English people called the Puritans. Like Wordsworth's dalesmen,

> "Pure livers were they all, austere and grave,
> And fearing God; the very children taught
> Stern self-respect, a reverence for God's word,
> And an habitual piety, maintained
> With strictness scarcely known on English ground."

Thus was the Puritan character a thing of slow and solid formation. It did not start into existence in an instant. Its beginnings must be traced to the union of the best elements of the British with the best elements of the Saxon nature; and its development is the history of the spiritualizing influence of Christianity upon these two excellent and prime ingredients, for eight hundred years. It grew with the growth, and strengthened with the strength, of the nation. In times of trial and danger it gave clearness to the head, determination to the will, and nerve to the arm, of the best of the people. It was ever on the side of liberty and law, of learning and religion. As it went along through the mutations of ages, it became more and more pure from foreign particles. Gradually narrowing the limits of its existence, by choosing for its residence the very soundest heads and the very purest hearts, in the age of Charles the First it exhibited as noble traits as ever have been seen in human beings.

England made the term "Puritan" a reproach, and took special pains to expel from itself this excellent character. Degenerate England drove out the Puritans. They sailed over the ocean which separates the two worlds. They put the Atlantic between them and their fatherland; and then calmly, proudly, piously deposited the elements of a great empire on the western hemisphere.

We now inquire, What is the prominent trait of the Puritan character? The fundamental trait of the Puritan character, upon which all its excellencies rest, and by which even its faults are to be explained, is *spirituality of mind*. By spirituality of mind, we do not now mean what is denoted by the theological definition of the phrase. Most of the Puritans were regenerated men, and were spiritually-minded in the New-Testament sense of the term. But, apart from this characteristic, which results only from the new birth, there was a peculiarity in the Puritan mind which perhaps cannot be denoted better than by the term "spirituality."

In accommodating the word to our present purpose, we mean by it that disposition which leads its possessor to believe in the invisible world, and to refer to it, both in his thoughts and actions. Though man, by creation, is a spiritual being, and is destined to spend the infinite part of his existence in the unseen world, yet he knows but little about that world, and it engages but little of his thought. Man generally has no sense of the reality of that sphere which is to be his eternal dwelling-place. Sin is the chief cause of this ignorance, and insensibility. If man were pure of heart, eternity would not be a dim or undiscovered country. It would have substantial reality for him, and he would think and act with reference to it, as the most permanent of all realities. But, besides this main and universal cause of man's ignorance of the spiritual world, there is a minor one arising from the mental constitution. We sometimes meet a person thoughtful by nature, serious-minded, and inclined to contemplate the mysterious and invisible. Unseen things have more reality to him than to the thoughtless and frivolous man

He naturally believes that there are more things in the universe than can be seen by the eye, or touched by the hand. Such a man differs from the mass, by this disposition to find reality behind the visible and material. It is not difficult for him to believe in the supernatural. He is, in this sense, spiritually-minded, and predisposed to believe in, and think about, unseen things.

The same difference of constitution appears in nations, as well as in individuals. We find some nations naturally inclined to believe in spiritual and unseen realities, while others are disinclined. The former do not need, or make use of, the visible symbol, but rest satisfied with the idea; while the latter find it difficult to apprehend the idea at all, and need and use a material sign, by which it shall be signified. The former are spiritual, the latter material, in their modes of thought. It has been observed by writers upon this subject, that, as a general rule, this difference of mental constitution follows, and accords with, the difference of climate. The nations of the torrid zone are sensuous in their conceptions, while those of the cold zones are spiritual. For this reason, the paganism of the south of Europe was very different from that of northern Europe. The southern heathen had gods many and lords many; but he must see them and handle them, in order to believe in their reality; and therefore he carved numerous idols, and builded many temples, in which his divinities should dwell. The northern heathen had fewer gods, and could believe in their reality without the aid of the visible form. He hewed no idol, and he erected no temple; he worshipped his divinity in spirit, beneath the open sky, in the free air. The keen vigor infused into the body by the northern winter, and the influences which rained down from the cold northern sky, glittering with intensely bright stars, and gleaming and flashing with the northern lights, seem to have induced spirituality of thought and conception in the northern heathen; while the languid air, and enervating influences, of the warm zone, tended to make the southern heathen sluggish, earthly, and sensuous, in his modes of thought.

From their northern extraction, the Puritans derived what we have styled, in an accommodated sense, spirituality of mind; or the disposition to believe in the supernatural, the ability to realize it without the aid of visible things, and the inclination to refer to it in thought and action. This, we think, is the ground, and native principle of the Puritan character. From this sprang the many virtues, and the few faults of the Puritans.

That we may more fully apprehend this their fundamental characteristic, let us contemplate it as we see its manifestation in the three main relationships of human life,—the social, civil, and religious.

1. Every one knows that the social life of the Puritans was extremely simple in its structure. Their customs, manners, and habits were singularly severe. They made little of fashions, and the outward appendages of society; and that long list of modes and conventionalities which is the sum and substance of much of modern social inter course was unknown to them. Their inborn disposition to believe that the inward and invisible is the substantially true and real led them, in their social relations, to regard the feelings and sentiments of the heart, rather than the actions and appearance of the body. Therefore, though the social life of the Puritans exhibits an exceedingly simple, in some respects a bald and uncouth appearance, it would be a great error to deny, that underneath the outward appearance there was a noble, kind, and generous courtesy. There has never been a human society in which there was more of genuine gentility, than there

was among them. The social charities and neighborly sympathies never had a more free play than in the Puritan heart. Good-will, which is the essence of politeness, animated the Puritan community; and exhibitions of kindness and courtesy in that society could be depended upon, as the manifestation and true index of its spirit.

This state of society was the natural growth of the disposition, native to the Puritan, to believe firmly in the unseen, and to make more of that than of the visible. The neighbor cared little for the outward demeanor of his neighbor, but everything for his inward temper. The friend took but little notice of the dress or manners of his friend, but directed a most keen and piercing glance to the tenor of his feelings. The citizen paid but little attention to the audible and outward professions of his fellow-citizen, but deemed the invisible and secret opinions of his mind to be the main object of attention. What cared the Puritan for the mean apparel and the rustic manner, if there were only an honest, upright, and kind heart throbbing in the bosom? And what cared the Puritan for the most gorgeous apparel and the most polite demeanor, if within the breast there were nothing but selfish indifference and hypocrisy?

Thus, there grew out of this disposition to regard the invisible, a singularly sincere and simple state of society. All of its arrangements referred to what is within, and unseen by the material eye. It is not denied that the Puritans, under the impulse of this strong tendency to regard the unseen, neglected, in too great a degree, to regard what is seen and outward. But this is always a minor fault, and one that is committed only by a very spiritual mind. It is better to go to this extreme than to the other; and it is more easy to reach the golden mean from this end than from the other. It is far more easy for the intensely spiritual man to cultivate himself into a due regard for the outward and apparent, than it is for the intensely earthly man to school himself into a spiritual way of thought. Indeed, it may be said of these two courses of cultivation, that the former alone is really feasible. Man can come down from heaven to earth, but he cannot go up from earth to heaven. He can fall, but he cannot rise.

Taken as a whole, therefore, the social life of the Puritans is a fair and admirable structure. If, in some minor respects, it is deficient; if there is not so much finish and adornment laid out upon the exterior as there might be; still the great plan of the edifice is noble, and the architecture lofty and beautiful. It has the beauties and faults of the great edifices of the natural world. Like the mountain, it rises into the clear sky in grandeur, and with a beautiful outline; like the mountain, it has spots that are rugged and bare.

2. We come, now, to the consideration of this trait of character, as exhibited in the Puritan government. The principles by which the Puritans were guided in the establishment and maintenance of government were in the highest degree rational. Those principles were spiritual; that is, they flowed from pure law and pure reason, and not from an earthly and material source. The Puritan felt that government is a great and solemn interest; that it is an ordinance of God; that its organizing principles must be drawn from the invisible world, and that its sanctions must come from heaven. All the reverence and fear that comes down upon man from the supernatural world, he felt, must be brought to bear in upholding human government. Thus, did the tendency of his mind lead him to refer to the unseen, in his civil relations, and

to found government upon purely rational and spiritual principles.

Hence, the spirituality of the Puritan government. As soon as we compare it with that of the European nations from whose atmosphere the Puritans had just departed, we see a striking difference. It is simple in its structure, its arrangements, and its working. The European mind, accustomed to a material and unspiritual mode of thought, because its faith in the invisible was weak, and its vision of pure principles was dim, had established government not mainly upon law and reason, but upon forms, precedents, arbitrary will, and absolute power. The structure of government in Europe was complicated, its arrangement irrational, and its working exceedingly despotic. It presented to the eye of an observer a long array of forms and ceremonies, under which it was difficult to discover the first principles of law and right, even if they were originally at the bottom, and by which those principles were straitened and hindered in their effectual working. A philosophical observer of the governments of Europe, at that time, would be led to suppose that man had either entirely lost sight of the pure, spiritual principles of government, or else, as was most probably the case, was unwilling to let them have a free and unhampered operation. Such an observer would see that there was but little faith, among the nations, in the great principles of reason and law, and that the state depended for security upon things seen and material; upon the trappings of royalty, the appendages of nobility, the pomp and circumstance of office, the sword and the cannon.

It was reserved for the Puritans to found a government on pure principle. They established but few offices. They stripped off from governmental institutions the forms in which they had been for so many centuries en cased, and let men see the steady and beautiful operation of just maxims, as applied to the regulation of human society. They were not afraid to rest so great a superstructure as the national government, upon what appears to the earthly-minded to be a very weak and unsafe foundation, a few invisible and rational principles. They had faith in the unseen, and knew that law and reason, though not visible to the outward eye, are full of " the power of an endless life."

The more we contemplate the system of government established by the Puritans, the more clearly shall we see the native spirituality of the Puritan mind exhibited in it. The disposition to appeal to what is within man, and so to subject him to wholesome restraint, by means of rational principles, is very apparent in it. Law, in its pure naked reality, was brought before the inward eye; and men obeyed freely, and like rational freemen, as they were. Throughout the whole Puritan commonwealth, so safely and beautifully did government do its perfect work, that peace and order prevailed; and the interference of the officer, the outward and visible representative of government, was rarely needed. Government was, in the best sense of the term, self-government; a voluntary subjection of self to those great maxims of reason and conscience which are invisible, and which connect man with the unseen world and the invisible God. Thus did the prominent trait in the Puritan character manifest itself in the Puritan government.

3. We pass now to the religion of the Puritans. In this, too, we find their fundamental characteristic manifesting itself with great power and intensity. Christianity never appeared in a more spiritual form, than it did in the first periods of the history of New England. It was despoiled entirely of all in which it had been clothed

by superstition and formalism, and stood out unencumbered by rites and ceremonies, a free, pure, and spiritual reality. New England felt that God is a spirit, and worshipped him in spirit and in truth.

But, let us scrutinize more narrowly the different parts of the Puritan religion, and we shall more clearly see their natural temper exhibited in it. For, be it ever remembered, that, although Christianity is a living principle coming down from heaven, and is therefore essentially one and the same in all men, yet it will receive some hues from the native traits of the mind in which it takes up its residence. Christianity in the French mind, though not essentially, yet in its manifestation, is different from Christianity in the English mind.

The Christian religion presented a remarkable appearance, when it lodged itself among the native energies of the Puritan character. Naturally inclined to regard the invisible as the chief reality, and disposed to make but little of things seen and material, it was natural that the Puritan should make religion a matter pertaining mainly to the unseen world, and should strip it, as far as possible, of all earthly conceptions, and all material forms. Hence, the spirituality of their mode of worship. They had no form of prayer, but spake as the spirit gave them utterance. They laid no stress upon postures, but let the body bend naturally to the movements of the soul. They were afraid, to a fault, of devotional music and poetry; for they feared lest their thoughts should be drawn away from the pure and naked realities of another world. They made much of the sermon, because they felt that truth is spiritual, and is a revelation from the invisible God.

Again, if we consider the scheme of doctrine received by the Puritans, we shall see their spiritual tendency. It was strict and pure. It was the theology of such spiritual men as Augustine and Calvin. This theology brings man into the immediate presence of God. It allows of no mediator between God and man, except Him who is God-man. The deity is thus brought into direct contact with humanity; heart to heart, spirit to spirit, life to life. Man is ushered directly into the eternal world; and, in view of its scenes and realities, is led to make his peace with God, through the atonement of God. This theology is exceedingly spiritual and soul-searching. It charges utter sinfulness upon man, convicts and eternally damns him, brings him trembling in his guiltiness to the foot of God, where he ought to be, and then bids him look up, to see if indeed there may be mercy for him.

There have been milder types of Christian doctrine than Calvinism. There were such in the times of the Puritans; but their native spirituality of mind, among other causes, led them to the reception of the strictest and purest theology in the Church. They desired to see the plain and naked truth of God. It was their disposition to remove all coverings, and get at the core. They did not shrink from the consequences of such thorough scrutiny, and they did not fear the results of seeing the bare, conscience-searching truths of the eternal world. Though the intolerable brightness should blind and blast them in that guiltiness which they shared in common with all men, they knew that in this way alone would they be prepared to stand the fires of the last day. Their spirits obtained no rest, until they had known the worst of their case, and the direst rigor of divine truth. And when they had once thoroughly known the whole pure truth of God, they stood firm. They could never again be moved; they could never again be terrified. They were ready, then, for the blast of the archangel's trump, for the resurrection of their own bodies, for the burning-up of the world, for the passing away of the heavens, and for the irrevocable sentence of the final day of doom.

Thus, possessing naturally a disposition to slight the formal and visible, and having this disposition intensified and energized by the indwelling presence of a most severely spiritual theology, is it any wonder that the Puritans abhorred formalism in religion ? Is it any wonder that they dissented, to the bottom of their souls, from all showy and seeming Christianity ? What satisfaction could men find in hollow rites and unmeaning ceremonies, whose spirits were hungering for pure spiritual food, for the living word of God ? What peace could men find in false and shallow exhibitions of truth, whose consciences had been set on fire by the clear vision of the Divine Law ? No ! these men had made thorough work in searching their own spirits; and now, nothing but the pure gospel could give them rest. These men had looked into the other world, and they felt that a formal religion and a lax theology cannot prepare a man to enter into its pure, soul-searching light.

Thus, by nature, by education, and by regeneration, the Puritans were spiritually-minded. That original trait in their character, of which we have spoken, reached its very height of life and absolute intensity of power, through the influences of the Holy Spirit. In society, and in government, we found them to be highly spiritual; in religion, we find them to be absolutely spiritual.

Having thus contemplated the prominent trait of the Puritan character, it is readily seen that all the excellence and glory of New England must be directly referred to it, as their source. Our present comparative simplicity of manners and purity of social life must be referred to it.

The freedom and beauty of our government must be referred to it. The spirituality of our mode of worship and the purity of our scheme of religious doctrine must be referred to it. That we are Protestants, is owing to our fathers. That, as a people, we dissent from formalism in religion, is owing to their instruction and prayers. Burke said of New England, when as a people it was still in the gristle, to use his own phrase, that it possessed "the dissidence of dissent, the Protestantism of the Protestant religion." * If that great statesman could rise from his grave, and look upon us now, when the gristle has become hardened into bones, well strung with thews and thickly netted with sinews, he could still say that New England is largely possessed of the very dissidence of dissent against all formalism in religion, and that the veriest Protestantism, the pure defecated essence of the Protestant religion, is its animating life and its actuating principle.

But, although we have reason to be thankful, that so much of the vigor of the Puritan character is still felt by us as a people, we have reason to fear lest that vigor wane away and die out, under the unfavorable influences to which it is exposed. That vigor, though it still animates us, is not so intense as it was two hundred years ago. We have lost too much of the spirit of our fathers. We have lost much of their faith in invisible things, and are greatly engrossed in things seen and temporal. Luxury and ease, the results of advancing civilization and improvement in the arts, are enervating us. False principles in social organization, in government, and in religion, are stealing, like slow poison, through our arteries. We are beginning to lose the Puritan reverence for the word of God, the church of God, and the sabbath of God.

---

* Speech on Conciliation with America.

It becomes us, therefore, to make the Puritan character a model for imitation. We ought to study it, until we see it in all its massive strength and simple beauty. We ought to invigorate ourselves, by drawing fresh life from the spirituality of our ancestors. Let us remember that our fathers were spiritually-minded, and were greatly under the influence of the other world; that they read God's word, kept God's sabbath, and feared God himself with a solemn awe. Their blood flows in our veins; let their spirit dwell in our breasts.

THE AFRICAN NATURE.*

Mr. President and Gentlemen:

On the 22d of March, 1775, Edmund Burke, pleading for the liberties of the American Colonies, in the British House of Commons, had occasion to allude to their marvellous growth, as outrunning everything of the kind in the then past history of England, or the world. In less than seventy years, he said, the trade with America had increased twelvefold. It had grown from a half-million of pounds per annum to six millions—a sum nearly equal to the whole export trade of England at the beginning of the eighteenth century. This rapid growth, he continued, might all be spanned by the life of a single man, " whose memory might touch the two extremities." Lord Bathurst was old enough in 1704, to understand the figures and the facts, as they then stood. The same Lord Bathurst in 1775 was a member of that parliament before whom the great orator was reciting the new facts that were stranger than fiction, in order to waken England to a consciousness that the colonies beyond the sea were bone of her bone, and flesh of her flesh, and must be treated accordingly. Warming from the gravity of his theme,

* An address before the Massachusetts Colonization Society, May 27, 1857.

and kindling in soul as the vision slowly evolved before him, he represents the guardian angel of the youthful Bathurst as drawing aside the curtain of the future, and unfolding the rising glories of his country; and, particularly, as pointing him, while absorbed in the commercial grandeur of England, to "a little speck scarce visible in the mass of the national interest, a small seminal principle rather than a formed body," and as saying to him: "Young man, there is *America;* which, at this day, serves for little more than to amuse you with stories of savage men and uncouth manners; yet it shall, before you taste of death, show itself equal to the whole of that commerce which now attracts the envy of the world." *

We have alluded to this well-known, but ever fresh and fine prosopopœia of the great Englishman, because it spontaneously comes into memory when one begins to read, to think, or to speak upon Africa. That tropical continent lies nearly as dim and vague before the mind of this generation, as the cold and cheerless America did before the mind of England when Johnson and Burke were boys. With the exception of a small strip of the Atlantic coast, the wilds of this Western world were as unknown to the Englishman of 1700, as the jungles of Soudan or the highlands of Central Africa are to us. And yet it may be, that there are youth of this generation who will live to see those dim beginnings of Christianity, of civilization, and of empire, which are now scarcely visible on the African Atlantic coast, expanded and still expanding into vigorous and vital churches, into strong and mighty states. The guardian angel, in this instance too, might with perhaps as much probability of verification, say to the youth whom he leads by the hand: "Young man,

* Speech on Conciliation with America.

THE AFRICAN NATURE. 247

there is *Africa;* which, at this day, serves for little more than to amuse you with stories of savage men and uncouth manners; yet it shall, before you taste of death, take its place among the continents, and be no longer an unknown world."

For, nothing is more wonderful than the changes and transformations of history. But, involved as every present generation is in the great stream, and whirled along by it, it is not strange that no generation of men are ever fully aware of the strength and rapidity of their own movement. He who belongs to another generation, and looks back, can sees that in such a century, and in such a quarter of the globe, a mighty current was running. The spectator always sees more than the actor. The rare prophetic mind, also, that beholds the future in the instant, may foresee and predict a history too great and grand for contemporaneous belief. The philosophic statesman is aware of what is going on in the struggling masses around him, and auspicates accordingly. But the common man, of the busy present time, never knows the rate he is moving; because he is himself absorbed and carried headlong in the movement. It is not strange, therefore, that all hopeful glowing vaticination, in respect to changes upon this sin-smitten planet, is regarded with distrust. Such anticipations are supposed to belong to the poet and the orator. They have no support in the data and calculations of the statistician or the statesman.

Called upon then, as we are at this time, to consider the present and prospective condition of the most wretched and unpromising quarter of the globe, by the voice of that Colonizing Society which has already done more than any other single association for the welfare of Africa, and which is destined, we believe, under that benign Providence which has protected and blessed it thus far, to see its own great ideas and plans realized; called upon to speak and to think for a hundred millions of our fellow creatures, by a small corporate body, not yet a half-century old, and annually disbursing only a few thousands of dollars, we desire to assign some reasons for believing that a career similar to that of the British colonies in America, and similar to that of all the great colonizing movements of the past, awaits the Republic of Liberia.

What, then, are the grounds for expecting that the plans and purposes of the American Colonization Society will be ultimately realized, in the Christianization of the African continent?

1. The first reason for this expectation is of a general nature. Africa has no past history. It is the continent of the future; for, it is the only one now left to feel for the *first* time the recuperating influences of a Christian civilization. Religion, law, and letters began their march in Asia, and a large part of that continent once felt their influence. From thence they passed into Europe; and Europe is still the stronghold of religion, law, and letters. Westward they then took their way; and the vast spaces of the American continent are still waiting for the Christianity and republicanism that have so rapidly, and firmly, taken possession of that comparatively small belt called the United States. It is true that these influences were, for a time, felt along the northern border of Africa. Egypt and Carthage were once civilized; and a very vigorous Christianity, for three centuries, erected its altar, and kept its fires bright, along the southern shore of the Mediterranean. But Egypt, though African in nature and blood, derived its ideas from Asiatic sources; and its place in history is Asiatic rather than African. That ancient and wonderful pantheistic civilization which built

Thebes and the pyramids, was but the corrupted remains of a yet more ancient Asiatic monotheism; as South tells us that "an Aristotle was but the rubbish of an Adam, and Athens but the rudiments of paradise." Carthage was Phœnician ; and when both Egypt and Carthage were absorbed into Rome, North-Africa belonged much more to the European than to the properly African quarter of the globe. The great continent, then, notwithstanding all these attempts at approach for thousands of years, lies lone and solitary. It is out of all historical connections ; so much so, that the generalizing Hegel, after a very brief characterization of it, in his Philosophy of History, dismisses it with the remark: "We now leave Africa, and shall make no further mention of it. That which we understand by Africa proper is totally destitute of a history ; is totally unopened and undeveloped ; and can, therefore, be merely hinted at, on the threshold of Universal History." *

Now, there is something in this fact that inspires expectation. It may be vague, but it is large and full. The mode and manner may be left to conjecture, or imagination ; but the fact that one whole quarter of the globe has *never* yet been visited by the great influences of religion, law, and letters, taken in connection with the fact that these influences are a part of the plan and destination of God in reference to the *whole* world, and the *whole* human family, lead to the confident faith that this will not always be so. Nature, it was said, abhors a vacuum. Empty spaces will be filled and peopled. History treads no step backward. Her voice cries, "Ever onward!" as the guiding Genius, according to Schiller, continually sounded in the ear of Columbus on the gray

* Hegel's Werke, IX., 123.

waste of waters, "Ever westward! Ever to the West!" Who expects that population, law, and manners will ever flow backward again, from the Alleghanies or the Rocky Mountains? Who expects that the great changes and alterations of the future are to take place on the old theatres of Assyria, Macedonia, Greece, and Rome; or on the more recent, yet already antiquated arenas of Modern Europe? The winds rush where there is vacancy. The great historic currents of the next half-millennium must disembogue where they find room.

The fact, then, that there is no pre-occupancy, and no effete civilization, in the African world, is a ground of expectancy and of courage in regard to it. It is a negative preparation for great results, when the time arrives.

2. A second ground of confident hope, in reference to the future of Africa, is found in the qualities of the African nature. The characteristics of the African man are still almost as unknown, as those of the African soil or the African flora. There are two reasons for this. In the first place, the African has never been in a situation where the depth and reserve of his nature has been drawn upon. Only the superficies of his being has been called into exercise; so that his real and true manhood lies as hidden as the sources of the Nile. In the second place, and as a consequence of this, only his surface-traits and characteristics have appeared in his portraiture. These, moreover, having been exorbitantly unfolded, because there has been none of the balance and moderation of a deeper education and culture, have been as extravagantly depicted. The black man in literature is, therefore, either a weakling or a caricature. The comic side of him, alone, comes into view. The single sonnet of Wordsworth upon the chieftain Toussaint, and the "sparkles dire of fierce, vindictive song," from the American Whittier, are almost the only

literary allusions to the sublime and tragic elements in the negro's nature and condition; certainly the only allusions that, without any abatement and introduction of ludicrous traits, ally him *solely* with human

> "exultations, agonies,
> And love, and man's unconquerable mind."

The African nature is the *tropical* nature. All the races that have hitherto struggled upon the arena of history have belonged to the temperate zone. The Egyptian, the Assyrian, the Babylonian, the Persian, the Greek, the Macedonian, the Roman, the Goth, the Frank, the Englishman, the Anglo-American—all lived north of Cancer. And the fact, that thus far the inter-tropical portion of the globe has furnished few or none of the elements of human history, is very often cited to prove that it can furnish none. It has almost come to be an axiom, that the hot zone cannot ripen man. Brazil may crystallize diamonds of the purest water, and Africa may distil the most elaborate juices and gums; but high intelligence and free will must grow up beneath northern skies.

Now, it is undoubtedly true that the *fallen* human being needs stimulation, and that *sinful* man has done best when he has been crowded from the outside. Easy and pleasant circumstances have always proved too much for his feeble virtue. Hence, though he was created in paradise, and lapped in elysium so long as he could bear it, yet, the very moment he unfitted himself for such perpetual peace and joy, he was driven out among the thorns and thistles, and compelled to eat his bread in the sweat of his brow. In consequence of human apostasy, then, and for no other reason, the general movement of human history has been in climes and under skies that have tasked man, and have fretted him to action. While, therefore, it is conceded that the colder zones and the harder soils have been favorable, like the primitive curse of labor itself, to the best unfolding of an *imperfect* and a *corrupt* humanity, it still remains true, that man was originally made for an outward world of genial warmth, of luxuriant growth, and of beauty. The primitive man was nude ; his light labor was merely to prune away luxuriance ; and his spiritual mind, sanctified by direct intercourse with angel, seraph, and the Eternal Mind, could both endure and profit by the otherwise enervating bliss and beauty of Eden. This original intent and adaptation of the Creator warrants the belief, that as there are some circumstances and influences under a temperate sky that are favorable to human development, so there are some, also, beneath a torrid one. Wherever man can go and live, there he can grow and thrive. Wisdom rejoiceth in all the *habitable* parts of the earth ; and her delights are with *all* the sons of men.

What, then, are the fundamental peculiarities of the African, or of man within the tropics, that afford ground for faith and confidence that human nature will here also, in due season, exhibit a culture and character unique and fine ?

Before proceeding to give only the very brief answer, which the time allows, to this question, it is necessary to direct attention to the comprehensiveness of the word " African." We mean by it, and it properly denotes, a physical and mental structure that belongs to the African continent as a whole, in the same sense that the Asiatic structure belongs to Asia, and the European structure belongs to Europe. The term, therefore, includes a variety of races ; all, however, characterized by certain common traits. From the mouths of the Nile to the Cape of Good

Hope, the observing traveller will find a primary type of mankind, different from the Shemitic, and different from the Japhetic; a style of man which is original and sui-generis; and the minor varieties of which can easily be accounted for, by the physical changes that are made by varieties in the modes of living, and particularly in the degrees of proximity to the burning equatorial line.

It is the misfortune of Africa, that only the most degraded portion of its population have been its representatives before the world. The enslaved, and thereby imbruted negro is the only specimen from which the civilized world obtains its ideas, and draws its conclusions, as to the dignity and capabilities of the tropical man. But, the coast negro, as we shall soon have occasion to see, is, in his best estate, merely the *extreme* of the African type; and even he has not yet been seen in his best estate. What would be thought of a generalization, in respect to the native traits and capacities of the whole Celtic stock—of the entire blood of polished France, and eloquent Ireland, and the gallant Scotch Highlands—that should be deduced from the brutish descendants of those Irish who were driven out of Ulster and South Down in the time of Cromwell; men, now, of the most repulsive characteristics; "with open projecting mouths, prominent and exposed gums, advancing cheek-bones, depressed noses, height, five feet two inches on an average, bow-legged, abortively featured, their clothing, a wisp of rags; spectres of a people that were once well-grown, able-bodied, and comely." But such a judgment would be of equal value with that narrow estimate of the natural traits and characteristics of the inhabitants of one entire quarter of the globe, which rests upon an acquaintance with a small portion of them, a mere infinitesimal of them, carried into a foreign land and reduced to slavery.

The African seems to differ from the European and the Asiatic, by a fuller, more profuse, and more sensuous organization. He is emphatically the child of the Earth and the Sun. His tissues are not compact, tough, and fibrous, like those of the more northern races. On the contrary, they are tumid, and betoken a luxurious soil. The organs of the senses—the eyes, nose, mouth, and ears —are "rich," in the technical phrase of the physiognomist; and in the extreme types are animal and coarse. Man is like the earth he lives upon; and the African man corresponds to that tropical soil and climate, in which every seed swells and sprouts with the rank luxuriance of a jungle. The great generical feature in the African, then, is *richness and fulness in the physical organization ;* and, in proof that it is so, we shall cite the testimony of travellers and physiologists.

The French Denon tells us, that "instead of the sharp features, the keen, animated, and restless visages, the lean and active figures of the Arabian," he finds "in the land of the Pharaohs, full but delicate and voluptuous forms; countenances sedate and placid; round and soft features; with eyes long, almond-shaped, half-shut and languishing, and turned up at the outer angles, as if habitually fatigued by the light and heat of the sun; thick lips, full and prominent; mouths large, but cheerful and smiling; complexions dark, ruddy, and coppery; and the whole aspect displaying, as one of the most graphic delineators among modern travellers has observed, the *genuine African character*, of which the negro is the exaggerated and extreme representation." Blumenbach's examinations of the Egyptian mummies led him to the belief, that there are three varieties in the physiognomy expressed in Egyptian paintings and sculptures. One of these was the Ethiopian, which, he says, "coincides with the descriptions given of the Egyptians by the ancients, and is chiefly distinguished by prominent jaws, turgid lips, a broad flat nose, and protruding eyeballs." "Among the modern Copts," says Prichard, " many travellers have remarked a certain approximation to the negro. Volney says that they have a yellowish, dusky complexion, resembling neither the Grecian nor Arabian; and adds, that they have a puffed visage, swollen eyes, flat nose, and thick lips, and bear much resemblance to mulattoes." Ledyard, whose testimony Prichard remarks is of the more value as he had no theory to support, says: "I suspect the Copts to have been the origin of the negro race: the nose and lips correspond with those of the negro. The hair, wherever I can see it among the people here (the Copts), is curled, not like that of the negroes, but like that of the mulattoes." *

But if the ancient Egyptians and modern Copts exhibit the full, sensuous, and luxurious organization of the African, and properly belong to the African race, it certainly will not be difficult to establish the same claim for all the remaining dwellers on the continent. The former were nearest to Asia and Europe, and were most affected by foreign influences; and yet the type could not be changed; the round cheek, the full protuberant eye, the dark hue, could not be converted into their contraries.

Passing southward, into the burning heart of Africa, we find the tropical man in yet greater intensity and power. The races of Soudan display the fervid type of humanity fully formed, and in the highest degree. There are varieties in this great central region; the lowest being found on the Guinea coast, and the higher ones meeting the traveller as he rises those great terraces by which the con-

---

* Prichard's Natural History of Man, pp. 151-159.

tinent lifts itself up from the sea. The negroes of the Gold Coast, though dwelling amidst miasm and fever, and feeling only the very worst influences of European intercourse, are nevertheless characterized by Barbot as "generally well-limbed, and well-proportioned; having good oval faces, sparkling eyes, eyebrows lofty and thick, mouths not too large, clean white and well-arranged teeth, fresh red lips, not so thick and pendent as those of Angola, nor their noses so broad." "Among the Ashantee tribe of this same Guinea race," says Bowditch, "are to be seen, especially among the higher orders, not only the finest figures, but, in many instances, regular Grecian features, with brilliant eyes, set rather obliquely in the head."

Of the Senegambian nations, the Mandingoes are remarkable for their industry; and, of all the inter-tropical races, have shown the greatest energy of character. Their features are regular, their character generous and open, and their manners gentle. Their hair is of the kind termed completely woolly. The Fulahs, another Senegambian people, forge iron and silver, and work skilfully in leather and wood, and fabricate cloth. An intelligent French traveller describes them as fine men, robust and courageous, understanding commerce, and travelling as far as to the Gulf of Guinea. The color of their skin is a kind of reddish-black, their countenances are regular, and their hair longer and not so woolly as those of the common negroes.*

These statements may be overdrawn in some particulars, and further exploration is undoubtedly required, in order to form a sure and completely satisfactory judgment respecting the tribes of Soudan. But, certainly, all the information thus far obtained, goes to evince that this

---

* Prichard's Natural History of Man, pp. 297-307.

Negro-land is filled up with no puny populations, but with barbaric races of a powerful structure—the bone and muscle out of which a Christian civilization shall hereafter form a powerful style of man.*

Finally, threading our way downward, from the terraces to the southern-ward slope of the African continent, we find the Hottentot and Kaffir, the most degraded of the African races,—yet owing the excess of their degradation, by which they fall below the other African tribes, to the contact and influence of a corrupt European civilization. Unless a genuine Christian influence shall eventually be thrown in upon them by missions, by education, and by commerce, it was, indeed, as one remarks, an ill-omened hour when a Christian navigator descried the Cape of Storms. The Hottentot, by war and vices, has to a great extent degenerated into the Bushman; but the Kaffir still retains his aboriginal traits. Professor Lichtenstein describes them as follows: "They are tall, strong, and their limbs well proportioned; their color is brown; their hair, black and woolly; they have the high forehead and prominent nose of the Europeans, the thick lips of the negroes, and the high cheek-bones of the Hottentots."†

This rapid survey of the inhabitants of the continent, from north to south, justifies us, then, in attributing a *common continental character* to them all; and a continental character that is neither feeble nor emasculated, but, on the contrary, one that is muscular, arterial, and prodigal. There is a generical type of the African nature, constituted by the assemblage of certain physical and mental characteristics, which may be found all over the

---

* Since this was written, twenty years of marvellous exploration, by Livingstone and others, has opened Central Africa in every direction, and this description of the African races has been abundantly confirmed.

† Prichard's Natural History of Man, p. 317.

African continent, whereby this portion of the globe becomes as distinct and peculiar as Asia, or Europe, or America. And it is from this inter-tropical humanity, that we are to deduce a ground of belief, and confidence, that Ethiopia will yet stretch out her hands to God, and that Africa is finally to acquire a place in the universal history of man on the globe.

The chief characteristic of the African nature is the *union of recipiency with passion.* The African is docile. He has nothing of the hard and self-asserting nature of the Goth. He is indisposed, like the dweller of the cold and stimulating zones, to stamp his own individuality upon others. On the contrary, his plastic, ductile, docile nature receives influence from every side, gladly and genially. It is not probable that great empires will be built up on the African continent, that will extend their sway over other parts of the globe—as the Persian sought to obtain rule in Europe, but was thwarted by Greece; or as the Roman extended his dominion over both Asia and Africa. The lust of empire will probably never run in African blood; for, foreign conquest requires a stern, self-reliant, indocile, ambitious nature, that would force itself upon other races and regions; and of this, the tropical man has little or nothing. It is rather to be expected that the African will confine himself to his own home, within the tropics, and will there take up, into his own rich and receptive nature, the great variety of elements and influences that will be furnished by other races and portions of the globe.

Under such circumstances, a unique and remarkable development of human nature must occur. A new form of national life will take rise. For, this plastic character, this deep and absorbing receptivity, will be an alluvium in which all seeds that are planted will strike a long root, and shoot up a luxuriant growth. National history, thus far, exhibits *stimulant* natures, and *stimulant* characteristics. The types of nationality that figure in the past, have generally been moulded from this sort of material—a species which has reached its height in the Anglo-Saxon. This quality is, indeed, a strong, intense, and grand one; and we are the last to disparage its worth. The triumphs of modern Christianity, and modern civilization, are intimately connected with its powerful and persistent action in individuals and nations. But, this tense and stimulant nature, characteristic of man in the northern zone, has its deficiencies, also, like everything human. In isolation, and after long strain, it becomes wiry, hard, brittle, broken. It would not be well that it should be the sole type of humanity; or that no other elements than it can furnish should enter into the texture and fabric of national or individual life, from generation to generation. The Saxon himself, in order to his own preservation even, as well as his own best development, needs some infusion of equatorial elements. It would be well, if his already overwrought stimulancy could be somewhat tranquillized and enriched by the languor and sluggishness of the tropics. It would be well, if the hollow features of the Anglo-American could assume somewhat of the rounded fulness of the Sphinx's or the Memnon's face; if his eager and too shallow eye could be made bulbous, and deep, like that of Soudan.

This, then, is the groundwork of the coming nationalities in Africa. It is a mild, docile, musing, and recipient nature, which is to drink in all the influences that shall pour forth from the old, and perhaps then declining civilizations of the other zones. It is the *artist's* nature, open at every pore, sensitive in every globule and cell of tissue, pulsing with a warm and somewhat slumbrous life—a deep base, for a high structure.

But, this lethargic quality in the tropical man is allied with an opposite one. He is also a creature of passion. In the phrase of Mark Antony, there is a "fire that quickens Nilus' slime." Like his own clime, the inhabitant of the tropics combines great antagonisms in his constitution. This slumber of his nature is readily stirred into wildest rage; as the heavy and curtained air of the equator, which has hung dense and still for days and weeks, is suddenly disparted by electric currents, and, in an instant, is one wide, livid blaze of lightning. This quality, like all counterbalancing ones, is not strictly *contrary* to the one that has just been described. Were it so, the one would neutralize and kill the other. There would be no interpenetration of the two, if nothing but the relation of sheer and mere contrariety, like that between fire and water, obtained between these two qualities in the African nature. It is antithesis, not contrariety. For, this very passion itself originates in, and springs directly out of, the lethargy. The nature has been slumbrous and dormant, only that it may, at the proper time, be fiery and active. The one balances, not neutralizes, the other. Were there an unintermittent draught and strain upon the entire man, there could never be this tropical vehemence. But the slumber is recuperative of the constitutional force; and, in and by the oscillations of passion and lethargy, the wondrous life goes on.

That the African is a passionate being, is attested by all history. No one can look at the features of the Memnon, without perceiving that beneath that placid contour there sleeps a world of passion. Shakspeare has given Cleopatra to us in her own proud words:

> "I am fire and air; my other elements
> I give to baser life."

The influences of Christianity do not destroy, but refine and sanctify, this quality. The North-African church of the first centuries was full of divine fire. It flashes in the laboring but powerful rhetoric of Tertullian. It glows like anthracite in the thoughts of Augustine, whose symbol in the church is a flaming heart; and over whose mighty and passionate sensualism the serene, spiritualizing, and divine power of Christianity ultimately, and only after an elemental war within like that of chaos, wrought out an ethereal and saintly transformation that has not yet been paralleled in the history of the church.

But we need not go into the distant past, or into the distant African continent, for evidence upon this point. We cannot look into the eye of the degraded black man who meets us in our daily walks, without perceiving that he belongs to the torrid zone. The eye, more than any other feature, is the index of the soul, and of the soul's life. That full, liquid, opaline orb, that looks out upon us from face and features that are stolid, or perhaps repulsive, testifies to the union of passion and lethargy in this fellow-creature. That large and throbbing ball, that sad and burning glance, though in a degraded and down-trodden man, betoken that he belongs to a passionate, a lyrical, and an eloquent race.

This tropical eye when found in conjunction with Caucasian features is indicative of a very remarkable organization. It shows that tremulous sensibilities are reposing upon a base of logic. No one could fix his gaze, for a moment, upon that great Northern statesman who has so recently gone down to his grave, without perceiving that this rare combination of the temperate with the tropical was the physical substrate of what he was, and what he did. That deep-black iris, cinctured in a pearl-white sclerotic, and more than all, that fervid *torrid* glance and gleam, were the exponents and expression of a tropical nature; while the thorough-bred Saxonism of all the rest of the physical structure indicated the calm and massive strength that underlay, and supported, all the passion and all the fire. It was the union of two great human types in a single personality. It was the whole torrid zone enclosed and upheld in the temperate.

It will be apparent from this analysis, that the African nature possesses a latent capacity equal, originally, and after its own kind, to that of the Asiatic or the European. Shem and Japhet sprang from the very same loins with Ham. God made of one blood those three great races by which he repopulated the globe after the deluge. This blending of two such striking antitheses as energy and lethargy, the soul and the sense; this inlaying of a fine and fiery organization into drowsy flesh and blood; this supporting of a keen and irritable nerve by a tumid and strong muscular cord—what finer combination than this is there among the varied types of mankind? The objection urged against the possibility of a historical progress in Africa similar to that in the other continents, upon the false ground that the original germ and basis was an inferior one—an objection that shows itself, if not theoretically yet practically, in the form of inaction, and an absence of enthusiasm and enterprising feeling when the claims of Africa are spoken of—this objection is invalid. The philosophic and the philanthropic mind must, both alike, rise above the prejudices of an age, and look beyond a present and temporary degradation that has been the result of centuries of ignorance and slavery. If this be done, the philosopher sees no reason for refusing to apply the same law of progress and development (provided the external circumstances be favorable, and the necessary conditions exist) to the tropical man, that he does to the man of the temperate or the arctic zones; and no reason for doubting that, in the course of time, and under the genial influences of the Christian religion—the mother of us all—human nature will exhibit all its high traits and qualities in the black races, as well as in the white. And, certainly, the philanthropist, after a wide survey of history; after tracing back the modern Englishman to the naked Pict and bloody Saxon; after comparing the filthy savage of Wapping and St. Giles, with the very same being and the very same blood in the drawing-rooms of Belgrave Square; has every reason for keeping up his courage, and going forward with his work. There have been much stranger transformations in history, than the rise of African republics, and African civilizations, and African literatures will be.

But, how is the way to be prepared for this? From what point or points, and through what instrumentalities, is the alteration to begin? It is this second branch of the subject which we now proceed briefly to examine.

1. It is natural to expect that the movements of God's providence, in the future, will be very much like those of the past; and that civilization and culture will, hereafter, pass into the unenlightened parts of the globe in very much the same way they have heretofore. But, history shows that this has uniformly taken place by the exodus of colonies. Religion, law, and letters are not indigenous, but exotic, in all the past career of man on the globe. One race hands the torch of science to another. One quarter of the globe is both the parent and teacher of another. There are autochthones nowhere. There are no strictly self-taught men anywhere. And in the last examination, and at the primary origin and source, we are compelled to rise above earth and man altogether, and find the first beginnings of knowledge and religion in the

skies. From first to last, there is an *imparting* act from the higher to the lower. The more intelligent makes revelations to the less intelligent. The genealogy cannot stop short of the Creator himself. Cainan was the son of Enos, " which was the son of Seth, which was the son of Adam, which was the son of God."

These changes and movements in human civilization are particularly visible at those points where civilization passes from one continent to another continent. The *knots* in the grape-vine reveal where the life gathers, and concentrates in order to a new expansion. Europe received letters and civilization from Asia. The little district of Greece was the radiating point; for, Rome received them from Greece, and gave them to all her empire. But, the original sources of Greek culture were colonists, few and feeble, from Egypt, Phœnicia, and Asia Minor. The Egyptian Cecrops and Danaus brought over the seeds of civility to Attica and Argos, fifteen centuries before our era. The Phœnician Cadmus carried over an Asiatic alphabet soon after. And the Lydian Pelops soon followed with his wealth, and knowledge of the mechanic arts.* But, the consequences of this immigration from another continent were not felt, to any great extent, upon Europe at large, until a thousand years had rolled by. The Greek, with all his treasures of wisdom and of beauty, was shut up from the "barbarian" world, until the Roman broke down the barrier, and Grecian culture then had free course. And if we should allow a millennium, for a colony upon the African coast to diffuse law, manners, letters, and religion, over the African continent, it would be as rapid a movement as that to which Ancient Rome and the whole Modern World owe their secular

---

* Heeren's Ancient Greece, Chapter III.

civilization. The radiating points for the Western Continent were the Spanish, and more especially the British colonies. The movement here has been much more rapid than anything in the history of the Old World. And yet, after more than two centuries, not one-quarter of this Western hemisphere is fully under the influence of Christian civilization.

The history of the past, then, indicates that Africa must receive religion, law, and letters in the same way that the other continents have received them. They must be *given* to her. The *colonist* must carry the seeds of civilization and of empire into the tropical world. Christendom owes colonies to the only portion of the globe that has never yet been a part of Christendom. Europe and America ought to adopt the utterance of the great apostle to Grecian and to barbarian Europe—an utterance to which both of them, under God, owe their religion and their culture, more than to any other single cause—and say: "We are debtors, as much as in us lies, to barbarian Africa." Each of them ought to prove its sincerity, by entering with energy upon a great colonizing movement, and planting Christian colonies all along the coast.

2. In the second place, it is the colonist of *African blood*, upon whom the chief reliance must be placed, so long as the colonizing period continues. For, the tropical climate necessitates the sluggish blood of the tropical man. It is certain death, to expose the nervous, high-strung, and never-relaxed nature of the Caucasian, to the fervors of the burning zone, and the damps of an equatorial night-fall. The dweller in this portion of the globe must be able to rise and fall, like a barometer, with the climate; to act and toil vehemently for a time, and then to pass into a recuperative inaction. All the colo-

nists of history have gone from temperate, to temperate regions. The true colonist for the tropics, then, is the man of the tropics. It may be, that the white man can live upon the high grounds of the interior, when the heart of Africa shall have been opened to commerce, and made yet more salubrious by agriculture and civilization ; but, for a long time to come, the black man must lay the foundations of empire and civilization, and build up the superstructure.

And, without intending to disparage in the least the other agencies that have been and will be employed, all present indications go to show that it is the *Liberian colonist* who must take the lead in this great movement. For, the Liberian is the tropical man more or less penetrated by the cold and calm ideas of the North. He carries with him some American discipline and education. He has not lost his ancestral traits ; for, while in bondage, he has still lived upon the borders of that great zone from which his forefathers were stolen. He can not only endure, but he loves a hot and languid clime. And yet, he has felt the stimulation of that active race among whom he has lived. The wrath of man has praised God. The American negro has been made aggressive, and enterprising, by his enslavement. He has been fitted to be a colonist, and to impress himself upon the passive and plastic millions of Africa, by a process that involves awful guilt in the human authors of it. The Liberian colonist has, thus far, obtained a firmer foothold than any other, upon the African continent. He has established a republic whose independence is acknowledged by the leading powers of the world; and whose nationality has now entered into the history of nations. There is a definite point of departure, and a living germ of expansion in Liberia.

Furthermore, this Liberian republic is a really *Christian state*. There is not now, probably, an organized commonwealth upon the globe, in which the principles of Christianity are applied with such a childlike directness and simplicity, to the management of public affairs, as in Liberia. New England, in the days of her childhood, and before the conflicting interests of ecclesiastical denominations introduced jealousies; Geneva, in the time of John Calvin, when the church and the state were practically one and the same body, now acting through the consistory, and now through the council; in fine, all religious commonwealths in their infancy, and before increasing wealth and luxury have stupefied conscience and dimmed the moral perception, furnish examples of the existing state of things in the African republic. Even the common school education, which the Liberian constitution provides for the whole population, has been given by the missionary, and in connection with the most direct religious instructions and influences. The state papers of the Liberian Executive and Legislature breathe a grave and serious spirit, like that which inspires the documents of our own colonial and revolutionary periods. It is not necessary, in the heart of New England, and before such an audience as this, to enlarge upon the significance of the fact, that the most influential radiating point for civilization in Western Africa is a *religious republic*. No reflecting man can ponder the fact, and think of all it involves, without ejaculating, from the depths of his soul: "God save the Commonwealth of Liberia."

Such, then, is the general nature of the argument for African colonies, and for the American Colonization Society. The race itself, which it proposes to elevate and Christianize, is one of the three great races in and through which God intended, after the total destruction of all antecedent ones by the flood, to re-people the globe and subdue it. The tropical man and the tropical mind is destined, sooner or later, to enter into human history, and to have a history. It is in this faith, that the Society whose anniversary we are celebrating toils and prays. It has been its misfortune, that its vision has been clearer than that of others, and that it has, consequently, cherished plans that have appeared impracticable. But, this is always the misfortune of faith within the sacred sphere, and of genius within the secular. Each of them may say to the torpid soul:

"I hear a voice thou canst not hear;
I see a hand thou canst not see."

Through good report, and through evil report, the American Colonization Society has pursued its straightonward course, and now begins to see what it foresaw. It sees four hundred miles of the African coast secured, by fair purchase and peaceble occupation, to the area of freedom. It sees this coast-line widened into a surface of fifty miles towards the interior, and destined to extend rapidly inland and coastwise. It sees the slave trade extinct not only within Liberian jurisdiction, but shrinking away from the remoter borders of it. It sees ten thousand colonists from America, with their descendants, mingling with, and giving tone to, three hundred thousands of native population. It sees a large annual commerce coming into existence, and one that is increasing in rapid ratio. It sees a regular republican government working firmly and equally through the forms of law, and administered with singular prudence and energy. It sees a system of education, from the primary to the collegiate, exerting its elevating influence upon the mass of the people, and an incipient literature, in state-papers and public addresses. It sees the church of Christ crowning all other institutions, and giving direction to the mind and heart of the rising state.

Looking back, then, over the brief forty years of its existence, and pointing to what God has wrought by it, is not the American Colonization Society justified in boldly appealing to the philanthropist, for the means of still greater benefits to the African, and to Africa? For, the time has now arrived for enlarged operations. Africa is evidently upon the eve of great events. The explorations of Barth, and Vogel, and Anderson, and Moffat, and Livingstone; the English Niger expeditions; the curiosity and courage of individual explorers, in search of the head-waters of the Nile; the discovery of fine stalwart races all through the interior; the very rapid growth of African commerce, at points upon both the Eastern and Western coasts; the very mystery, itself, which overhangs this part of the globe, the more stimulating because all the rest of the world lies in comparative sunlight—all these things combined tend to the belief that, comparatively, more will be discovered, and more will be done, in and about Africa, within the coming century, than in and about any other quarter of the globe. The other continents have had their hour of deliverance. The hour for Africa has now, for the first time, come. Her scores of races prove to have capacities for Christianity and self-government. The American emancipationist is ready and waiting to send out, among them, hundreds and thousands of Americanized colonists. Shall not the philanthropists of this land now make full proof of the colonizing method? —that method which was employed with such vigor by Rome in Romanizing the barbarians whom she conquered; that method by which Britain, the modern Rome, has made her drum-beat to be heard round the globe? And, especially, shall not the church of Christ secure a foothold and a protection for its missionaries in Africa, by helping to extend the influence of those Christian colonies which have hitherto been their best earthly protection, and in connection with which, alone (so the history of past missions in Africa, for four hundred years, plainly shows), can missionary operations be carried on with permanent success?

COLERIDGE AS A PHILOSOPHER AND THEOLOGIAN.*

THE epithet "myriad-minded," which Coleridge applied to Shakspeare, is applicable to himself. He possessed an almost universal capacity. The elements of the poet, the philosopher, the theologian, the critic, and the artist, were mingled in his constitution. The only important branch of human knowledge for which he had little inclination was mathematics; and even this had its equivalent, in that tendency to subtle and scholastic ratiocination so characteristic of him. "I have known," said Wordsworth, "many men who have done wonderful things, but Coleridge is the only wonderful *man* that I ever knew." This breadth and opulence of endowment accounts, in part, for the diversity of judgment passed upon him. From the first appearance of this author down to the present time, he has been the subject of analysis and criticism, both offensive and defensive, to an extent unparalleled in the instance of any other literary man within the same length of time. Critics themselves have been embarrassed by the universality of his genius, and the variety of his productions, and have generally confined themselves to one side

* Published in 1852, as an introduction to Harper's edition of Coleridge's Works.

of his mind, and one class of his works. The result is,
that one gift of the man has been extolled to the deprecia-
tion of another. Those, and they are the great majority,
who have been impressed by the rich and exhaustless
imagination of Coleridge, and by his contributions to the
lighter and more beautiful forms of literature, have la-
mented that so much of the power and vigor of his intellect
should have been enlisted in philosophy; while the lesser
number, who have been stimulated and strengthened by his
profound speculations as they have been by no contemporaneous English writer, have regretted that the poetic nature prevented that singleness of aim, and unity of pursuit,
which might have left as the record of his life a philosophic system, to be placed beside those of Plato and Kant.
With the exception of the clear and masterly essay, prefixed to his edition of the *Aids to Reflection*, by the late
Dr. Marsh, whose premature decease, in the full vigor of
his powers, and the full maturity of his discipline and
scholarship, is the greatest loss American philosophy has
yet been called to meet, we recollect no thoroughly elaborated, and truly profound estimate of the philosophical
opinions of Coleridge. There are two reasons for this.
In the first place, the speculative opinions of Coleridge
were a slow formation, and although they finally came to
have a fixed and determined character, yet during the first
half of his literary career he was undoubtedly not clear
in his own mind. The consequence therefore is, that the
philosophy of Coleridge must be *gathered* from his writings, rather than *quoted* from them, and hence the difficulty, for the critic, which does not exist in the instance
of a rounded and finished treatise, to determine the real
form and matter of his system. In the second place, the
literary world has not been interested in the department
of philosophy. Those problems relating to the nature of

man, the universe, and God, which in some ages of the world have swallowed up in their living vortex all the best thinking of the human mind, and which in reality have been the root whence have sprung all the loftiest growths of the human intellect, have been displaced by other and slighter themes, and hence the English philosopher of this age has been a lonely and solitary thinker. There have been times, when the striking expression of Hazlitt would apply with literal truth to the majority of the literary class: "Sir, I am a metaphysician, and nothing makes an impression upon me but abstract ideas." But the age in which one of the most subtle and profound of English minds made his appearance, and cast his bread upon all waters, was the least abstract in its way of thinking, the most concrete and outward in its method and tendency, of any. These two causes combined will account, perhaps, for the fact that while the poetical and strictly literary productions of Coleridge have, on the whole, met with a genial reception and an appreciative criticism, his philosophical and theological opinions have been at the best imperfectly understood, and, more often, much misunderstood and misrepresented. While, therefore, Coleridge has done more than any other man, with the exception of Wordsworth, to form the poetic taste of the age, and to impart style and tone to the rising generation of English poets, and as a literary man has done more by far than any other one, to revolutionize the criticism of the age—while, in this way, "he has been melted into the rising literatures of England and America"—Coleridge as a thinker has accomplished less.

And yet it is our belief, that in this latter character, in the capacity of a philosopher and theologian, Coleridge is to exert his greatest and best influence. After his immediate influence upon poetry and belles-lettres shall have disappeared in the ever-shifting development of national literature, the direction and impulse which his speculative opinions have given to the English thinking of the nineteenth century will, for a long time to come, be as distinct and unmistakable as the gulf-stream in the Atlantic. It is for this reason that we shall, in this introductory essay, confine our remarks to the philosophical and theological opinions of Coleridge; and it will be our aim, as fully as our limits will permit, to contemplate him as a thinker, the main tendency of whose thinking is in the right direction, and the general spirit and influence of whose system is profound and salutary. It will be our object to justify to the general mind that respectful regard for Coleridge's philosophical and theological views, and that confidence in their general soundness, which is so marked a characteristic of that lesser but increasing public who have been swayed by him for the last twenty years. In doing this, however, we mean not to appear as the mere passive recipient of his opinions, or as the blind adherent of each and every one of them. How far we are disposed to look upon Coleridge as an original thinker, in the high sense in which the phrase is applied to such philosophers as Plato and Aristotle, as Des Cartes and Kant, and to what extent we think he may be regarded as the author of a system, and the head of a school in philosophy, will appear in the course of our remarks.

And we would here, in the outset, direct attention to the manner in which the opinions of Coleridge originated. It is unfortunate that no biography at all worthy of the man is in existence; his own most interesting, but most fragmentary *Biographia Literaria* still being the best account of his intellectual and moral history yet given to the world. With the aid, however, to be derived from the biographical materials now before the world, a careful study of his writings themselves will enable the discerning student, not only to gather the general system finally adopted, and to some extent developed by Coleridge, but also to trace the origin and growth of it. A full account, however, of the inward as well as outward life of Coleridge, by a congenial mind, would be, in many respects, the richest contribution to psychology that could be made.

For, the mental development of Coleridge was eminently an historic process. He did not, as do the majority of thinking men, begin with the same general system and method of thought with which he ended, but, like the age in which he lived and upon which he impressed himself, he passed by a slow and most thorough process from a sensuous to a spiritual system of speculation. Bred up in the reigning empirical philosophy of the eighteenth century, it was, only gradually, and as we think, through the intermediate stage of pantheism, that he finally came out, in the maturity of his powers, upon the high ground of a rational and Christian theism. In like manner, and parallel with this, he went through a great theological change. Beginning with the Socinianism which, at the close of the last century, existed not merely in an independent and avowed form of dissent from the Established church of England, but also to some extent in the clergy of this church itself, Coleridge, partly from the change in his philosophic views, and still more as we believe from severe inward struggles, and a change in his own religious experience, in the end embraced the Christian system with a depth and sincerity, a humility and docility of spirit rarely to be found in the history of philosophers and poets, of whom "few are chosen." And, finally, the same revolution, the same change for the better, and growth, appears in his political opinions. Embracing with "proud precipitance of soul" the cause of a false freedom, he gradually moderated his views, grew conservative, and in the end settled down upon the principles of the majority of cultivated Englishmen, and rested in them.

Now, this peculiarity in the origin and formation of the system of opinions finally adopted by Coleridge, and by which alone he ought to be known and will be known to posterity, deserves serious and candid attention for several reasons. In the first place, the student will thereby be saved from the errors into which many individuals, and to some extent the age itself, have fallen, of attributing to Coleridge, as the ultimate and fixed view of his mind, opinions that had but an early and transient existence in it, and which sustain about the same relation to his final system, that the pang and the throe do to the living birth. The question for the student in relation to Coleridge is not: What did he believe and teach on this point, and on that point, in the year 1800? but, What did he teach and believe in the fulness of his development, and in the maturity of his ripened reason? The question is not: What can be logically deduced, and still less what can be twisted and tortured, out of this or that passage in his writings? but, What is unquestionably the strong drift and general spirit of them as a whole? No writer more needs, or is more deserving of a generous and large-minded criticism than this one. Without reserve, he has communicated himself to the world, in all the phases of experience and varieties of opinion through which he passed—in all his weaknesses and in all his strength—and such an exposure as this surely ought not to be subjected to the same remorseless inference as that to which we of right subject the single treatise on a single doctrine, of a mind made up.

Again, this recognition of the manner in which the opinions of Coleridge were formed will, at the very same time that it opens the eye to all that is true and sound in them, also open it to whatever is defective or erroneous. How much there is of the latter, is a point upon which each mind must judge for itself, and such freedom of judgment is one of the plainest lessons and most natural fruits of the general system contained in these volumes. Provided only the judgment be intelligent and free from bigotry, we believe Coleridge will suffer no more than the finite human mind must suffer, when it allows itself to expatiate in all regions of inquiry, and attempts to construct a system of universal knowledge. If we remember the immense range of Coleridge's studies and the vastness of his schemes, and also remember that though he had not the constructive ability of an Aristotle or a Hegel, and did not fairly and fully realize a single one of his many plans, he yet has left on record some expression of his mind, upon nearly or quite all the more serious and important subjects that come before the human understanding, we shall not be surprised to find some misconceptions and errors in his multifarious productions. But, these mistakes and deficiencies themselves will be the most unerringly detected, and the most effectually guarded against, by him who is able to view and criticise them from the very vantage-ground itself, to which his mind has been lifted by the principles of the general system of Coleridge. Having made these "the fountain-light of all his day, the master-light of all his seeing," the inquirer after truth will be able to detect the errors to which the human mind is always liable, and which in the present instance are, as we verily believe, the excrescences merely.

But, however it may have been with Coleridge himself, it is plain that this slow process of renunciation of erroneous systems, and reception of more correct ones, is one of increased interest and worth for the inquirer. Like the *Retractations* of Augustine, the retractations of Coleridge, if we may call them such, have a negative worth almost equal to that of the positive statements to which they lead. This rise of the mind through doubts and prejudices to a higher and more rectified position; this nearing the centre of absolute truth, by these corrections; is always one of the most instructive passages in literary history. And especially is it so in the case of Coleridge. We see, here, one of the most capacious and richly-endowed minds of the race, after a slow and toilsome course, first through materialism, the less profound, and lastly through pantheism, the most profound of the two erroneous systems of speculation in which many of the most gifted intellects contemporaneous with him were caught and stopped, ultimately and with a deep and clear consciousness finding rest in Christianity, as the eternal ground not only of life but also of truth, not only of religion but also of philosophy. Coleridge lived contemporaneously with that most wonderful, and for the speculative intellect most overmastering of all mental processes, the pantheistic movement in the German mind. But while he was at one period of his life—the heyday of hope and aspiration—involved in it so far as to say that his head was with Spinoza, we find him freeing himself from it, at an after-period, when the whole continental mind was drawn within reach of its tremendous sweep as within the circles of a maelstrom. He worked his way through and out of a system the most stupendous for its logical consistence, and the most fascinating for the imagination, of any that the world has yet seen, and undoubtedly stablished and settled his own mind, whether he may have done the same for others or not, in the Christian theism, at a time when the speculation and philosophizing of his day were fast departing from the centre of truth, and drawing nearly all the inquiring intellect of Germany and France with them. During the last quarter of his life, as matter of fact, Coleridge was the oracle and the teacher for many minds who were seeking rest and finding none in the sphere of philosophy, and whether he relieved their doubts and cleared up their difficulties or not, no one of them ever seems to have doubted that he was clear and settled in his own mind, and that though he might not succeed in refuting the positions of atheism and pantheism, he was himself impregnable to them. But, there is reason to believe that many minds were strengthened and armed by him, and that the philosophy and theology of England is at this very moment very different from what it would have been, had the thinking of Coleridge not been working like leaven in it.* It is a remark of Goethe, that our own faith is wonderfully increased on learning that another mind shares it with us; and perhaps one of the strongest reasons for a wavering soul, for believing in the highest truths of philosophy and religion, and for rejecting the skepticism of the human understanding, lies in such examples as that of Coleridge. His belief was not hereditary and passive. He was not ignorant of the arguments and gigantic schemes which the speculative reason has constructed in opposition to the truth. He had painfully felt in his own being the difficulties and doubts to which man is liable, and to which

* Even the recent picture of Coleridge by Carlyle unconsciously betrays a sense of the superiority of this intellect, in reference to the deeper problems of man's existence and destiny; while Sterling seems to have derived from the oracle at Highgate, most of that struggling faith in God, and in man's freedom and immortality, which throws such a sadly-pleasing air over his biography.

the acutest intellects have too often succumbed. He had been over the whole ground from Pyrrho to Hegel, and, after all his investigation, saw his way clear into the region of Christian revelation, and rested there. Surely, such an example is an argument and an authority for the doubting mind. All that Burke * says of the relation of the culture of Montesquieu to the Constitution of England, in that splendid passage, at once the most magnificent rhetoric and the strongest logic, applies with fuller and far deeper force, to the relation of an endowment, a discipline, and an acquisition, like that of Coleridge, to philosophy and Christianity.

It is in reference to this historical formation and enunciation of the opinions of Coleridge that this, so far as we know, first *complete* collection of his works finds its justification and recommendation. It has been said in respect to the publication of such portions of his writings as the *Table Talk* and the *Literary Remains*, that their extremely fragmentary character ought to exclude them from a permanent collection of a great writer's works, and that, at least, they should be subjected to a revision that would strike out the less important matter, the sometimes hastily conceived and rashly uttered remark. But, in the light of what has been said, the value of every jot and tittle of what Coleridge and his friends for him have ever printed is clearly apparent. Not that everything he has left on record has high intrinsic worth; not that everything he has written can be regarded as the pure product of his own brain; not that everything contained in his writings is to be received as truth by the reader; but each and everything has value and interest, if for nothing else, as exhibiting the course and development of his intellect.

* Appeal from the New to the Old Whigs, *sub fine.*

In this reference, the volumes containing the *Table Talk* and *Literary Remains* are of the highest value, not only for the wonderful pregnancy and suggestiveness of his remarks upon all things human or divine, but for the acquaintance they give the reader with the interior process and change going on within him. A careful perusal of these, in connection with the dates, throws great light upon the history of Coleridge's mind. Aside, however, from the importance of these productions in this respect, they have great intrinsic worth. Besides the profound and piercing glances into the highest truths of metaphysical philosophy, scattered throughout the *Literary Remains*, unquestionably the best philosophy of art and of criticism, and the very best actual criticism upon the great creative minds in literature, that is accessible to the merely English reader, are to be found in this same miscellany.

It is of course impossible in an essay, to attempt a criticism in detail upon all the principal topics upon which Coleridge has philosophized, even if we were competent to the task, and we shall therefore confine ourselves to a few points which we think are deserving of consideration, and which will tend to place their author in a just and fair light as a thinker.

1. And in the first place, we think this author is to be recommended and confided in, as the foremost and ablest English opponent of pantheism. We do not speak of formal opposition to this the most powerful and successful of all systems of false philosophy, for Coleridge has left on record no professed and finished refutation of Spinoza or Schelling, but we allude to the whole plan and structure of the philosophy which he finally adopted and defended, as in its own nature the most effectual preventive of the adoption of pantheism, and the best positive remedy for it when adopted, to be found out of that coun-

try which has furnished both the most virulent bane and the most powerful antidote. The distinctions lying at the foundation of his whole system, if recognized and received, render it impossible for the recipient to be diverted from the true method of thinking, into one so illegitimate as the pantheistic, to say nothing of their incompatibility with the fundamental positions of pantheism. No ingenuity whatever, for example, can amalgamate the doctrine, of which Coleridge makes so much, of an *essential* distinction between nature and spirit, with the doctrine of the *substantia una et unica*. If the natural is of one substance, and the spiritual is of another; if the distinction is not merely phenomenal but metaphysical, and no possible heightening and clarification of the former can result in the latter; then there is a gulf between nature and spirit, between matter and mind, that cannot be filled up. This distinction, moreover, not only permits, but naturally conducts to, the conceptions of an uncreated and a created substance—conceptions that are precluded by the assumption which the pantheist supposes he must make in order to introduce unity into the system of the universe, that there is ultimately only one substance, uncreated, infinite, and eternal. The very moment that the materialism which is to be found in ideal pantheism, notwithstanding its boast of spirituality, as really as in material pantheism, is eliminated and precluded, by the recognition of a difference in *kind* between nature and spirit, the inquirer is left alone with the self-determined, *personal* spirit, the contrary and antithesis of nature and of matter, with its reason and its conscience, and thereafter may be safely left to answer the questions: Is there an uncreated personal God? am I a created and accountable being? am I destined to a conscious immortality of existence? But if this distinction is denied, and nature and spirit, matter and mind, the world and God, are all one essence and substance, and the distinctions denoted by these terms are merely formal, subjective, and phenomenal, then such questions as the above are absurd and impossible.

We are aware, that in these pantheistic systems the terms nature and spirit, the world and God, are as freely employed as in theistic systems, and that in the last and most remarkable of them all, that of Hegel, philosophy itself is divided into the philosophy of nature and the philosophy of spirit. But, on the hypothesis of a one sole substance, the subject-matter of each must be one and the same, and the inquirer in the latter department is only investigating a mere *modification* of the same thing which he has just investigated in the former. Metaphysics are nothing but physics, and *vice versa*. He has risen into no *essentially* higher sphere of being or of cognition, by passing from the philosophy of nature to that of spirit, as he understands and employs these terms, because he has not passed into any *essentially* different sphere. The vice of the whole system is in the fatal error, the pantheistic postulate, at the outset. There is and can be but one substance, and, notwithstanding all the modification it may undergo in infinite space and everlasting time, it remains but one substance still. But, this vice is impossible in any system of philosophy, or in any method of thinking, that starts with the fundamental hypothesis of a difference in *kind* between the substance of the natural and the substance of the spiritual, or between matter and mind.*

Now, the earnestness and force with which this distinction, so fundamental to theism and preclusive of pantheism, is insisted upon by Coleridge, particularly in the *Aids*

* We use matter in a somewhat loose way in this connection, in order to illustrate the technical use of the word nature as the contrary of spirit, and not because it contains all that is meant by nature.

to *Reflection*, the most complete and self-consistent of his strictly philosophic writings, will strike every reflecting reader. It is not merely formally laid down, but it enters so thoroughly into his whole method of philosophizing, that it can be eliminated from it only as oxygen can from atmospheric air, by decomposition and destruction. And especially are all pantheistic conceptions and tendencies excluded by the distinction in question, when it is further considered that the constituent element in the spiritual is freedom, as that of the natural is necessity. In nature, as distinguished from spirit, there is no absolute beginning, no first start, consequently no self-motion, and consequently no responsibility. Nature, says Coleridge, is an endless line of antecedents and consequents, in continuous evolution. To be in the middle of an endless series, is the characteristic of a thing of nature, says Jacobi, * between whose statements regarding this general distinction, in the last part of his *Von göttlichen Dingen*, and those of Coleridge in the *Aids*, there is a striking coincidence. In the mental and spiritual realm, on the contrary, this law and process of continuity by which we are hurried back from the effect to its foregoing cause, and from this foregoing cause to *its* foregoing cause, and so backward forever into an infinite series, and can never reach a point where a movement has no antecedent, because it really *begins*, by *self*-movement—that point where a *responsible* movement is first found, and which is to be reached, not by a gradual ascent within the sphere of the natural to the highest degree of the same kind, but by a leap over the gulf that divides the two great domains from each other—this law of continuous cause and effect, we say, is excluded from the sphere of the spiritual, by

---

* Werke, III. 401. Leipsic Ed. 1816.

virtue of its differing in *kind* from the natural; by virtue of its being of *another substance*, and, consequently, of having an essentially different function and operation from nature and matter. It is true, that we speak of a continuous evolution and development, and properly too, within the realm of spirit as well as of nature, but the continuity in this instance is not continuity without beginning, or the continuity of the law of cause and effect, which is the only law in the natural world, but continuity that has a true beginning or first start, or the continuity of self-determination. Development in the mental or spiritual world—that of the human will, for example—begins with the creation of the will, and proceeds freely and responsibly so long as the will exists. The development or movement, in this instance, is not, like that of a movement in nature, a mere and pure *effect*. If it were, a cause must be found for it antecedent to, and *other* than it; and this would bring the movement out of the sphere of the spiritual or *self*-moved, into the sphere of nature and matter, and make it a necessitated unit in an endless series of movements, to the destruction of all responsibility. But we have no disposition to repeat what has been so clearly expressed by Coleridge on this point, and reaffirmed and explained by Dr. Marsh in his preliminary essay to the *Aids*. The distinction itself, never more important than at this time when materialism and naturalism is so rife, cannot, after all, be taught in words, so well as it can be thought out. It is a matter of direct perception, if perceived at all, as must be the case with all *a priori* and fundamental positions. Man's immediate consciousness is the most convincing, because the most vital of all evidence, that mind is not a mode of matter, or spirit a phase of nature, or voluntary agency a necessitated series of concatenated causes and effects.

Now, on the pantheistic system, there is really nothing but nature; there is nothing absolutely mental or spiritual. The one substance, of which all things are modifications and developments, is nothing but a single infinite nature. From eternity to eternity, the process of emanation and evolution goes on, and the result is, all that was, is, and is to come. Though the terms God and man, spirit and nature, mind and matter, may be employed, yet the objects denoted by them are of one and the same substance, and therefore have the same primary attributes. The history of the universe is the history of a single Being, and of one, merely natural, necessitated process, slowly and blindly evolving from that dark ground of all existence, the one aboriginal substance. There is no creation out of nothing of a new and secondary substance, but merely the shaping of the old and only substance. There is, except in a phenomenal and scenic way, no finite being. The All is one, and infinite. The self-consciousness of the finite subject which the pantheist recognizes does not help the matter. This consciousness itself is but a mockery, by which a modification of the one and only Being is made to suppose for a little time that it has a truly individual and responsible existence. The only *reality*, on this scheme, is a single universal nature with its innumerable processes, and all the personal self-consciousness that is recognized by it is a deceptive and transitory phenomenon, for the reason, that there is, in an essence which is not simply under and through all things, but *is* all things, no basis for distinct personality, free self-determination, and permanent self-consciousness, either in God or man. For, there must be logical coherence between attributes and their substance, and it is absurd to endow with the attributes of freedom and responsibility a substance, or a subjective modification of a substance, whose whole history is in fact a necessitated and blind evolution. In order to an infinite personality, there must be an infinite personal Essence or Being. In order to finite personality, there must be a finite personal essence or being. And these two cannot be or become one Essence or Being, without destroying the peculiar basis for the peculiar consciousness belonging to each. Pantheism has, therefore, no right to the terms of theism, for the simple reason that the objects denoted by them are not recognized by it as metaphysically and absolutely real. Pantheism is but a philosophy of nature, and as matter of fact it has accomplished more, or rather has done least injury to the cause of truth and true philosophy, when, as in the case of the earlier system of Schelling, it has been confined mainly to the sphere of nature. It would be unjust to deny that the pantheism of Schelling has done something toward destroying the mechanical theory and view of nature and natural science ; while the fact that he proceeded no farther with it in its application to the philosophy of spirit and of intelligence, and is understood to have renounced it in his late attempt to construct a system that will solve the problems of intellectual and spiritual existence, seems to corroborate the position here taken, that pantheism can never at any time, or under any of its forms, rise out of the sphere of nature, because it, in reality, recognizes the existence of nothing but nature.

It has been asserted, we are aware, and perhaps it is still to some extent believed, that the matured and final philosophy of Coleridge is itself liable to the charge of pantheism. The warm admiration with which he regarded Schelling, and the reception at one time of Schelling's doctrine of the original identity of subject and object, have given some ground for the assertion and belief. We shall, therefore, dwell briefly upon this point of Coleridge's relation to Schelling, because, while we are clear that the earlier system of this philosopher, whatever his later system shall prove to be, is nothing but Spinozism, we are equally clear that Coleridge freed himself from it, as decidedly as he did from the mechanical and sensuous philosophy of his youthful days.

After all the study and reflection which Coleridge expended upon the systems of speculation that sprang up in Germany after that of Kant, it is very evident that his closest and longest continued study was applied to Kant himself. After all his wide study of philosophy, ancient and modern, the two minds who did most toward the formation of Coleridge's philosophic opinions were Plato and Kant. From the Greek, he derived the doctrine of ideas, and fully sympathized with his warmly-glowing and poetic utterance of philosophic truths. From the German, he derived the more strictly scientific part of his system—the fundamental distinctions between the understanding and the reason (with the sub-distinction of the latter into speculative and practical), and between nature and spirit. With him also, he sympathized in the deep conviction of the absolute nature and validity of the great ideas of God, freedom, and immortality, of the binding obligation of conscience, and, generally, of the supremacy of the moral and practical over the purely speculative. Indeed, any one who goes to the study of Kant, after having made himself acquainted with the writings of Coleridge, will be impressed by the spontaneous and vital concurrence of the latter with the former—the heartiness and entireness with which the Englishman enters into the method and system of this, in many respects, greatest philosopher of the modern world. For, to say that Coleridge was the originator of the distinctions above-mentioned, in the sense that Kant was, is to claim for him what will never be granted by the holar; and, on the other hand, to say that Coleridge was a mere vulgar plagiary, copying for the mere sake of gratifying vanity, is not to be thought of for a moment. The plagiary is always a copyist and never an imitator, to use a distinction of Kant,* also naturalized among us by Coleridge. There is no surer test of plagiarism, therefore, than a dry, mechanical, and dead method, by which the material handled becomes a mere *caput mortuum*. But who would charge such a method upon Coleridge? Whatever else may be laid to his charge, there is no lack of life, and life, too, that organizes and vitalizes. Much of that obscurity charged upon him is owing to an excess of life; the warm stream gushes out with such ebullience that it cannot be confined to a channel, but spreads out on all sides like an inundation. Had there been less play of living power in his mind, he would have been a more distinct thinker for the common mind, and, as we believe, less exposed to the charge of plagiarism. This power of sympathy with the great minds of the race, in all departments of mental effort—this opulence and exuberance of endowment, coupled with an immense range of reading, and a brooding contemplation that instantaneously assimilated every thing brought into his mind—put him *unconsciously, and in spite of himself*, into communication with all the best thinking of the race; and hence it is, that while the beginner in philosophy finds the writings of Coleridge full to bursting, with principles, and germs of truth, freshly presented and entirely new to him, his after-study of the great thinkers of ancient and of modern times compels him to deduct from Coleridge's merits on the score of absolute discovery and invention, though not an iota from them on the score of originality in the sense of original

* Urtheilskraft, § 32.

treatment. It is for this reason, that the writings of this author are the very best preparatory exercise for the student, before he launches out upon the "mighty and mooned sea" of general philosophy. One who has thoroughly studied them is well prepared to begin his philosophical studies; and, we may add, no one who has once mastered this author can possibly stop with him, but is urged on to the study of the greatest and choicest philosophic systems themselves.

But, returning to the relation of Coleridge to Schelling, we think that it is very evident that his reception of the doctrine of the identity of subject and object, of which he gives an account in the *Biographia Literaria* that is mainly a transfusion from Schelling, was temporary. In the year 1834, we find him speaking thus of this account: "The metaphysical disquisition at the end of the first volume of the *Biographia Literaria* is unformed, and immature; it contains the fragments of the truth, but it is not fully thought out."* This, taken in connection with the general drift of Coleridge's annotations upon Schelling, contained in the appendix to the latest edition of the *Biographia Literaria*, we think is nearly equivalent to a distinct verbal renunciation of the theory in question. † At any rate, his rejection of the system of

---

* Table Talk, Works, VI., 520.

† "Spite of all the superior airs of the *Natur-Philosophen*, I confess that in the perusal of Kant I breathe the air of good sense and logical understanding, with the light of reason shining in it and through it: while in the physics of Schelling I am amused with happy conjectures, and in his theology I am bewildered by positions which in their first sense are transcendental (überfliegend), and in their literal sense scandalous." Biographia Literaria, Appendix, Works, III.,; 709.—"The *Spinozism* of Schelling's system first betrays itself." Biographia Literaria, Appendix, Works, III., 707.—"Strange that Fichte and Schelling both hold that the very object which is the condition of self-con-

Spinoza is expressed often and with emphasis in his writings,* although, in common with all who have made themselves acquainted with the works of this remarkable mind, he expresses himself in terms of high admiration respecting the loftiness and grandeur of many of his sentiments and reflections, even on subjects pertaining to ethics and religion. But what is Schelling's identity of subject and object in their ultimate ground, but the reappearance of the one substance of Spinoza with its two modifications, thought and extension? The theory which teaches that the subject contemplating and the object contemplated are in reality but one substance, and that the consciousness we have of things without us "is not only coherent, but identical and one and the same thing, with our own immediate self-consciousness," † plainly does not differ in matter, however it may in form, from the theory of the *substantia una et unica*. What is gained by saying that Spinoza started with an unthinking substance, but that the system of Identity starts with a thinking subject, ‡ when the position that *One is All, and All is One* is the fundamental postulate of both systems alike? This position, common to both, renders both sys-

---

sciousness is nothing but the self itself, by an act of free self-limitation. P. S. The above I wrote a year ago; but the more I reflect, the more convinced I am of the gross materialism which lies under the whole system." Biographia Literaria, Appendix, Works, III., 701.— This last remark, it deserves to be noticed, is a note upon Schelling's Briefe über Dogmatismus und Criticismus: an attack upon the Kantean philosophy. The earnestness with which Coleridge, in these annotations upon Schelling, sides with Kant, shows that neither his head nor his heart was with the system of Identity, at the time when he wrote them.

* Aids to Reflection, Works, I., 211. Table Talk, Works, VI., 301, 302.
† Biographia Literaria, Works, III., 340.
‡ Hegel's Phänomenologie, s., 14.

tems alike pantheistic, because it precludes that duality—that difference in substance between God and the world, and that distinction between an uncreated and a created essence or being—which must be recognized by a truly theistic philosophy. The only difference between the two systems is adjective: Spinozism being material, and the system of Identity ideal pantheism. If the postulate in question were limited, in its application, to the sphere of the finite alone, there might be a shadow of reason for saying that the doctrine of Identity does not annihilate the deity as other than the world. If an identity of substance were affirmed only between the human mind and the material universe, a supramundane deity, other than and above all this finite unity, might still be affirmed without self-contradiction; though, even in this case, this limited annihilation of the essential distinction between nature and spirit would result in its universal and absolute annihilation, so soon as it became apparent that the finite spirit, though not of the *same*, is yet of *similar* substance with the Infinite Spirit. But there is no limitation of this sort in the system, neither can there be, for it is its boast that it reduces the All to a One. It is the *universal* subject and the *universal* object between which an identity of substance is affirmed.

But, we lay much stress upon the indirect evidence in the case. It is perfectly plain, as we have already remarked, that the philosophy of Kant is the modern system with which Coleridge finally and most fully sympathized. If he is to be called after any one of the great founders of philosophical systems among the moderns, Coleridge was a Kantean. Not that he pushed his inquiries no further than Kant had gone, for there is abundant evidence on many a page of the *Literary Remains*, that the highest problems of Christianity, during the last period of his life, were themes constantly present to his deep and brooding reflection, and that whatever it shall be found that he actually accomplished, in the way of distinct statement, in the unfinished work which was to put the crown upon his literary life, he did satisfy his own mind upon these subjects, and was himself convinced of the absolute rationality of the highest mysteries of the Christian faith. Yet the groundwork of all these processes, the psychology and metaphysics from which they all started, was unquestionably the theistic method of Kant, and not the pantheistic method of his successors Even supposing that Coleridge at one time may have gone so far as to regard the system of Schelling (with the still more remarkable one of Hegel, he does not seem to have been acquainted, for we do not recollect any allusion to him throughout the whole of his works) as a positive and natural advance upon that of Kant, there is sufficient reason for saying that he saw the error, and fell back upon the old position of Kant, as the farthest point yet reached in the line of a true philosophic progress, regarding the systems that sprang up afterward as an illegitimate progeny. And in so doing, he only exhibited in an individual, the very same process that has gone on, and is still going on in the Germanic mind itself. There was a time, when even the serious theist was inclined to regard with favor at least, that wondrous evolution of the theoretic brain, the three systems of Fichte, Schelling and Hegel, as a natural and normal development from Kanteanism, and so to regard the four systems as being in one and the same straight line of advance. It is true, that at the very time when these later systems were rising into existence "like an exhalation," a man like Jacobi was found, to protest against the deviation and error, and to proclaim, with a serious and deep-toned eloquence that will ever endear him and his opinions to every serious-minded scholar who feels that his own mental repose, with that of the reflecting mind generally, is bound up in the ideas of theism, that these later systems were not genuine offshoots from Kant, but wild grafts into him. But, at the time, the national mind was caught in the process, and it was not until the speculative enthusiasm had cooled down, and the utter barrenness of this method of philosophizing, so far as all the deeper and more interesting problems of philosophy and religion are concerned, had revealed itself, that men began to see that all the movement had been off and away from the line of true progress, and that the thinker who would make real advance must join on where Kant, and not Hegel, left off.

In thus siding ultimately with the Kantean Philosophy, rather than with the system of Identity that succeeded it, Coleridge had much in common with Jacobi. Indeed, it seems to us that, speaking generally, Coleridge stands in nearly the same relation to English philosophy, that Jacobi does to that of Germany, and Pascal to that of France. Neither of these three remarkable thinkers has left a strictly scientific and finished system of philosophy, but the function of each was rather an awakening and suggestive one. The resemblance between Coleridge and Jacobi is very striking. Each has the same estimate of instinctive feelings, and the same religious sense of the pre-eminence of the moral and spiritual over the merely intellectual and speculative. Each clings with the same firm and lofty spirit to the ideas of theism, and plants himself with the same moral firmness upon the imperative decisions of conscience and the moral reason. But, in no respect do they harmonize more than in their thorough rejection of the pantheistic view of things; of that mere naturalism which swallows up all personality, and, thereby, all morality and religion. In reading Jacobi's *Von göttlichen Dingen,* one is struck with the great similarity in conception, and often in statement, with remarks and trains of discussion in the *Aids to Reflection.* The coincidence in this case, it is very plain to the reader, does not arise, as in the case of Coleridge's coincidence with Schelling, from a previous study and mastery of a predecessor, but from sustaining a similar relation to Kant, together with a deep sense of the vital importance and absolute truth of theism in philosophy. The coincidence in this case is not a mere genial reception, and fresh transfusion, of the thought of another mind, but an independent and original shoot, in common with others, from the one great stock, the general system of theism. Add to this, that both Coleridge and Jacobi were close students of Plato, and by mental constitution were alike predisposed to the moulding influence of this greatest philosophic mind of the pagan world, and we have still another ground and cause for the resemblance between the two.

Now, in this resemblance with Jacobi, we find still another indirect proof of the position, that Coleridge's adoption of the system of Schelling was temporary, and that he returned, with still deeper faith and clearer insight, to the theistic system. For, no mind of the age in which he lived, or of any age, was more decidedly and determinedly theistic, than Jacobi. His *Letters to Mendelssohn upon the system of Spinoza,* and still more, because more regularly constructed, his treatise on *Divine Things and their Revelation,* are among the most genial, certainly, and we think among the most impressive, and practically effective, of all attacks upon the pantheistic naturalism. We know that it was fashionable, especially when the hard logical processes of Hegelianism were more influential and authoritative as models than they now are, to decry the method of Jacobi as unscientific, and to endeavor to weaken the force of his views, by the assertion, that his is the mere "philosophy of feeling." But there is reason to believe, that this same thinker, though deficient as must be acknowledged in the logical and systematizing ability of Kant and Hegel, has done a giant's work, in aiding to bring the German mind back to the position of theism in philosophy. His influence, healthful and fruitful, is to be traced through the whole of the spiritual school of theologians. If there is any one of the many philosophers of Germany, who is regarded with admiration and veneration by this class of reflecting men—a class which shares largely in the disposition of its great head, Schleiermacher, to establish theology upon an independent basis, and thereby divorce it altogether from philosophy—it is Jacobi; and this, principally on the ground of his earnest religious abhorrence of that speculation of the mere understanding which, under the name of philosophy, has so invariably ended in the overthrow of the foundations of ethics and religion.

We have dwelt the longer upon this point of Coleridge's relation to Schelling, because we believe it to be the fact that the philosophic system which he finally adopted, and which is the prominent one in his writings, is irreconcilable with the system of Identity, and if so, that it is of the highest importance that the fact be known and acknowledged. Moreover, the establishment of the position we have taken acquires some additional interest, in relation to the charge of plagiarism which has of late been frequently urged. This charge becomes of little importance, so far as the question of Coleridge's original power as a philosopher is concerned, so soon as it appears that this reception of the views of Schelling was only one feature in the temporary pantheistic stage of his mental history, and of still less importance, when it is further considered, that Schelling himself is entitled to but small credit on the score of absolute invention—the philosophy of Spinoza being "the rock and the quarry," on and out of which the whole system of Identity was constructed. Indeed, in leaving this system, Coleridge has been imitated by Schelling himself, if, as there is reason to believe, the later system of this philosopher is a renunciation of his earlier, and not a mere development of it. How far either of these two minds possessed that highest, and most truly original philosophic power—the power of forming an era in the history of philosophy, by carrying the philosophic mind onward through another stadium in its *normal* course and development—remains yet to be seen. This point cannot be settled, until the publication of the *Logosophia* of Coleridge, and the recent system of Schelling.

The influence, however, of this pantheistic system upon Coleridge was for a time undoubtedly great, harmonizing as it did with the imaginative side of his nature, and promising, as it always has done, to reduce all knowledge to a unity—that promise always so impressive and fascinating for the human intellect, and which moreover addresses, though in this instance by a false method, one of the necessary and organic wants of reason itself. Besides the disquisition in the twelfth chapter of the *Biographia Literaria*, there are some statements in the *Friend*, * respecting the mutual relations of nature and the mind of man, and trains of reflection, that spring, as it seems to us, from the pantheistic intuition, and which, run out to their legitimate consequences, would end in a mere naturalism, of which all of Coleridge's more matured, and more

---

* See Essays X. and XI. of the Friend, Works II., 448-472.

strictly scientific views are a profound and powerful refutation, and against which, his own moral and spiritual consciousness, certainly for the last twenty years of his life, was one loud and solemn protest. *

* Mrs. H. N. Coleridge, in a note to Chapter IX. of the Biographia Literaria, remarks that her father, "soon after the composition of the Biographia Literaria, became dissatisfied with Schelling's system of philosophy, considered as a fundamental and comprehensive scheme, and objected to it as essentially pantheistic." She then adds, that she is "not aware, however, that he at any time altered or set aside the doctrine of Schelling, put forth in the Biographia Literaria, on nature and the mind of man, with their mutual relations; or, indeed, that he discovered any positive error, or incompatibility with higher truth, in such parts of Schelling's system as are adopted in the Biographia Literaria, and which he believed himself, in the main, to have anticipated."

It is difficult to reconcile this last statement with the preceding remark, that Coleridge finally regarded the system of Schelling as "essentially pantheistic." The doctrine of Schelling, on "the mutual relations of nature and the mind of man," which Coleridge has reproduced in Chapter XII of the Biographia, is, that there is originally an *identity* of substance between them, and that both are only different modifications, or phases, of one and the same substance or being. According to this scheme, commonly called the system of Identity, that which in one of its aspects is nature, in the other aspect is spirit; and it is the peculiar power and prerogative of the philosophic as distinguished from the spontaneous or common consciousness, to perceive this identity, and thus to reduce back all the manifoldness in the spheres of both nature and spirit, or matter and mind, to the absolute and primary unity whence it all emanated, and which it all is—to the one substance, in the phraseology of Spinoza; to the absolute subject-object, in the phraseology of Schelling; to the absolute conception, in the phraseology of Hegel.

Now, we see not on what possible ground Schelling can be charged with pantheism, if not on that of this doctrine of the original identity of subject and object,—a doctrine which Schelling applied to the universal object and the universal subject; asserting identity of substance not merely between nature and the mind of man, but between nature and all mind. It is certainly the ground upon which both his and Hegel's systems are now generally regarded as pantheistic, and is the doctrine by which the later German philosophy differs from the earlier toto genere.

In this connection, also, it may be proper to speak of the objection made to the system of Kant himself, that it is essentially skeptical. This objection is founded upon

Kant, with Des Cartes, affirmed the old doctrine of a duality between nature and spirit, matter and mind. He left the subject and object apart from each other when contemplated back of consciousness, and in their original metaphysical relations. And it is the standing objection of the system of Identity to the Kantean philosophy, that it is dualistic; that it does not reduce all things, both natural and spiritual, material and mental, to unity of essence; while it is the constant reply of the latter, that there can be no reduction of all things to this speculative and pantheistic unity, for the good reason that there *is* no such unity. God and the universe are not one substance. Mind and matter differ in essence. In other words, the dogmatism of the pantheist affirming a single substance, of which both God and the world (so called) are alike modifications, is met by the dogmatism of the theist affirming a supramundane and spiritual Being who creates the world out of nothing,—thus affirming a primary and a secondary substance, the latter *im*manent in the former, it is true, but not *e*manent from it, or identical with it. And the question as to which of these two dogmatisms is legitimate ; which of these two postulates—that of one, or of two substances—is valid ; must be settled by a psychological method. That postulate is the true one which harmonizes best with the various forms of human consciousness, especially those relating to ethics and religion; which best explains them all; and best solves the various problems that arise in human consciousness.

It may be said, and it has been, that the system of Identity admits distinctions in the one universal substance, and only denies division or literal duality. But, a mere distinction in one and the same essence does not constitute another essence or being. To illustrate by reference to the Christian doctrine of the trinity—the distinctions that subsist in the one single essence of the Godhead do not constitute three essences or beings. The distinctions are consubstantial, and are in, and of, one substance only. Unless, therefore, the distinction between God and the world is founded in an absolute duality of essence ; unless the distinction is ἄλλο καὶ ἄλλο, and not merely ἄλλος καὶ ἄλλος ; it is no such distinction as theism affirms, and religion must affirm, between the Creator and creation. It would be impossible that the self-consciousness of God and that of man should be different and diverse from each other (and they must be, in order to the existence of the relations

the fact, that the Critical philosophy denies the possibility, *within a certain sphere*, of an absolute knowledge on the part of the human mind, because its knowledge is conformed to forms and modes of cognition that pertain to the human understanding, and are peculiar to it. The thing *in itself* is not known, but only the thing as it *appears* to the finite intelligence. An absolute knowledge, true intrinsically, and irrespective of the subjective laws of human intelligence, is therefore impossible within *this sphere*.

If this theory were to be extended over the *whole* do-

and affections of religion), if the essence which underlies each, when traced to its lowest metaphysical ground, is one and identically the same essence.

We are aware of the alleged difficulty of accounting for a knowledge of the objective world, on the dualistic hypothesis that there is no identity of substance between it and the subjective intelligence, and of the confidence with which it is assumed that the mystery of cognition vanishes, as soon as it is shown that all consciousness is in reality self-consciousness. But, self-consciousness is more mysterious and difficult to explain, than mere consciousness. It is easier to apprehend how the ego can cognize an object that is other than the ego, than to apprehend how the ego can cognize the ego ; even as it is easier to understand how the eyeball can see a tree, than to understand how the eyeball can see the eyeball. How the great problem will ultimately be solved, and how much Coleridge and Schelling have contributed toward the true solution, will be answered variously. But it seems to us, that neither of these minds ultimately rested in the doctrine of Identity, as the means of arriving at the true theory of perception. Schelling is understood to have renounced his earlier system, and to have verged toward theism, in his later views. And, certainly, all such teaching of Coleridge as that the *moral* reason is the highest form of reason, and that no merely speculative decisions can set aside those of *conscience*, are in the vein and spirit of the Kantean philosophy, and a protest against a theory that obliterates all the fixed lines and immutable distinctions of theism. Such teaching could not have come from a mind included in the slowly-evolving, and blindly-groping processes of the philosophy of Identity.

main of knowledge, spiritual as well as natural, it is plain that it would end in universal skepticism. If, for instance, the knowledge which the human mind has of right and wrong, of its own freedom and immortality, of the divine attributes and the Infinite One in whom they inhere, is no real and absolute knowledge, but is merely subjective, the foundations of all morals and religion would sink out of sight immediately, and the human mind would be afloat upon the sea of doubt, conjecture, and denial. This was the identical skepticism against which Socrates and Plato waged such serious and successful war. But Kant, by his distinction of the speculative and practical reason, intended to *confine*, and actually does confine this doctrine of a subjective and conditional knowledge to the sphere of the natural and the sensuous. Within *this* sphere, there is no absolute knowledge, for the good reason that there is no absolute object to be known. Absolute and necessary truth is not within the domain of nature, but above it altogether, in the domain of spirit.* All things that are sensuous, and cognized by the understanding with its subjective forms, are in continual flux; and even in regard to the immaterial principles beneath them, even in regard to the laws of nature themselves, we cannot conceive of their being of such a necessary and immutable quality, as we cannot but conceive moral and spiritual laws and realities to be. For, they are creations ex nihilo, and, as such, are only one out of the infinitely various manners in which the Divine Mind can express itself in a material universe. The whole domain of nature and of matter is itself but a means to an end, and therefore cannot, like the domain of the spiritual which is an end, have absolute

---

* See Cudworth's Immutable Morality, passim; where this same view is maintained.

and necessary characteristics, and therefore cannot be the object of an absolute knowledge. All this domain of the conditional, therefore, legitimately comes before the understanding, with its categories or subjective forms of cognition.

But, there is another and a higher realm than that of nature, of another substance, and therefore not merely a higher development of the natural. The moral and spiritual world, as it is not subject in its functions and operations to the law of cause and effect, but is the sphere of freedom, so it is not cognizable under the forms of the understanding, but by the direct intuitions of reason. It is no mere afterthought, therefore, as has been charged, but a most strictly philosophic procedure in the system of Kant, by which, after the whole domain of the natural and the conditioned has been legitimately brought within the ken of the understanding, the domain of the spiritual and the absolute is assigned to a higher, even the very highest faculty of the soul, as the proper organ and inlet of knowledge regarding it. It is because such an object of knowledge as God, *e. g.*, cannot be truly known by being brought within the limitations of time and space, and under the categories of quantity, quality, &c., that Kant affirmed the existence of a power in man, not hampered by these subjective forms of the understanding, through which, by an act of direct spiritual intuition, this highest of all objects is known. Not *fully* and *completely* known, as some have falsely asserted that he taught; for, the object in question is infinite, and reason in man is finite; but truly and absolutely known, so far as the cognition does extend. Kant, unlike Fichte, Schelling and Hegel, never claimed for the finite reason of man that *plenitude* of knowledge which belongs only to the infinite reason, but he did affirm, that so far as the reason in man does have any knowledge of

God, and of spiritual objects generally, it has an absolute and not relative knowledge. God is not thus, for one man's reason, and thus, for another man's, as a color is thus, for the sense of one man, and thus, for the sense of another; but, so far as his infinite fulness *is* known by the finite reason, it is known *as it really is*, and is therefore known in the same way by all rational beings, and is the same to all. The same is true of all the ideas and objects of the spiritual, as distinguished from the natural world. In the former, the human mind has an absolute, *i. e.* unconditionally true knowledge, so far as it has any at all (for there may be no development of reason, and no use of the faculty at all), while in the latter, its knowledge is merely subjective and conditional. Hence the prominence, the supremacy, assigned in Kant's system to the moral or practical reason. This is reason in its highest and substantive form, and no decisions of any other faculty of the human soul have such absolute authority respecting moral and spiritual problems, as distinguished from problems of nature and matter, as those of this faculty. It stands over against the moral and spiritual world, precisely as the five senses stand over against the world of sense, and there is the same *immediateness* of knowledge in the one case as in the other. In the phrase of Jacobi, reason, *i. e.* the moral reason, is the *sense* for the supernatural,* and therefore we have, in fact, the same kind of evidence for the reality of spiritual objects, that we have for that of objects of sense—the evidence of a direct intuition.

There is, therefore, no room for skepticism, on this system, within the only sphere in which the philosopher and the theologian have any *vital* interest in keeping it out—

---

* Von den göttlichen Dingen, Beilage A.

the sphere of the moral and spiritual. However subjective and relative may be our knowledge of the material and natural, coming to us as it does through the mechanism of the understanding, and shaped by it into conformity with our subjective structure as creatures of sense and time, our knowledge of the supernatural, so far as we have any at all, is absolute and unconditional. We may doubt in regard to the real nature of matter, but we cannot doubt in regard to the real nature of right and wrong. We may grant that our knowledge of an object of sense is conditional, and not absolutely reliable, but we may not grant that our knowledge of a moral attribute of God is conditional, and not absolutely reliable. The skepticism of the human mind, on this system, is confined to the lower and less important sphere of nature, while the "confidence of reason," the faith that is insight and the insight that is faith, can exist only in relation to the moral and spiritual world; only in relation to moral and spiritual objects.

Kant's treatise on the practical reason, therefore, though from the very nature of the subject (it being that mode of reason which is intuitional, and freest from the complexity of logical forms) not so artificially constructed as that upon the theoretic reason, and seemingly occupying a humbler place in his general system, should be regarded as the sincere and serious expression of his real views upon the highest form of reason, and upon the very highest themes of reflection. Certainly, no one can peruse those lofty and ennobling enunciations, respecting the great practical ideas of God, freedom, and immortality, and those grand and swelling sentiments regarding the nature of duty and the moral law, that are contained in this treatise, without a deep conviction that this part of Kant's system was by no means an afterthought, or contrivance to save himself from universal skepticism.* If the cold and passionless intellect of the sage of Königsberg ever rises into the sphere of feeling, and ever exhibits anything of that real enthusiasm by which a *living* knowledge is always accompanied and manifested, it is in this, the most practical and serious-toned of all his productions. And if it is objected, as it has been, that this knowledge of the spiritual is rather a belief, than a knowledge, and that the function of this so-called practical reason is that of feeling rather than scientific cognition, the objection must be acknowledged to have force, *provided*, that that only is scientific which is the result of logical deductions, and that alone is know ledge which comes mediately into the mind by processes of comparison and generalization. But, on the other hand, if it is proper to call that, knowledge, which by virtue of its *immediateness* in the rational consciousness is a most original and intimate union of *both* cognition and feeling, of *both* reason and faith, of *both* the scientific and the moral, then, the knowledge in question is the absolutely highest of all, for, it contains the elements of both forms of perception; and is the most truly scientific of all, because, in the form of first principles, it lies at the foundation of all the processes of logic, and all the structures of science.

But, whatever may have been the relative position of the practical reason and its correspondent ideas, in the general system of Kant, or in Kant's own mind, no reader of Coleridge can doubt that for him, and his system, this form of reason and these ideas are paramount. Coleridge had a special interest in developing this part of philosophy, and establishing an absolute validity for the decisions

* Kant himself asserts this. See Kritik der practischen Vernunft, s. 110. Rosenkranz's Ed.

of the moral reason and conscience, superadded to that which actuated Kant. The former had received into his soul the peculiar doctrines of Christianity, while the latter, so far as we have had the means of judging, stood upon the position of the serious-minded deist, and was impelled to the defence of the foundations of ethics and natural religion, by no other motives than such as actuated minds like the emperor Marcus Aurelius and Lord Herbert of Cherbury. Coleridge had more than a merely moral interest, in saving the fundamental principles of ethics and religion from an all-destroying skepticism, or an all-absorbing naturalism, in philosophy. And hence the positiveness, and, in the best sense of the word, the dogmatism, with which he iterates and reiterates his affirmation, that " religion, as both the corner-stone and the key-stone of morality, must have a *moral* origin : so far at least, that the evidence of its doctrines cannot, like the truths of abstract science, be wholly independent of the *will*." *

Now, as the defender and interpreter of this decidedly and profoundly theistic system of philosophy, we regard the works of Coleridge as of great and growing worth, in the present state of the educated and thinking world. It is not to be doubted that pantheism is the most formidable opponent which truth has to encounter in the cultivated and reflecting classes. We do not here allude to the formal reception and logical defence of the system, so much as to that pantheistic way of thinking which is stealing into the lighter and more imaginative species of modern literature, and from them is passing over into the principles and opinions of men at large. This popularized naturalism—this naturalism of polite literature, and of literary society—is seen in the lack of that depth and

* Biographia Literaria, Works, III. 297.

strength of tone, and that heartiness and robustness of temper, which characterize a mind into which the personality of God and the responsibility of man cut sharply, and which does not cowardly shrink from a severe and salutary moral consciousness. There is no remedy for this error of the brain and of the heart, but in the resolute and positive affirmation (worthy of the name of *virtue* wherever found) of a distinction in essence between the natural and the spiritual, with its implication of a supreme and infinite Spirit, the first cause and last end of both the finitely spiritual and the natural. For all philosophy, false as well as true, must begin with an affirmation—a postulate upon which all else rests, and which is itself unsusceptible of proof, because it is the ground of proof for all other affirmations. Pantheism itself starts in dogmatism: starts with postulating, not proving, the existence of its one only substance. It has an interest in so doing. The evidence of this its so-called first truth "is not altogether independent of the *will*." Here too, the voluntary and the theoretic, the practical and the speculative, are, though illegitimately, in one act of the intellect. In respect therefore to the logical necessity, the compulsory necessity, of its first premise, we see not the advantage which it boasts of having over a theism which does not reject all aid from the moral side of the human soul, or regard all evidence as not truly scientific and absolute that is not of the nature of mathematical. Since, then, there must be a postulate to start from, in either or any case, let the individual mind imitate that justifiable postivity, that rational dogmatism, of the general human mind (which the soundly philosophizing mind only repeats with a fuller and distincter consciousness of the meaning and contents of the affirmation) by which the absolute existence of a personal supra-mundane God is affirmed. This Being styles Himself the I AM—the self-affirmed self-existence; and what is left for the human reason but to imitate this positive affirmation, and steadfastly to assert that "HE IS, and is the rewarder of them that diligently seek him."

In driving the hesitating mind over its hesitancy, and urging it up to that moral resoluteness, which is at the same time the most rational freedom, whereby it takes sides with the instincts of reason and the convictions of conscience, rather than with the schemes and fictions of the speculative understanding and the unethical deductions from them, we esteem the writings of Coleridge to be of great worth. Apart from the influence of the example of this most learned and most contemplative mind, the clearness and profundity with which the doctrines of theism are enunciated, and their mutual relation and dependence explained, is admirably fitted to propagate the living process of insight and of faith into the mind of the student. For it is one great merit of this author, that when his views are once mastered, they become inward and germinant. The consciousness of the teacher becomes that of the pupil. "You may," he says with perfect truth, " you may not understand my system, or any given part of it, or by a determined act of wilfulness, you may, even without perceiving a ray of light, reject it, in anger and disgust. But this I will say—that if you once master it, or any part of it, you cannot hesitate to acknowledge it as the truth. You cannot be skeptical about it."* And we appeal with confidence to those who have had opportunities for observing, whether, as matter of fact, those minds, and especially those young minds, (ever most liable to be misled by the imposing pretensions

---

* Table Talk, Works, VI., 519, 520.

of a false and miscalled spiritualism in philosophy) who have once come fairly and continuously under the influence of the opinions of Coleridge, have not been, not only shielded from error, but also, fortified in the truth. Are those who have been educated and trained in this general method of philosophizing liable to be drawn aside from it? Does not the method itself beget and nurture a determined strength of philosophic character, which obstinately refuses to receive the brilliant and specious theories that are continually arising in the speculating world?

This self-conscious and determined spirit, in the recipient of the general system promulgated by Coleridge, springs naturally from its predominantly moral and practical character. The staple and stuff of this philosophy are the great moral ideas, and the faculties of the human soul most honored and developed by it are the moral reason, the conscience, and the will. The purely speculative *matériel* of philosophy is made to hold its proper subordinate place, and the merely speculative and dialectic faculty is also subordinated along with it. By recognizing the absolute authority of conscience, not only within the domain of religion but also of philosophy, and by affirming that the will itself, being the inmost centre of the man, and, ideally, conjoint and one with reason, ought not to stand entirely aloof, while, by a compulsory logical process, the first truths of philosophy and religion are attempted to be forced upon the mind with the same passivity and indifference with which its belief of abstract axioms is *necessitated*—by regarding, in short, the moral reason and the free-will in their living synthesis, as the dominant faculty and seat of authority in the human soul, this system of philosophy not only secures a belief in the truths of theism, but at the same time builds up and strengthens the human mind. Mental belief, in this system, has the element of will in it. The doctrine of the Divine existence, e. g., is believed not merely passively and from the mere mechanic structure of the intellect, as the axioms of geometry are, but to a certain extent by free self-determination. The individual believes in the essential difference between right and wrong, partly because he is *inclined* to believe it, and not because it is impossible to sophisticate himself into the disbelief of it. On this theory, man becomes responsible for his belief, even in respect to the first principles of morals and religion, and thus feels all the stimulation of a free and therefore hazardous position.

And this brings us back again, to the intensely theistic character of this philosophy. It is rooted and grounded in the personal and the spiritual, and not in the least in the impersonal and the natural. Drawing in the outset, as we have remarked above, a distinct and broad line between these two realms, it keeps them apart from each other, by affirming a difference in essence, and steadfastly resists any and every attempt to amalgamate them into one sole substance. The doctrine of creation, and not of emanation or of modification, is the doctrine by which it constructs its theory of the universe, and the doctrine of responsible self-determination, and not of irresponsible natural development, is the doctrine by which it constructs its systems of philosophy and religion.

2. In the second place, we think that this author is worthy of study, for his general method of theologizing, and as an able defender and expounder of the doctrines of Christianity on grounds of reason and philosophy.

In treating of this point, we shall be led to speak of Coleridge in his other principal character of a theologian. In regard to his general merits under this head, there is, both in this country and in Great Britain, more difference of opinion than in regard to his general merits as a philosopher. We are inclined to the belief, however, that there is a growing confidence in the substantial orthodoxy of his theological opinions, and that it is coming to be the belief even of those who do not sympathize with his philosophical opinions, and of course not, therefore, with his method of unfolding and defending the truths of Christianity, that the name of Coleridge deserves to be associated with those of the great English divines of the seventeenth century, and that his views do not differ fundamentally from that body of Christian doctrine which had its first systematic origin in the head and heart of Augustine. We are ourselves firm in the belief, that the theology of Coleridge, notwithstanding variations on some points, of which we shall speak hereafter, and which we are by no means disposed to regard as insignificant, is yet heartily and fully on the Augustinian side of that controversy which, after all, makes up the pith and substance of dogmatic church history. Even in relation to the difference between the Calvinistic and Arminian schemes, —schemes which, though essentially the same with the Augustinian and Semi-Pelagian, yet have a narrower sweep, and allow their adherents less latitude of movement—even in relation to these two schemes, respecting which there is such a shrinking in the English clergy, notwithstanding the strongly-pronounced tone of the Thirty-nine Articles, from a clear expression of opinion, Coleridge has not hesitated to say, that "Calvinism (archbishop Leighton's, for example), compared with Jeremy Taylor's Arminianism, is as the lamb in the wolf's skin, to the wolf in the lamb's skin: the one is cruel in phrases, the other in the doctrine." *

* Literary Remains, Works, V. 200.

If the reader will peruse the Confession of Faith drawn up by Coleridge as far back as 1816,[*] he will find that he expresses his solemn belief in the personality and tri-unity of God, the free and guilty fall of man, the redemption of man by the incarnation and death of the Son of God, and the regeneration of the human soul by the Holy Spirit; and if he will further peruse the development of Coleridge's views, in the *Aids to Reflection* especially, on these cardinal doctrines of Christianity, he will find that, with the exception of that part of the subject of redemption technically denominated justification, Coleridge did not shrink from the most thorough-going statements. No divine, not even Calvin himself, ever expressed himself more decidedly than this author, in respect to such points as the divinity of Christ, the depth and totality of man's apostasy, and the utter bondage and helplessness of the fallen will: and the mere novice in theology knows that profound and thorough views of sin lie at the foundation of all depth, comprehensiveness, and correctness, in a general theological system.

It is rare, very rare, in the history of literature, to find a mind so deeply interested in the pursuits of philosophy and poetry as was that of Coleridge, at the same time deeply and increasingly interested in theological studies and speculations; and still more rare, to find the philosopher and the poet so thoroughly committed to the *distinguishing* doctrines of the Scriptures. Compare Coleridge, for example, with his learned and able contemporary in philosophy, Sir James Mackintosh, and observe the wide difference between the two men, in respect to the relation of each to the so-called evangelical system. Compare him again with his contemporary and friend, the poet Southey,

---

[*] Literary Remains, Works, V. 15.

and notice the same wide difference, in the same respect. Neither Mackintosh nor Southey seem to have had that profound and living consciousness of the truth of such doctrines as those of sin and redemption, which imparts so much of the theological character to Coleridge, and which would justify his being placed among the divines of England, were not theology, in this as in too many other instances, thrown into the shade by the less noble but more imposing departments of philosophy and poetry. He tells us that he was drawn off from poetry by the study of philosophy; and the account we gather of his studies and reflections during the last quarter of his life shows, that he was drawn off—so far as the nature of the case permits this—from philosophy itself by theology: or, rather, that the one passed over into the other.

Now, it seems to us that this mind, having received such a profound discipline in philosophy, and that too a spiritual and theistic philosophy, and being led both by its original tendency and the operation of divine grace to the study and defence of the truths of the Christian religion on grounds of reason, is eminently fitted to be a guide and aid to reflection in this direction. We do not recommend Coleridge to the student as the author of a theological system, but rather as the defender and expounder of a general method of inquiry and reflection upon theological doctrines, in the highest degree fruitful and sound. Indeed, what we have said of Coleridge's lack of constructive ability in the department of philosophy applies with still more force to him as a theologian. The longest and most continuous statements, that Coleridge has made upon the doctrines of Christianity, are to be found in the *Aids to Reflection*, and yet the general character of this, the most elaborate and valuable of his prose productions, is aphoristic. The aphoristic method is, obviously, not the best by which to convey opinions upon so intrinsically systematic and actually systematized themes as the doctrines of Christianity; much less, therefore, can this method be employed successfully, in constructing a whole theological system. Still, as an *aid* to reflection, as inducing a general style of thinking, and manner of unfolding and defending truth, this method has some decided advantages over that of the connected treatise. It allows of more mental freedom on the part of the pupil, and fosters original reflection, more than a work finished in all its parts and details. "For," says Lord Bacon, " as young men, when they knit and shape perfectly, do seldom grow to a further stature, so knowledge, while it is in aphorisms and observations, it is in growth; but when it is once comprehended in exact methods, it may perchance be further polished and illustrated, and accommodated for use and practice; but it increaseth no more in bulk and substance." *

We regard the general method of theologizing induced by the reflections of Coleridge upon theological doctrines, as eminently profound and comprehensive. It leads the student to prize first of all, depth, breadth, and certainty of view, in this department of knowledge. It does this,

* Advancement of Learning, Book I.—Consonant with this, are the following remarks of Schleiermacher: "Denn erinnert Euch nur, wie wenige von denen, welche auf einem eigenen Wege in das innere der Natur und des Geistes eingedrungen sind und deren gegenseitiges Verhältniss und innere Harmonie in einem eigenen Lichte angeschaut und dargestellt haben, wie dennoch nur wenige von ihnen gleich ein System ihres Erkennens hingestellt, sondern vielmehr fast alle in einer zarteren, sollte es auch sein zerbrechlicheren Form, ihre Entdeckungen mitgetheilt haben. Und wenn Ihr dagegen auf die Systeme seht in allen Schulen, wie oft diese nicht anders sind als der Sitz und die Pflanzstätte des todten Buchstabens; weil nämlich, mit seltenen Ausnahmen, der selbstbildende Geist der hohen Betrachtung zu flüchtig ist und zu frei für die strengen Formen."—Reden über die Religion. Erste Rede.

by teaching as its first and great lesson, that "the scheme of Christianity, though not discoverable by human reason, is yet in accordance with it," * and that all reflection upon the truths of Scripture ought, therefore, to carry the mind down into deeper and deeper depths of its own being, and result in the absolute and unassailable conviction that divine revelation is likewise divine reason. The influence of Coleridge's speculations is to produce and establish the belief that there is no inward and necessary contradiction between faith and reason, but that when both are traced to their ultimate and central unity, faith, in the phrase of Heinroth, † will be seen to be undeveloped and unconscious reason, and reason, again, this same faith, developed, self-conscious, and self-intelligent: in other words, that when the believer shall have been raised by the highest grade of Christian consciousness to the highest grade of Christian knowledge, he will see that the unquestioning and childlike docility with which he trusted and rested in the truths and mysteries of Christianity, was the most rational of all mental acts, and the most philosophic of all mental processes. That this absolute consciousness can be perfectly reached, even by the most profound and holiest mind while in the flesh, we for one deny; for the same reason that, within the sphere of life and practice, we deny the doctrine of spiritual perfection here on earth. But, that this knowledge, this insight into the identity of the revelation of God with the reason of God, is a reality, and may be striven after, and that in its perfect completeness it will be attained by the human spirit when it has ceased to see through a glass darkly, has been the steadfast belief of the holy and the wise, in all ages of the Christian church. There is a point, a final centre, where

* Biographia Literaria, sub fine.
† Anthropologie, s. 219.

faith and insight meet, even in regard to the mysteries of Christianity; and to this point, the earnest straining eye of Christian speculation has in all ages steadily turned. This point is at once the mysterious power that attracts, and the goal where the whole mighty tendency is to come to a rest. Only on the hypothesis that the problem is not in its own nature absurd and insoluble, but that by a legitimate method Christian philosophy may draw nearer and nearer its solution, even here in space and time, can we account for the existence of a Christian theology at all. How far Coleridge has contributed, in the employment of this method, to the scientific statement and philosophical defence of the doctrines of Christianity, and, generally, what his positive merits are in respect to this relation of philosophy to revelation, is a question to which we would devote a short space.

In respect to the doctrine of the *Trinity*, upon which his thoughts seem to have centered during his latter life, the position which he took, that this doctrine though mysterious is yet rational, and is therefore a legitimate object of investigation for a rational mind, at first sight seems to extend the sphere of Christian speculation beyond its proper limits. For the last two centuries, it has been customary among English and American theologians to receive the doctrine of the Trinity purely on the ground of its being revealed in Scripture, and attempts to establish its rationality and intrinsic necessity have, in the main, been deprecated. It has not always been so. In some ages, the doctrine of the triunity of the Divine Being was the battle-ground of the church, and we are inclined to think that the Christian mind has never reached a deeper depth in metaphysical philosophy, than that to which it was compelled to sink by the acute objections of Arianism and Sabellianism. Let any one thoughtfully peruse the creeds that had their origin in these controversies, and see with what masterly care and ability the orthodox mind, in spite of all the imperfections of human language, strove to express the idea with which it was laboring, so as to avoid the Arian, the Sabellian, and Tritheistic ideas of the Divine Nature, and then ask himself if there is not something of the mental, something of the rational, in the doctrine of the Trinity, by virtue of which it becomes a legitimate object of contemplation for the human mind, and to some extent a guide to its inquiry. How could a man like Athanasius, for example, contend so earnestly, and with such truth of counter-statement, *against* a false idea, unless he had the true idea somewhat clear in his own mind to contend *for*. And if it be said that this was derived from the bare letter of the Scriptures, and that the whole controversy between the contending parties hinged upon the citation of proof texts, the question arises: How came Athanasius to see such a different truth in these texts from that which his opponents saw in them? Suppose a transfer of consciousness—suppose that the inward convictions and notions, upon the subject of the Trinity, possessed by Arius, could have been carried over into the mind of Athanasius—would the letter of these proof-texts have contained the same spirit, or meaning, for him that they actually did? For it must be recollected that the Scriptures do not furnish, ready-formed, a systematic and scientific statement of the doctrine in question. How, then, came the orthodox mind to derive its own sharply-defined dogma from the Scriptures, and the heterodox mind its own equally sharply-defined dogma from the very same Scriptures, unless each brought an antecedent interpreting idea into the controversy? We do not by any means suppose that this orthodox idea of the Trinity sprang up in the orthodox mind at this particular instant in the history of the church, and entirely independent of the Scriptures. It was a slow formation, and had come down from the beginning, as the joint product of scriptural teaching and rational reflection, but was brought out, by this controversy, into a greater clearness and fullness than it had ever before appeared in, outside of the circle of inspired minds. But that the doctrine of the Trinity was now *an idea in the mind of the church*, and therefore contained a mental element, by virtue of which it was a legitimate object of rational contemplation, and not a mere letter upon the page of Scripture, is the point we wished to bring out.

Now we think it a return to an older and better view of the subject, and not a mere novelty, that Coleridge was disposed to affirm, that whether it can be distinctly and fully shown or not, the doctrine of the Trinity *is* a rational doctrine, and is not, therefore, a theme altogether forbidden to the theologian because it stands in no sort of relation to a human intelligence. We believe that the position taken by him in common with the spiritual school of theologians in Germany, between whose general views in theology and those of Coleridge there is much affinity, that the doctrine of the Trinity contains the only adequate and final answer to the standing objection of pantheism —viz., that an Infinite Being cannot be personal, because all personal self-consciousness implies limitation — is a valuable one for both philosophy and theology. It proposes a high aim for both of these sciences, and provided the investigation be conducted in the light of Scripture and of the Christian consciousness, and for the very purpose of destroying the pantheistic conception of the Deity, into which such abstruse and recondite speculation we confess is very apt to run,* we have little fear that the

---

* The Trinity of Hegel is an example.

cause of true philosophy and religion will suffer from the attempt. Whether the attempt be successful or not, surely it is honoring divine revelation, and that body of systematic knowledge which has sprung up out of it, to affirm with Julius Müller, that " the Christian religion, as it lies in the New Testament, contains the fundamental elements of a perfect system of philosophy in itself; that there cannot be a real reconciliation between philosophy and Christianity, if such reconciliation must come in from without, and that such a reconciliation is possible only as it is merely an unfolding of that which is already contained by implication in Christianity: and hence, that it must be possible to find, from the immediate contents of the Christian religion, *as its metaphysical complement, ulti-, mate and absolutely scientific statements* relative to the existence of God and the world, and their mutual relations, in such way as that they shall of themselves constitute a system of Christian philosophy." *

Furthermore, whether the attempt to construct philosophically the doctrine of the Trinity succeed or not, the assertion that it is grounded in reason, and the necessity of the Divine Nature, logically cuts the root of the doctrine of a merely modal Trinity: a heresy that was revived by the contemplative Schleiermacher. If the doctrine of the Trinity has a rational necessity, i. e., a necessity in the Divine Essence itself—if God, *in order to be personal and self-conscious*, and not merely that he may manifest himself, must be triune—then it follows that a trinity of mere manifestation, whatever it may do for other beings than the Deity, leaves the Deity himself destitute of self-consciousness. The position of the Christian theology is, that irrespective of his manifestation in the

* Lehre von der Sünde, Bd. I. ss. 7, 9.

universe, antecedent to the creation, and in the solitude of his own eternity, God is personally self-conscious and *therefore* triune—absolutely self-sufficient, and therefore needing to undergo no process of development and manifestation, in order to absolute plenitude and perfection of existence. By affirming that the doctrine of the Trinity is an absolutely rational and necessary one, because the Divine Nature is *essentially* and *necessarily* trinal, the doctrine of a relative and modal trinity is logically precluded.

So far as concerns the speculations themselves, of Coleridge, upon this doctrine, he undoubtedly received the theological statement of it, contained in the Nicene Creed, as the truth, and endeavored, from this as a point of departure, to originate a corresponding philosophical determination of the doctrine. How much he has actually contributed to the scientific solution of the problem, each reader will decide for himself. We are free to say for ourselves, that we think Coleridge committed an error in leaving the scheme of the triad for that of the tetrad, in his construction. The symbols of the Church proceed upon the hypothesis of a simple triad, which is *also* a monad, and hence teach a trinity *in* unity and a unity *in* trinity. Coleridge, on the other hand, proceeds upon the scheme of the Pagan trinity, of which hints are to be found in Plato, and which can be traced back as far as Pythagoras —the scheme, namely, of a monad logically anterior to, and other than, the triad ; of a monad which originally *is* not a triad, but *becomes* one ; whereby four factors are introduced into the problem. The error in this scheme consists in this its assumption of an aboriginal unity existing primarily by itself, and, in the order of nature, *before* a trinity—of a *ground* for the trinity, or, in Coleridge's phrase, a *prothesis*, which is not in its own nature either trinal or personal, but is merely the impersonal base from which the trinality is evolved. In this way, we think, a process of *development* is introduced into the Godhead that is incompatible with its immutable perfection, and with that golden position of the schoolmen, that God is *actus purissimus sine ulla potentialitate*. There is no latency in the Divine Being. He is the same yesterday, to-day, and forever. We think we see in this scheme of Coleridge the influence of the pantheistic conception of potentiality, instead of the theistic conception of self-completeness, and that if he had taken the distinct and full personality of the finite spirit as the image and likeness of the Infinite Personality, and, having steadfastly contemplated the necessary conditions of self-consciousness in man, had merely freed them from the limitations of the finite—of time, and degree—he would have been more successful, certainly more continuous and progressive. While we say this, however, we are far from believing that Coleridge's practical faith, as a Christian, in the Trinity, was in the least affected by this tendency to modalism in his speculative construction of the doctrine—a modalism, too, which, as we have remarked above, is logically, and ought actually to have been, precluded by the position which he heartily adopted, of the intrinsic rationality and necessity of the doctrine. Few minds in the whole history of the Christian church, as we believe, have had more awful and adoring views of the Triune God, or have bowed down in more absolute and lowly worship before the Father, Son, and Holy Ghost.

The reflections of Coleridge upon the great and important doctrine of *Sin*, we regard as of the highest worth both in a practical and speculative respect. Indeed, a profound consciousness of sin in the heart, and a correspondingly profound theory of it in the head, are fundamental to all depth and soundness of view in the general domain of theology. Coleridge speaks, in several places, of his renunciation of Socinianism and reception of Trinitarianism as resulting from a change in his philosophical opinions: of a spiritual philosophy as the means of bringing him to a spiritual religion. Without denying the co-operation of this influence, we are yet inclined to the belief, that in his case, as in that of Augustine and of men of a strongly contemplative bent generally, the change from error to truth had its first and deepest source in that profound and bitter experience of an evil nature which every child of Adam must pass through before reaching peace of soul, and which, more than any other experience, carries the mind down into the depths of both the nature of man and of God. The biographical materials, for forming an estimate of the spirituality and religious experience of Coleridge, are somewhat meagre, but there is full reason for believing, from the gushes of tender devotional feeling that burst up spontaneously, and with the utmost unconsciousness, on the slightest hint or occasion, that a most profound Christian experience lay warm and tremulous under the whole of his culture and character.* We think we can see plainly in those most touching expressions of a sense of bondage which sometimes escape from him, that Coleridge, in common with the wise and the holy of all ages, was slowly but triumphantly fighting through that great fight between the flesh and the spirit, which, far more than the splendor of a merely human en-

* See Table Talk, Works, VI. 323 (Note), 327 (Note), 478 (Note), 527; and Literary Remains, Works, V. 19–21, 368, 372, 290.—These passages should be read by any one who would know how lowly and penitential, how filial and trustful a Christian this "logician, metaphysican, and bard," as Lamb called him, had become.

dowment, is the secret of the lofty and melancholy interest with which, even if personally unacquainted with the struggle, every thoughtful mind contemplates the lives of those elect spirits whom God's grace has chosen as its distinguished organs of manifestation—that unearthly contest which, more than all else, is the secret of that superior charm which sets the *Confessions* of Augustine as high above the *Confessions* of Rousseau as the heavens are above the earth. In this connection, we believe that the opium-eating of Coleridge, about which so much has been said in a pharisaic spirit, by those who had small if any knowledge of that publican-like humility, and lowly self-despair, which is the heart and kernel of a Christian as distinguished from a merely pagan or ethnic character, was the occasion, as are all evil habits in the regenerate soul, of this deep and continually deepening religious consciousness; and that if that peculiarity which resulted from this struggle with an evil habit were to be taken out of Coleridge's experience as a Christian, it would lose much of its depth, expanse, and true elevation. We have not the slightest doubt that, when told, "the tale of his long and passionate struggle with, and final victory over, the habit, will form one of the brightest, as well as most interesting traits of the moral and religious being of this humble, this exalted Christian." * The pious-minded believer who finds in his own experience a fac-simile of this struggle with the relics of an evil nature, and the philosophic inquirer who traces the Christian life to its hidden and lowest springs, are both of them, alike, far better qualified to be judges and censors over such a frailty and sin as the one in question, than those moralists who are precluded, as of old, from both the reception and

---

* H. N. Coleridge's Preface to the Table Talk, Works, VI. 252.

the apprehension of an evangelical spirit, by their self-righteousness, and whose so-called religion is that merely negative thing which owes its origin not to the conflict of grace with sin, but to an excess of lymph in the blood.

Coleridge's view of sin, which is to be found the most fully expressed in the *Aids to Reflection*, is so intimately connected with his view of the will, that it is necessary to direct attention to the nature and functions of this important faculty. The place which the will holds in his system of philosophy was briefly alluded to under that head. As the spiritual, i. e., self-determined, principle in man, it stands over against all that is strictly and merely natural in him, in the sharpest opposition. In the idea and plan of the human soul it was intended to control and subject to its own rational self-determination all the functions and operations, all the appetencies and tendencies, of a nature which unallied with such a higher spiritual power would be as irresponsible, because as necessitated in its development, in man, as we find it to be in the brute. All *radical* deterioration, therefore, in the human soul, must begin in the *self*-determined part of it, for this is the only point at which a *radical, responsible* change can be introduced, and from which it can evolve. A mere nature, as in the case of irrational and irresponsible existences, is not capable of either a radical deterioration or a radical improvement. It must develop itself, in the main, and substantially, in accordance with what has been inlaid in it. There are, therefore, in the world of nature as distinguished from that of spirit, no *radical* changes—no terrible catastrophes like the fall of the human will, no glorious recoveries like its renovation. There is, and must be, within the realm of the strictly natural, only one uniform evolution, in one continuous and endless line, because mere development cannot, by a free act, go behind itself, and alter the basis from which it proceeds.

Sin, therefore, as involving a radical change in the character, development, and history of the human soul, originates in the will. If man were a mere creature of nature, his development would go on with the same necessary uniformity with which a crystal or a tree is built up in accordance with the law of nature. But he is also a spiritual, i. e., *self*-determined, creature, and hence that possibility of sinning which has become a dreadful actuality. By virtue of this power, man is capable of throwing himself out of the normal line of development prescribed for him by his Creator, and of beginning, by an absolute beginning, a character, a course, and career, the precise contrary to the right and ideal one.

Without going into further detail in regard to sin as originating within the sphere of freedom—a point upon which there is no controversy among those who hold to the existence of sin at all—we wish to allude, as concisely as possible, to the idea of the will itself as held by Coleridge, and as it is found generally, we think, in the Platonic as distinguished from the Locke Calvinism. For, the doctrine of sin assumes a very different form, and is accompanied with totally different results, both in speculative and practical theology, according as the idea of the will is capacious, deep, and exhaustive, or the contrary. If the will is regarded as merely the faculty of single choices, or particular volitions, the sin that has its origin in it must necessarily be atomic—a mere series of single and isolated acts, or, in the technics of theology, actual and conscious transgressions. If, on the other hand, the will is regarded as the power of determining the *whole* soul, and the soul as a whole, to an ultimate *end* of living, the sin that has its origin in it is dynamic—an immanent process or *state* of the will, having the unity, depth and totality of a nature, and, in theological phraseology, is an evil nature, from which all actual and volitionary transgressions proceed. This distinction between the volitionary and the voluntary or self-determining power—a distinction plainly marked by the Latin *arbitrium* and *voluntas*, and equally plainly by the German *Willkühr* and *Wille*—is important not only intrinsically, but also in order to an apprehension of Coleridge's view of the doctrine of original sin, which, we think, does not differ materially from that of Augustine and the Reformers. For, although Coleridge insists earnestly and at length upon the doctrine of free self-determination, he is equally earnest and decided in affirming the absolute bondage and helplessness of the *fallen* human will. According to him, the will is capable of originating its states —its holy state only in concurrence with, and aided by, the one Holy Will which is the ground and support of all finite holiness, and its sinful state without any aid or co-operation on the part of the Infinite Will—but when an evil moral state has once been originated, and the will has once responsibly formed a sinful character and nature, a central radical change in the direction and tendency of this faculty is, from the very nature of the case, then out of its power. For the will is not merely the surface-faculty of single volitions, over which the individual has arbitrary control, but also that central, and inmost active principle into which all the powers of cognition and feeling are grafted, as into the very core and substance of the personality itself. So that when the will, in this *full* and adequate sense of the word, puts forth its sinful self-determination, it takes the whole soul along with it from the centre to circumference, leaving no remainder of power in reserve, by which the existing direction of its movement can be reversed. The fall of the will, therefore, though a free and self-moved procedure, brings this faculty into such a relation to holiness, that it is utterly impossible for it to recover itself back into its primitive state : it being a contradiction, to attribute a power of originating holiness, to a faculty, the *whole* of whose power is already absorbed in an unintermittent determination to sin. The will, as thus conceived, is a unit and a unity, and having once freely set itself in the direction of evil, it thereby, and in the same proportion, becomes powerless in respect to a contrary direction ; not because, be it observed, of any compulsion from without, but because of the obstinate energy and overmastering momentum within. It is an impossibility for Satan to cast out Satan, because it is an incompatibility.

Coleridge, in brief, while holding to the doctrine of free self-determination with the serious earnestness of a philosopher who well knew the vital importance of it in a system of theism — the doctrine of responsible and personal free-will being the very and only corrosive of all pantheistic naturalism — at the same time agreed with the oldest and soundest theology of the Christian church, in not affirming the existence of positive and efficient power in the *fallen* will, either to recover itself, or to maintain itself in holiness after recovery. "The difference," he says, " between a Calvinist and a Priestleyan materialist-necessitarian consists in this : the former not only believes a will, but that it is equivalent to the *ego ipse*, to the actual self, in every moral agent ; though, he believes that in human nature it is an enslaved, because a corrupt will. In denying free-will to the unregenerate, he no more denies will, than in asserting the poor negroes in the West Indies to be slaves, I deny them to be men. Now the latter, the Priestleyan, uses the word will — not for any distinct correspondent power, but — for the mere result and aggregate of fibres, motions, and sensations ; in short, it is a mere generic term with him, just as when we say, the main current of a river." * In fine, the fallen will in relation to a holy state—in relation to the "new heart" of the Scriptures—is a capability and not an ability, a recipiency and not a self-sufficient power, because the decided and positive energy of the faculty, its actual and actuating force, is entirely enlisted and swallowed up in the process of a sinful self-determination. This sinful self-determination, involving the whole soul into itself, and implicating all the energies of the inward being of man with itself, constitutes that evil nature, below the range of distinct consciousness, from which all conscious transgression proceeds, and of which it is the phenomenal manifestation. In this way, sin is seen to be a single indivisible nature, or disposition, and not merely an innumerable series of isolated acts, and this nature again is seen to be essential guilt, because, as originated in a will and by a will, it is self-originated and self-determined. In the phrase of Coleridge, man " receives a nature into his will, which by this very act becomes a corrupt will ; and *vice versâ* this will becomes his nature, and thus a corrupt nature ; " and, bearing in mind the distinguishing characteristics of nature and spirit, the reader will see the meaning of the further position of this author, "that a nature in a will is as inconsistent with freedom, as free choice with an incapacity of choosing aught but evil ; and that a free power in a nature to fulfil a law above nature is a startling paradox to the reason." †

Respecting the doctrine of Original Sin, therefore, we

---

* Literary Remains, Works, V. 448 ; compare, also, Aids to Reflection, Comment on Aphorism X., Works, I. 271-291.

† Aids to Reflection, Works, I. 281 (Note). See also Notes on Jeremy Taylor's Unum Necessarium. Literary Remains, Works, V. 195.

think there is a substantial agreement between Coleridge and that form of doctrine which has come down in the Christian church as the best expression of both the Christian experience, and the Christian reflection upon this momentous subject; and, as we have already remarked, a profound view of sin is the deep and strong soil from which all sound, healthy, and healing growths in theological speculation shoot up. Depth and truth of theory here is the very best preventive of errors and misconceptions elsewhere, and the very best mitigation and remedy for them, if they exist.

We have thus far spoken of the soundness and fruitfulness of Coleridge's general method of theologizing; of his profound belief in the inward harmony of reason and revelation, and of that instinctive and irresistible desire which he shared with the profoundest theologians of all ages, to exhibit and establish this harmony. We have also dwelt upon his views upon the fundamental doctrines of the Trinity and the Fall of man, selecting these out of the great circle of Christian doctrines, because they are fundamental, and in their implication contain the whole Christian system. It is impossible, however, within the space of an essay, and it is not perhaps desirable, to pursue the opinions of this author through the whole series of individual doctrines, and having, as we think, shown his substantial agreement, so far as the general type and character of his theology is concerned, with the Augustinian, we pass now to a brief consideration of some erroneous and defective views that cling to it.

Notwithstanding Coleridge's earnest advocacy of the doctrine of the self-determining power of the human will, whereby the origin of sin is taken out of the course of nature, and merely natural processes, and brought within the sphere of freedom and amenability to justice, we think that the idea of *guilt*, though by no means denied, or unrecognized, either in his personal experience or his speculations, was not sufficiently deep, clear, and impressive for him. Sin, for him, as for many contemplative minds in the Christian church—as it was for Origen in the early church, for the mystical theology of the middle ages, for the school of Schleiermacher at the present time—was too disproportionately the corruption and disharmony of the human soul, and not sufficiently its guilt. Now, the strongest motive which the theologian, as distinguished from the philosopher, has for maintaining the doctrine of free will, is to find an adequate and rational ground for the responsibility and criminality of the human soul as fallen and corrupt. He is not so anxious to establish the doctrine of self-determination in reference to the origin of holiness (though in this reference the doctrine is important), as in reference to the origin of sin: knowing that while there is little hazard in attributing too much to the divine agency in the production of moral good, there is the greatest hazard in implicating the deity in the origin of moral evil. It would seem, therefore, that so determined an advocate of the doctrine of human freedom as Coleridge was, should not only have seen that the very essence of sin, as *self-determined*, and thereby distinguished from all other forms of evil, consists in its ill-desert and penality, and that therefore its first and most important relation is to law and justice, but should, especially, have allowed this view to have moulded and shaped in a proper degree his theory of *Redemption*. But, the scheme which Coleridge presents in the *Aids to Reflection* is defective in not insisting with sufficient emphasis upon the truth, that as the essential nature of sin (by virtue of which it is different in kind from all other forms of evil, and becomes, strictly speaking, the only evil, per se) is *guilt*, so an essential element in any remedial plan must be *atonement*, or *expiation*. The correlate to guilt is atonement, and to attempt to satisfy those specific wants of the sinful soul which spring out of remorse of conscience, which is the *felt* and *living* relation of sin to law and justice, by a mere provision for spiritual sanctification, however needed and necessary this may be in its own place, must be like the attempt to satisfy thirst with food. Coleridge was repelled from the doctrine of vicarious atonement, by some of the mechanical schemes and forms under which it has been exhibited; but if, as the best theology of the church has generally done, he had looked at it from the view-point of the *absolute nature of justice*, and had brought it under the category of want and correlate—one of the most vital of all, and one with which Coleridge's own mind was thoroughly familiar—it seems to us that he would have seen, that, although the terms *ransom* and *payment of a debt*, when applied to the agency of the Redeemer, are indeed metaphorical, the term *expiation* is not.* If he had steadfastly contemplated the subjective wants of the human soul while filled with the consciousness of guilt, and before that sense of corruption and those yearnings for holiness of heart which are the consequent rather than antecedent of regeneration have sprung

---

* See Aids to Reflection, Aph. XIX., Comment, Works I. 306–321. We never read this ardent but merely analogical argument against substituted penal suffering within the spiritual sphere of justice, founded upon the merely natural, and wholly unjudicial, relation of a son to his mother, without thinking of the words in Wallenstein :

"O thou art *blind*, with thy deep-seeing eyes."

There is no inward and real analogy between the two spheres. There can be no legitimate arguing from a sphere from which the *retributive* is altogether excluded, such as that of the mother and child, over into a sphere in which the *retributive* is the principal element, such as that of God the just and man the guilty. It is μετάβασις ἐις ἀλλο γένος.

up in it, and then had gone still farther, and contemplated the dread objective ground of this remorseful and guilty conscience, in the divine justice, which, through this finite medium, reveals itself against all unrighteousness, he would have seen as the Augustines, the Anselms, the Calvins, and the Howes have seen, that there is a rational necessity for the expiation of guilt—a necessity founded in the rational nature and moral wants of man, and therefore primarily in the nature and attributes of that infinitely Holy Being who made man in his own image, and after his own likeness.

Moreover, in taking the position which he does—viz., that the real and absolute relation of the Passion of the Redeemer to the divine attributes is a mystery, in such sense that nothing can be affirmed concerning it that can be intelligible to the human intellect, or edifying to the human heart (for this is said, when it is asserted that the subjective consequences in the redeemed are *all* that can be known upon the subject), Coleridge stands in remarkable inconsistency with himself. We have seen that even the Trinity was not by him regarded as a mystery, in the modern but really improper sense of standing in no sort of relation to a rational intelligence—in the sense of containing no rational and intelligible element, upon which the human mind can seize as a point of contact and communion. And yet, one whole side of the work of Redemption—that side, too, which stands in the very closest connection with the deepest and most awful sense in the human soul, the sense of guilt, and ministers to the deepest and most awful craving that ever emerges into the horizon of consciousness, the craving for a deliverance from guilt on *real* grounds, i.e., on grounds of *justice:* (a craving that lies at the bottom of the whole system of sacrifices, Pagan as well as Jewish, and is both their rational justification and explanation)—this whole side of the work of Redemption is thrown utterly out of, and beyond, the range of the human mind; so that although its consequences in the redeemed may be known, its own inward nature, the ground and cause of these very consequences, is as utterly unknown and unknowable as that of a "gorgon or chimæra dire!" But, aside from this inconsistency, it is a fatal objection to this theory, that these consequences themselves—this Christian peace of conscience, and sense of reconciliation with a Holy Lawgiver —cannot come into existence through such an ignorant and blind faith as the soul is shut up to on this scheme. Such effects cannot proceed from such a cause. Here, if anywhere in the whole field of the Christian consciousness, there must be the union of faith with insight. There must be some knowledge of the *purpose*, and *purport* of the death of the Son of God—some knowledge of the inward and real relation which the substituted sufferings of Christ sustain to divine justice—before the guilt-stricken spirit, looking about instinctively for an atonement of guilt, can confidently and calmly rest in them for purposes of justification. At the very least, their intrinsic *adaptation* to the end proposed and desired, their *adequacy*, must be recognized by the mind; and what is such recognition but a species and a grade of knowledge respecting their nature, fitness, and rational necessity? The faith of the common Christian contains implicitly the rationale of the doctrine of atonement; for, the origin and existence of this faith itself is explicable, only on the hypothesis that there is reason or fitness in the doctrine; and if it is rational, it is apprehensible.

While, however, we are noticing this defect in Coleridge's statement of the doctrine of Redemption, it ought at the same time to be observed, that he was not impelled to the view he took, by a morbid and feeble moral sentiment, or from any disposition to merge all the divine attributes into an irrational and blind benevolence. It was an intellectual, more than a moral defect, with him; for when he is himself opposing Socinianism—and few minds have been more heartily opposed to it than his—we find him employing the very same objections to a scheme of salvation that makes no provision for the guilt of man, and the justice of God, which the orthodox mind has urged in all ages. "Socinianism," he says, "is not a religion, but a theory, and that too, a very pernicious, or a very unsatisfactory theory. Pernicious—for it excludes all our deep and awful ideas of the perfect holiness of God, his justice and his mercy, and thereby makes the voice of conscience a delusion, as having no correspondent in the character of the legislator ; regarding God as merely a good-natured pleasure-giver, so happiness is produced, indifferent as to the means—unsatisfactory, for, it promises forgiveness, without any solution of *the difficulty of the compatibility of this, with the justice of God*." *

In other places,† on the other hand, we find him expressing himself respecting the more mechanical view of this doctrine, with an impatience and rashness which a deeper, calmer, and more truly philosophic insight into it would have precluded. For, he who has meditated profoundly upon the Divine Being, and has thoughtfully asked himself the question : Has the Deity affections in any sense, and what solid meaning have such biblical terms as *anger* and *propitiation*, when applied to Him? will not be in haste to condemn even the most inadequate statement upon this "abyssmal subject," provided he sees

---

* Literary Remains, Works, V. 552, 553; and compare Works, V. 446-448.

† Literary Remains, Works, V. 74, e. g.

that its general meaning and purport is on the right side of the great controversy. That Coleridge had not speculatively reached the bottom of this doctrine, and acquired a view of it as profound and comprehensive as that of Anselm, e. g., in his *Cur Deus homo?* or as that to which a tract like Owen's on the *absolute* nature of divine justice leads, is evident from the irresolution of his mind, and the unsteadiness of his attitude.* In fine, as we remarked at the outset, the defect in Coleridge's view of this subject is traceable to a deficiency in his theoretic view of sin, in one of its two main aspects. The idea was not full. And perhaps the cause of this speculative deficiency was a practical one at bottom. Like many other contemplative spirits, Coleridge came into Christianity gradually, and not through a violent inward crisis, and hence his experimental consciousness of sin, though not by any means entirely lacking the element of remorse, was yet predominantly a sense of bondage and corruption. We doubt not that Coleridge's exposition of the doctrine of Redemption (as would that of Schleiermacher) would have been different from what it now is, by a very important modification, had his own Christian consciousness been the result of such an inward conflict with guilt as Luther's was, or such a keen insight into the nature of law and justice as Calvin had, instead of being, as it was, the result of a comparatively quiet transition into Christianity and growth therein; in which process, the yearning after holiness and purity, instead of the craving after atonement for agoniz-

---

* When himself attacking Socinianism, Coleridge employs the phraseology of the Calvinist, and seems thereby to reserve the attacking of Calvinism as a *peculium* of his own; as Johnson allowed no one but himself to abuse Goldsmith. See Literary Remains, passim; and observe the general animus of the notes on *Jeremy Taylor*, and on *A Barrister's Hints.*

ing guilt in the conscience, was the predominant, though not *sole* feeling.

In respect to the views of Coleridge upon the subject of *Inspiration*, it is not our purpose to enter into any detail, but simply to notice the defect in the general principle adopted by him. This principle, to state it in a word, is as follows: In determining the absolute truth and authority of the Scriptures, the objective, generally, is subordinate to the subjective. With the exception of those particular instances in which the objective revelation explicitly claims a paramount superiority to the subjective intelligence, by asserting a direct dictation from God, the former has intrinsic authority or validity, only so far as it *acquires* it before the bar of the individual judgment. The subjective reason, with the exception specified, is placed first, as the fixed and absolute norm or rule to which the objective reason is to be brought up and conformed. Now, the strongest objection to this theory of Revelation is to be derived from the very principles of the philosophy adopted, as we have endeavored to show, by Coleridge himself. But, even if we should regard him as an adherent of the later German philosophy, the absolute and fixed truth would not lie in the subject alone, but in the *identity* of the subject and the object—in a common ground that contains *both* factors. And even this position would be more sound, and less objectionable, when applied to the mutual relations of the individual mind and divine Revelation, than the one which we have mentioned above, which is really tenable only by an adherent of Fichte's system, in which the truth is laid in the subject wholly. Even on the principles of the philosophy of Identity, the truth would not be wholly and ultimately in the subjective, nor would the objective Revelation be so passively exposed to the fluctuations of an individual consciousness; because, at the very least, there would be room for action and *re*action, for correction and *counter*-correction.

But, we think it has been made out, that Coleridge, on this point of the relation of the subject to the object, ultimately adopted the view of the Kantean philosophy, substantially that of all theistic systems, which explains the possibility of knowledge by a preconformity of the subject to the object, instead of an identity of substance between them. On this system, there is a dualism between the object and the subject. Of the two, the former is the unlimited and the universal, and stands over against the latter as the limited and particular. It is the *objective*, therefore, which possesses the fixed and uniform character (in this instance, the infallibility), to which the subjective comes up with its preconformed powers of apprehension; and the function of the latter, consequently, is a recipient one, instead of an originant or creative one as in the system of Fichte, or a self-developing one as in the system of Schelling and Hegel.

We are aware that Coleridge believed that the Scriptures are, as matter of fact, infallibly true on all fundamental subjects, and that those doctrines which he, in common with the Christian church, regarded as *vital* to human salvation, are all plainly revealed in them. This ought to be noticed, because this of itself separates him heaven-wide from a mere rationalist, and places him in the same general class with the evangelical school of theologians in Germany, in respect to this doctrine of Inspiration. Still, we regard it an error in him, and in them, that the canon is not contemplated as a complete whole in and by itself, having a *common* origin in the Divine Mind, in such sense, that as a body of information it is infallibly correct on all the subjects that come within its scope and purpose. There must be truth *somewhere*, in regard to all, even the most unimportant, particulars of history, biography, and geography, that enter into the subject matter of the sacred canon, and it seems to us altogether the most rational, to presume and assume that it lies in the canon itself—in the written Revelation considered as a finished and inspired unity. These secondary matters are always an important, and sometimes vital part of the great whole,* and as they are so integrated into the solid doctrinal substance of the Scriptures that they cannot be taken out of it, any more than the blue veins can be from the solid marble, why is it not rational to believe that they had the same *common* origin with the doctrines and fundamental truths themselves which are encrusted and crystallized in them—in other words, that the Divine Mind, whether as positively revealing, or inspiring, or superintending, is the ultimate Author of the whole? There are but two objections to this position. The first is, that the inspired writers become thereby mere amanuenses and automata. This objection has no force for one who believes that the Divine can, and does, dwell and work in the human, in the most real and absolute manner, without in the least mutilating or suppressing the human, and ought not to be urged by one who believes in the indwelling of the Holy Ghost in the regenerate soul. As,

---

* In *some* instances at least, a vital part; as e. g., the biographic memoirs of the Redeemer by the evangelists. If these are not infallible as history, then the whole Christian religion instantaneously disappears: for then the Personage in whom it centres and rests cannot be proved to have had an actual existence in space and time, and the forecasting intimations which the human soul (of a Plato, e. g.) has had of a future Redeemer would not save it from skepticism and despair. Hence, in the contest between rationalism and supernaturalism in Germany, the historical narratives in the four gospels have been the hottest part of the battle-field.

in this instance, the human cannot be separated from the Divine, in the individual consciousness, and all "the fruits of the Spirit" seem to be the very spontaneity of the human soul itself, so, in the instance of the origination of the body of Holy Writ, while all, even the minutest parts have the flexibility, freshness, and naturalness of purely human productions, there is yet in and through them all, the unerring agency of the Supreme Mind. In other words, the Supreme Intelligence is *the organizing principle* of that outstanding body of information which is called the Bible, and, working like any other organizing principle with *thoroughness*, produces a whole that is characterized by its own characteristic — perfection of knowledge — even as life in the natural world diffuses itself, and produces all the characteristic marks of life, out to the rim of the tiniest leaf. The second objection, and a fatal one if it can be maintained, is, that there are actual errors in the Scriptures, on points in regard to which they profess to teach the truth. Let this be shown, if it can be; but until it has been shown, without possibility of contradiction, the Christian mind is certainly rational in continuing to assume and affirm the infallibility of the written word. We say this with confidence, because, out of the great number of alleged errors and contradictions that have been urged against the plenary inspiration of the Scriptures, there is not a single one established as such upon grounds that render it absurd for a defender of the doctrine to take the opposite side. There is no list of conceded and acknowledged errors in the Scriptures. There are many difficulties still remaining, we grant, but while there is not a case in which the absolute and unappealable settlement has resulted in establishing the fact of undoubted error, there are many in which it has resulted in favor of the doctrine of plenary inspiration. No one acquainted with the results of the severe and skeptical criticism, to which the canon has been subjected for the last half-century in Germany, will deny that the number of apparent contradictions and errors is smaller now than it was at the beginning of this period, and that the remainder of the series is diminishing. And, had Coleridge himself kept up with the progress of Biblical Criticism in that country where the foundation of his views on this subject seems to have been laid, he would undoubtedly have seen reasons for rejecting some erroneous hypotheses which, though exploded in the land of their birth, clung to him to the end of his life. He seems in regard to such an important point, as the inspiration and canonical authority of the *Christopædia* in both Matthew's and Luke's gospels, e. g., not to have made any advance upon the general views of the brilliant but superficial Eichorn, who was his teacher in 1799.*

This whole subject of Inspiration, a most important and difficult one in some respects, turns upon the true relation of the subjective to the objective, and particularly of the human to the Divine Reason. We cannot but regard this middle theory of Inspiration, set forth by Coleridge in common with that spiritual school of theologians in Germany which is destined to exert a great, and we believe on the whole salutary influence upon the theology of this country and Great Britain, for some time to come, as in direct opposition to that sound and rational philosophy which regards the objective as fixed, reliable, and absolute, and conceives of the subjective as designed to receive this into itself with intelligence and freedom, and as really free from fluctuation and error, only so far as it partakes of the fixedness and truth of the objective. The finite rea-

---

* Literary Remains, Works, V. 76, 78, 79, 532.

son is rather a recipiency than a self-subsistent power, according to Kant and Jacobi, and there are many passages in Coleridge's writings that endorse this. The human mind is rather a capacity, than a self-sufficing fulness like the Divine Mind ; and therefore the only rational attitude of the subjective intelligence towards the objective Revelation, and towards all revelation of the Supreme Reason, is that of intelligent and living receptivity. The Christian consciousness itself cannot safely be left to its own independent movement, without any moulding and modifying influence of the written word. The outward, fixed, and self-included Scripture must go down through all the ages and changes of the Christian experience and Christian reflection, as the absolute norm by which the whole process of practical and speculative development is to be protected from deviations to the right hand and to the left. The inspired Canon is to steady and solidify that living process of thinking and of feeling which is embodied and manifested in the Christian church, and keep it from the extremes on either hand, to which a finite mind and a living process are ever liable. Neither the practical nor the scientific form of a particular doctrine, or of Christian theology generally, may be sought for in the Christian consciousness, except as this has been rectified and purified by the Scriptures—in the subjective, except as it has been rectified from its errors and purified from its foreign elements, by the conscious reception into itself of the objective which is absolutely free from both. There would be more weight in the doctrine of the authority of the finite reason, and the Christian consciousness, than there now is, if all the processes of the human soul, even the regenerate human soul, were *normal* processes. But he has studied the history of even Christian speculation to little purpose, who has not learned from it the need of an objective and fixed authority for the *fallen* human mind. Taken as a whole, the thinking of the human mind has never been nearer the central line of truth, than while it has been under the influence and guidance of Christianity. Christian philosophy is far nearer this centre than the best schools of merely Pagan philosophy. And yet, how fluctuating has been the movement, and what constant need there has been of an absolute standard by which to determine and correct the aberrations of the human mind! We think that in his strong belief that Christianity is absolutely rational, and in his earnest desire to exhibit it as such, Coleridge was led, at times certainly, to attribute a greater power of *origination* to the finite reason than it really possesses, and to forget, that as an endowment superinduced, and not as the whole essence of the finite mind, reason in man, though the same in kind with the Supreme Reason, is not that infinite *plenitude* of wisdom which is incommunicable to a created spirit.*

We have been the more free and full, in speaking of the views of Coleridge upon the two topics of vicarious *Atonement*, and *Inspiration*, because we believe that the defect in them originated not so much from a moral as from a speculative source. We have already spoken of the manner in which he identifies himself with the orthodox feeling and view, in relation to the doctrine of atonement, when himself opposing Socinianism, and any one who will carefully peruse the expressions of reverence for the Scriptures which spontaneously break from him, and bear in mind that whatever may be the actual *influence*, the serious and solemn *purpose* of his little tract was to strengthen the Bible in its claims upon the human intellect as the source of religious knowledge, cannot doubt

---

* Compare the author's Theological Essays, pp. 2 4–210.

that Coleridge was induced to reject the common theory of Inspiration from a conviction that it really defeated its own end, and not because he wished to weaken, in the least, the belief of Christendom in the divine oracles. While, therefore, we have distinctly expressed our convictions on these points, we wish at the same time to remind the reader that these defects, though important, are not the substance and staple of the theological opinions of this author. Notwithstanding a partial disagreement with the Christian mind upon these subjects, there is a positive and profound agreement with it on all the other important doctrines of Christianity; and it should be remembered that, in a fundamental agreement with such a body of truth as the Christian religion, a basis is laid for the ultimate correction of views and opinions not in consonance with it. When a mind has once received into itself the substance of Christianity, it is its tendency to deepen and widen its religious consciousness, and in this process foreign and contradictory elements are finally cast out of it by its own saliency and vitality. In the case of Coleridge, it should moreover be observed, that he was compelled to clear himself of systems of philosophy and religion inimical to a theistic philosophy and a spiritual Christianity, in and during the development of his positive and final opinions; and hence, that it is not to be wondered at, that these latter should, here and there, exhibit the vanishing hues of the former. It is not to be wondered at, that some particles of the chaotic slime should have cleaved to him, compelled as he was to paw himself out of ground, like Milton's first lion.*

* Now half appeared
The tawny lion, pawing to get free
His hinder parts; then springs, as broke from bonds,
And rampant shakes his brinded mane.
Paradise Lost, VII. 463-466.

We have now, as briefly as possible, touched upon the leading points in the philosophy and theology of Coleridge, thereby to show what are the general drift and spirit of his speculations in these two highest departments of knowledge. We have not been anxious to defend this author upon each and every one of the various topics on which he has given the world his thoughts, believing that on some of them he is indefensible. At the same time, we have expressed a decided opinion, that in respect generally to the highest problems of philosophy and theology, the opinions of Coleridge are every way worthy of being classed with those of the master minds of the race. We are confident that his writings contain, after subtracting the subtrahend, a body of thought upon the highest themes of reflection well worthy of the study of every mind that is seeking a deep, clear, and exhaustive development of itself. Into the great variety of philosophical theories, and the great diversity in the ways and methods of thinking, characteristic of this age, we think the speculations of Coleridge deserve to be cast, and believe that just in proportion as they are thoroughly apprehended, and thereby enter vitally into the thinking world, will they allay the furious fermentation that is going on, and introduce unity, order, serenity, and health, into the mental processes of the times. We believe that they will do still more than this. We believe that they will help to fortify the minds of the rising generation of educated men in that Platonic method of philosophizing which has come down through all the mutations in the philosophic world, which has survived them all, which more than any other method has shown an affinity with religion, natural and revealed, and which, through its doctrine of seminal and germinant ideas, has been the fertile root of all the finest growths and fruitage of the human mind.

THE CONFESSIONS OF AUGUSTINE.*

THERE are a few autobiographies that challenge and receive a special attention from age to age, because they possess characteristics that are not found in the common mass of such productions. They are the unreserved delineation of an extraordinary intellect and of a remarkable experience. They embody the thoughts of a deep mind in its most secret and absorbed hours, the emotions of a vehement soul in its most critical and impassioned moments. In them, the experiences of human life reach such a pitch of intensity, and such a breadth, range, and depth, as to strike the reader with both a sense of familiarity and a sense of strangeness. It is his own human thought and human feeling that he finds expressed; and yet it is spoken with so much greater clearness, depth, and energy, than he is himself capable of, or than is characteristic of the mass of men, that it seems like the experience of another sphere and another race of beings. The *Confessions of Augustine* is a work of this class; and upon sending forth another edition of it, we seize the opportunity to notice some of its more distinguishing and remarkable features.

* Published in 1859, as an introduction to the writer's revision of the translation of Augustine's Confessions.

1. The first characteristic that strikes the reader is, the singular *mingling of metaphysical and devotional elements* in the work. The writer passes, with a freedom that often amounts to abruptness, from the intensely practical to the intensely speculative. In the very midst of his confession of sin, or rejoicing over deliverance from it, his subtle and inquisitive understanding starts a question the answer to which, if answer were possible, would involve the solution of all the problems that have baffled the metaphysical mind from Thales to Hegel. In the very opening of the work, for example, when the surcharged and brimming soul is swelling with its thick-coming emotions, and is seeking vent for its sense of the divine mercy which has saved it from everlasting perdition, it slides by an unconscious transition to the question: "*How* shall I call upon my God, my God and Lord, since when I call for Him I shall be calling Him into myself? And what room is there within me, whither my God can come into me? Whither *can* God come into me, God who made heaven and earth." * At the very moment when Augustine is enjoying the most heartfelt and positive communion with God, his intellect feels the pressure of the standing problem respecting the possibility of such an intercourse—the problem which Howe has discussed with such ability in that part of the Living Temple where he treats of the "conversableness" of God. Such transitions are perpetually occurring, until, in the eleventh book, the author leaves his autobiography altogether, and devotes the remainder of the work to an interpretation of the opening chapters of Genesis, in which he debates the most recondite questions respecting time and eternity, the Creator and creation, and the triunity of the Divine Essence.

* Confessions, I. 2.

It is not, however, from any open or lurking skepticism, or even from any mental unrest, that Augustine raises such inquiries. The great men in the Christian church have been little troubled by skeptical doubts. Their faith was too strong, their spiritual insight too clear, and their work too pressing, to be involved in that languid infidelity which assails a sentimental religiousness. Who can think of the Augustines, the Anselms, the Luthers, the Calvins, the Knoxes, and the Bunyans, as dallying with divine truth instead of grasping it; and uttering, instead of the clarion tones of an assured and triumphant faith, the weak moan of

> "An infant crying in the night;
> An infant crying for the light;
> And with no language but a cry."

These questions, so numerous and so searching, in these Confessions, are not the issue or the index of a mind tormented by doubts. They are only the exuberant play and careering of a subtle and thoughtful intellect, from the vantage-ground of a living and victorious trust. Conscious of being now, at last, at rest in God, the centre of being and blessedness, Augustine allows his mind to pose itself with the infinite truths that are involved in the childlike faith of the Christian. His purpose is not to unsettle his own belief, or that of his reader; but by the mere immensity of truth to stagger and overwhelm the understanding, and thereby fill the soul with that sense of mystery which is at once the constituent element of awe and the nutriment of worship. Nothing can be farther from infidelity than the spirit with which Augustine raises these inquiries respecting time, eternity, the nature of God and the human soul, the possibility and manner of creation from nothing, the nature of matter, and the origin of evil. Neither is there anything of gnostic curiosity and

pride, in his approaches to the frontiers of this realm of
mystery. He merely desires, by this tentative method,
to fill his own mind, already believing, hoping and rejoicing in divine realities, with a more distinct consciousness
of the infinitude of the world beyond space and time, and
of those facts and truths which, in his own phrase, cannot
enter by any of the avenues of the flesh. Hence, his
questionings leave him humble, while they leave him more
self-intelligent. His speculation issues from his religious
life and feeling, and helps both to clarify and deepen
it. In other words, Augustine is here practising upon
his own celebrated dictum, that *faith precedes scientific
knowledge.* The practical belief of the truths of Christianity contains much that is latent and undeveloped. The
Christian is wiser than he knows. The moment he begins to examine the implications of his own vivid personal
experience, he finds that they contain the entire rudimental matter of Christian science. For example, he believes
in the one living and personal God. But, the instant he
commences the analysis of this idea of ideas, in the construction of the ontological argument, he discovers its profound capacity and its vast implication. Again, he believes in God incarnate. But, when he endeavors to com-
prehend what is involved in this fact and truth, he is
overwhelmed by the richness of its contents, and the
multitude of its relations. His faith has positively and
strongly grasped these ideas of God and the God-man;
but, to employ an illustration of Bernard, it has grasped
them in their closed and involuted form.* If he would
pass, now, from faith to scientific reason, he needs only to

---

* "Intellectus rationi innititur, fides authoritati, opinio sola veri-
similitudine se tuetur. Habent illa duo *certam* veritatem, sed fides
clausam et involutam, intelligentia nudam et manifestam."—Bernar-
dus, De Consideratione, Lib. V. cap. 3.

reflect upon the intrinsic meaning of these ideas, until they open along the lines of their structure, and are perceived philosophically, though not exhaustively. But, in this process, faith itself is reinforced and deepened by a reflex action, while, at the same time, the intellect is kept reverent and vigilant, because the cognition, though positive and correct as far as it reaches, is not exhaustive and complete, only by reason of the immensity and infinitude of the object.

Holding such a theory of the relation of reason to faith, Augustine never shrinks from making excursions into the region of metaphysical truth. Although he uniformly approaches the problems of theology upon their most difficult side, and never attempts to become clear by becoming shallow, yet there is little fear of philosophy, and still less disparagement of reason in the writings of the bishop of Hippo. And this, because of the above-mentioned theory. Always making his own vital and confident faith the point from which he departs, and to which he returns, he is at once bold and safe. Go where he may, he cannot lose sight of his pole-star; and thus he always keeps his northing. Like the mariner far out at sea, and with a strong ship under him, he careers courageously over the waste of waters, with no dread of a lee shore or of sunken rocks. Hence the frequency, and oftentimes the strange abruptness, of his metaphysical queryings. He knows that all truth is consistent with itself, and that the philosophical answer, if it come at all, must come out of the material furnished by the Christian consciousness. His reason cannot contradict his faith, because it is homogeneous and consubstantial with it. The former is the evolution, the latter is the involution.

2. A second characteristic of Augustine's Confessions is the *union of a minute and exhaustive detail of sin, with*

the most intense and spiritual abhorrence of it. The only work in any language that bears any comparison with this of the North African Father, is that in which Rousseau pours out his life of passion and evil concupiscence. There is the same *abandon* and unreserve in each; the same particularity in recounting the past conduct; the same subtle unwinding of the course of transgression. Each absorbs himself in his own biography, with an entireness and simplicity that precludes any thought for a spectator or a listener, any regard for either an unfeeling or a sympathizing world of readers. Augustine and Rousseau, both alike, withdraw into the secret and silent confessional of their own memories and recollections, and there pour out their confidences with utter self-abandonment.

But, the resemblance ceases at this point. The motive prompting the confession, and the emotions that accompany it, are as different as light from darkness, as Christ from Belial. Augustine's confession is really such—an acknowledgment to God. Rousseau's recital is a soliloquy that never goes beyond himself. The Christian bishop confesses his past sinful life, only that he may magnify and make his boast in that unmerited grace which plucked him " from the bottom of the bottomless pit." * He brings out his secret and scarlet sins into the light of his memory, that he may praise the God of his salvation for his marvellous pity. "I will now call to mind," he says, " my past foulness, and the carnal corruptions of my soul; not because I love them, but that I may love Thee, O my God. For love of Thy love, I do it; reviewing my most wicked ways in the very bitterness of my remembrance, that Thou mayest grow sweet unto me." † The minute-

* Confessions, II. 4.
† Ibid., II. 1.

ness, the plainness, and the exhaustiveness of his account of his sinful life, only sets in stronger relief the strangeness of the mercy that lifted him out of it; only fills him with a delirium of joy and love towards his redeeming God. How different all this is from the motive and the feeling of Rousseau, it is needless to say. It is not necessary, perhaps, to affirm the existence of a deliberate intention to debauch the world by those impenitent and shameless confessions of sin and guilt, though such is unquestionably the inevitable tendency of them. It is enough to say, that there certainly was no intention to waken abhorrence of evil by means of them; and still less to reflect any light upon the Divine character and government. The impelling motive probably was, to relieve an ungoverned and restless nature, by a simple overflow of the pent-up elements. Rousseau merely followed that impulse of a burdened soul which necessitates self-utterance; that law of both mind and matter which inexorably forbids the perpetual suppression of struggling elements and forces. All the devices of man cannot choke down even the smallest spring of water, so that it shall *never* come to the surface; and all the efforts of men and angels combined cannot keep under, in *eternal* burial, the emotions and passions of an inordinate and billowy spirit. Under this stress and pressure, the "self-torturing sophist" enters into the detail of his unworthy and unhappy life, without the slightest recognition of the claims of law, and apparently without the slightest fear of its retributions. The wild and passionate rehearsal goes on, but with no reference either to the holiness or the mercy of the Supreme; with no allusion to the solemn relations of an immortal spirit either to time or to eternity.

Again, while Augustine relates the sins of his youth, and his transgressions, with a plainness which the factitious modesty of an inwardly impure mind has sometimes condemned, it is always with the most genuine and unaffected sorrow and abhorrence. A more sincere book than the Confessions of Augustine was never written. Every statement of sin is a wail over it. Rivers of water run down the relator's eyes, because he has not kept the divine law. The plainness of this book is like that of the prophecy of Ezekiel; the vileness is brought out into sight, only that it may be trampled and stamped upon. The ethical indignation is like that of Moses, when he ground the golden calf to powder, and mingling it with water made the people drink it down. And yet it is not a spasmodic or an affected reprobation. From the depths of a now spiritualized mind, Augustine abhors his past iniquity. He is a new creature ; old things have passed away, and all things have become new. With the clear and crystalline eye of the cherubim, he looks into the hole of the pit whence he was digged, and beholds according to truth. There is no furtive glance towards the past voluptuousness. It is seen to be sin and guilt, meriting the wrath and curse of God, and fit only to be burned up in the consuming fire of the Divine immaculateness. All this is perceived with calmness and certainty ; so that the judgment of damnation, which is passed by this autobiographer upon his personal corruption, is deep and tranquil, like that of the bar of final doom.

3. But this is only a negative excellence. A third characteristic of this work is that it palpitates with the *positive love of God and goodness.* The writer does not merely look back with aversion and abhorrence, but he looks forward with aspiration and longing. He gazes with a steady and rapt eye upon the supernal Beauty—the heavenly Eros. His spiritualized perception reposes with joy unutterable and full of glorying upon the perfections

of God, and the realities of eternity. Hear his impassioned utterance: "Not with doubting, but with assured consciousness, do I love Thee, Lord. But what do I love, when I love Thee? Not the beauty of bodies, nor the fair harmony of time, nor the brightness of the light so gladsome to our eyes, nor sweet melodies of varied songs, nor the fragrant smell of flowers, and ointments, and spices, not manna and honey, not limbs acceptable to the embracements of flesh. None of these do I love when I love my God. And yet, I love a kind of light, a kind of melody, a kind of fragance, a kind of food, and a kind of embracement, when I love my God—the light, the melody, the fragrance, the food, the embracement of the inner man: where there shineth unto my soul what space cannot contain, and there soundeth what time beareth not away, and there smelleth what breathing disperseth not, and there tasteth what eating diminisheth not, and there clingeth what satiety divorceth not. This is it which I love when I love my God." The entire emotiveness of that deep, passionate, North-African nature has been transferred from sense to spirit, from time to eternity, from earth to heaven, from the creature to the Creator, and now flows on like the river of God which is full of water. Indeed, the feeling which Augustine bears towards the blessed triune God cannot be better expressed than by the word *affectionateness*. There is in his experience awe " deep as the centre;" there is humility absolute; there is the reverential fear of the wing-veiled cherubim; but there is also, in and through it all, that confiding, childlike love which is both warranted and elicited by the dying prayer of the Redeemer. This man, who so often denominates himself "abominable," "miserable," and "godless;" who prostrates his whole being in shame and grief unspeakable before the infinite and adorable majesty of God; yet finds an answer in his own regenerate consciousness to the wonderful supplication of the Redeemer, that his redeemed "all may be one, as Thou Father art in me, and I in Thee; that they may be one even as we are one; I in them, and Thou in me, that they may be made perfect in one."

This sense of union with God is very vivid in this Latin Father; as it is, also, in some of the more spiritual of the schoolmen—particularly Anselm and Bernard. It is very different, however, from that vague feeling of the mystic theologian which, even in its best forms, sometimes hovers upon the borders of pantheism, and in its worst forms, as in Eckart and Silesius, is little better than the Hindoo absorption in the Deity. On the contrary, it is that intelligent consciousness of union with God which issues from the evangelical sense of *reconciliation with Him through the blood of Christ*. The ideas of incarnation and redemption shape the whole experience of Augustine, and his communion with God has its root in the sense of sin and the sense of mercy. But these two utterly preclude the pantheistic intuition. He who feels himself to be guilty knows most piercingly that God and man are two distinct beings. And he who has rejoiced in the manifested pity of the Creator towards the creature cannot possibly confound the two, either in philosophy or theology. And such is the foundation upon which Augustine's filial and affectionate communion with God rests. He knows that if God spared not his own Son, but freely gave him up a sacrifice for a guilty creature like himself, he will surely, after this transaction, freely give him all things. Springing from this evangelical root, the affectionateness of Augustine, whereby he cries, Abba, Father, is totally different, also, from that fatal form of self-deception seen in the sentimentalist's love of God. He does not presume to cast himself upon the Divine mercy, until he has first recognized and acquiesced in the Divine justice. These Confessions contain none of that religiousness to which the intrinsic and eternal damnableness of sin is an offensive truth, and which avoids all the retributive and judicial aspects of revelation. Augustine never shrinks from the fact, that a creature's free and wilful transgression in its own nature merits, and, without faith in Christ's blood of atonement, will receive, an everlasting punishment from the living God. He knows that the doctrine, of *genuine unselfish* penitence for sin stands, or falls, with that of an absolute ill-desert and an everlasting penalty; that every species of religious anxiety which reluctates at Christ's representations of the final doom, and at the scripture doctrine that only Christ's atonement stands between a sinner and eternal perdition, is spurious; and that he who would " climb up some other way " to throw himself into the arms of the Redeemer, before he has knelt with a broken heart at the bar of the Judge, will ultimately meet a terrific rebuke to his presumption and moral worthlessness. Augustine's trust in the compassion of God has for its antecedent the distinct consciousness of the " wrath to come." The Divine love is, for his mind, a *self-sacrificing* pity that " bore his sins on the tree," and thereby delivered him from an infinite infliction that was merited and actually impending, or it would not have been vicariously endured by incarnate God. "I was going," he says, in reference to a dangerous sickness in his youth, " I was going down to hell, carrying all the sins which I had committed both against Thee and myself and others, many and grievous sins, over and above that bond of original sin whereby we all die in Adam. For, Thou hadst not forgiven me any of these things in Christ, nor had He abolished by His cross the enmity which by my sins I had incurred with Thee. And, now, the fever heightening, I was parting and departing for ever. For, had I then parted hence, whither had I departed but into fire and torments such as my misdeeds deserved in the truth of Thy appointment." *

Such thoroughness in Augustine's experience of both the justice and the mercy of God resulted in an undoubting confidence in God. The trustfulness of his feeling towards the Dread Supreme exhibits itself, sometimes, like the prattling of a child: "I beseech Thee, my God, I would fain know, if so Thou willest, for what purpose was my baptism then deferred? Was it for my good that the rein was laid loose, as it were, upon me, for me to sin?" † "Bear with me, my God, while I say something of my talents—Thy gift—and on what dotages I wasted them." ‡ In fact, the whole life, the entire experience of Augustine, with all that is insignificant equally with all that is great in it, is poured into the ear of the Divine Confessor. To God there is nothing great and nothing small; and this penitent, childlike, and affectionate soul passes from point to point in its detail, without stopping to measure or compare. The Divine ear is not heavy that it cannot hear even the minutest items of the penitential record, and the filial, grateful heart is never tired of the exhaustive confession and rehearsal.

Such an experience of both the law and the gospel brought Augustine into most intimate relations with God. "Sometimes," he says, "Thou admittest me to an affection very unusual, in my inmost soul; rising to a strange sweetness, which, if it were perfected in me, I know not what in it would not belong to the life to come." §

* Confessions, V. 9.
† Ibid., I. 11.
‡ Ibid., I. 17.
§ Ibid., X. 11.

The Modern Church is too destitute of this child-like affectionateness and this fervor of love. It is certainly striking to pass from the more formal and reserved types of religious experience, characteristic of an over-civilized Christendom, to the simple and gushing utterances of Augustine, Anselm, and Bernard. "Too late I loved Thee, O Thou Beauty of ancient days, yet ever new! Too late I loved Thee. Oh, that I might repose on Thee! Oh! that Thou wouldest enter into my heart, and inebriate it. O Thou sweetness never failing, Thou blissful and assured sweetness." * In one of the Soliloquies ascribed to him, Augustine addresses God as both father and mother: "Et tu Domine Deus pater orphanorum, et tu mater pupillorum tuorum, audi ejulatum filiorum tuorum." The soul follows hard after God, and its pantings often find a natural expression in language and terms as fervid as those which we are wont to associate only with the most absorbing and consuming of earthly passions. The rhythmical and sonorous Roman speech becomes yet more deep-toned and sounding in its note, as the rapt mind rises upon the wings of spiritual intuition and ecstasy. The superlative becomes the positive. "Dulcissime, amantissime, benignissime, preciosissime, desiderantissime, amabilissime, pulcherrime; tu melle dulcior, lacte et nive candidior, nectare suavior, gemmis et auro preciosior, cunctisque terrarum divitiis et honoribus mihi carior, quando te videbo? Quando apparebo ante faciem tuam? Quando satiabor de pulchritudine tua?" †

---

* Confessions, X. 27; I. 5; II. 1.

† Augustini, Opera, VI. 874, 928, sq. Ed. Migne. The Soliloquies and Meditations, from which these extracts are taken, are probably ungenuine, but the remark of Erasmus respecting them is true: "Auctorem esse vel Augustinum, vel qui ejus libros non indiligenter legit." They bear the marks, however, of Romish interpolation.

This language, it should be remembered, flows from a mind that is naturally speculative and dialectic; that has meditated not merely profoundly, but systematically, upon the being and attributes of God. It is not the utterance of a sentimentalist, but of a robust understanding, out of which issued the most logical and severe of the ancient types of Christian theology. When we find the most abstract and intellectual of the Christian fathers dissolving in tears, or soaring in ecstasy, we may be certain that the emotion flows from truth and reality. When the rock gushes out water, we may be sure that it is pure water. Were it not that we find the systematic writings of Augustine, which constitute the great bulk of his works, calm as reason itself, consecutive as logic itself, and entirely free from extravagance, we might query whether a sinful mortal, an imperfectly sanctified man, could use such language as the above, without a latent insincerity; or, at least, without running far in advance of his real emotions. But such soliloquies and meditations are the moments of Christian and saintly inspiration; hours when the deep and subtle reasoning of the renewed mind, having reached its term, becomes hushed and breathless in the spiritual intuition, and passes over into awe and worship. The knowledge of the cherub becomes the love of the seraph. The one is the dark root, the other the bright consummate flower of religion.

One who imbues his mind with the spirit of Augustine's Confessions finds no difficulty, therefore, in understanding the Song of Solomon—the figures and phrases of which are so frequently employed in the meditations and prayers of the great fathers and schoolmen. An earthly exegesis can interpret this song of songs only from its own point of view. The conceptions, figures, and terms of the spiritual lyric are instinctively referred to earthly relationships. An unspiritual mind cannot, by any possibility, rise into the pure ether and element of incorporeal and heavenly Beauty, in which the writer of this canticle moves his wings. But not so the Augustines, the Anselms, and the Bernards. These purged and clear eyes were granted, at certain favored hours, and as the result of their long vigils and meditations, the immortal vision of the pure in heart. And the immortal vision wakened the immortal longing. The environment of earth and time became a prison to the now illuminated spirit, and it pined for the hill of frankincense and the mountains of myrrh. Having seen the King in his beauty, the holy and ethereal soul fell into love-longing.*

4. A fourth striking characteristic of these Confessions is, the insight which they afford into the *origin and progress of the Christian experience.* They are the best commentary yet written upon the seventh and eighth chapters of Romans. That quickening of the human spirit, which puts it again into vital and sensitive relations to the holy and the eternal; that illumination of the mind, whereby it is enabled to perceive with clearness the real nature of truth and righteousness; that empowering of the will, to

* The experience of the elder Edwards exhibits these same characteristics. "I began," he says, "to have a new kind of apprehension and idea of Christ and the work of redemption. My mind was greatly engaged in meditations on Christ, on the beauty and excellence of his person. These words used to be abundantly with me: 'I am the Rose of Sharon, and the Lily of the valleys.' These words seemed to me sweetly to represent the loveliness and beauty of Jesus Christ. The whole book of Canticles used to be pleasant to me, and I used to be much in reading it. The sense I had of divine things would often, of a sudden, kindle up as it were a sweet burning in my heart; an ardor of soul that I know not how to express."—This rapt, exulting vision of the Divine beauty and majesty, which fell upon him like the dawn, in the beginning of his Christian life, would, in the middle ages, have given him the title of the "angelic," or the "seraphic" doctor.

the conflict and the victory—the entire process of restoring the divine image in the soul of man—is delineated in this book with a vividness and reality never exceeded by the uninspired mind. And particularly is the bondage of the fallen will brought to view. Augustine, though subject to pangs of conscience, and the forebodings of an unpardoned soul, from his earliest years, did not, nevertheless, attain evangelical peace until the thirty-second year of his life. He died at the age of seventy-six; so that nearly one-half of his earthly existence was spent in unregeneracy. He was born and bred in the midst of paganism, and his tropical North-African nature immersed itself in the ambition and sensuality of his clime and his race, with an intensity to which the career of a Rousseau, a Byron, or a Heine, affords a nearer parallel than does anything that meets the eye in the externally decent and restrained life of modern society. To such a soul of flame, was uttered in tones that startled, and tones that shattered, and tones that for a moment paralyzed, the solemn words: "Not in rioting and drunkenness, not in chambering and wantonness, not in strife and envying; but put ye on the Lord Jesus Christ, and make not provision for the flesh." It was, at first, like the giving up of the ghost. The effort to obey was convulsive. "Thou, O Lord, didst press upon me inwardly with a severe mercy, redoubling the lashes of fear and shame lest I should again give way, and not bursting that slight remaining tie it should recover strength, and bind me faster. For I said within myself, 'Be it done now, be it done now.' And as I spake, I all but performed it. I all but did it, and did it not; yet sunk not back to my former state, but kept my stand hard by, and *took breath*. And I essayed again, and lacked somewhat less of it, and somewhat less, and all but touched and laid hold upon it; hesitating to die to death, and to live to life. And the worse, whereto I was accustomed, prevailed more with me than the better, whereto I was unused; and when the moment approached when I was to become other than I was, the greater dismay did it strike into me; yet did it not strike me back, nor turn me away, but held me in suspense." * What a subtle and most truthful glimpse into the workings of inveterate sin, which has grown with his growth, and strengthened with his strength, is afforded in the petition of his early manhood: "Give me continence, only *not yet*." † These, and a hundred others like them, bring the whole inward struggle into plain view. It is a real conflict in which the kingdom of heaven suffers violence, and the violent take it by force. We know of no other religious book, except the Bible and Pilgrim's Progress, that makes so deep an impression of *reality* as this one. Religion, in the experience here delineated, is veritable. The fears and forebodings that herald it are actual. The pangs and throes that bring it to the birth are actual. The joys and sorrows, the assurance and the doubts that accompany its growth are actual. As the doctrinal system of Augustine rests upon a basis of realism, so does his practical life and history. There is nothing, upon either side, that is nominal, fictitious, ideal.

But, the whole excellence of this delineation of the bondage of the apostate will, which is the cause of all this struggle, will not be perceived, unless it be noticed that Augustine continually refers the enslavement to the creature himself, and never to the Creator. It is the product of man's self-determination, and not of that creative fiat by which man was originally made a holy, and an *un*-enslaved spirit in the image of God. "My *will* the enemy held, and *thence* had made a chain for me, and bound

---

* Confessions, VIII. 11.
† Ibid., VIII. 7.

me. For, of a perverse will comes *lust;* and a lust yielded to becomes *custom;* and custom not resisted becomes *necessity.* By which links, as it were, joined together as in a chain, a hard bondage held me enthralled. And that new will, to serve Thee freely and to enjoy Thee, O God, which had begun to be in me, was not able to overcome my former long-established wilfulness." * Thus, the bondage is guilt; and at the very instant when the soul is weighed down with a sense of utter impotence to holiness, it is also prostrate before the judicial bar with the consciousness of deserved condemnation. The enslavement is not pleaded in excuse of sin, because it is perceived to be a *part* of sin. "All wickedness is weakness," says Milton's helpless Samson Agonistes. The element of servitude, like the element of blindness, or of hardness, is part and particle of that evil and abominable thing which the soul of God hates. The *reflex* action, or reaction, of transgression, upon the understanding, is spiritual blindness; upon the heart, is spiritual hardness or insensibility; upon the will, is spiritual bondage, or inability to do good. The voluntary faculty cannot, any more than any other faculty of the soul, escape the reaction of its self-action. Suicide is as total an extinction of life as homicide. Whosoever commits sin, by and in this very voluntary act, becomes the slave (δοῦλος) of sin. The cause inevitably carries its consequence. That which is done cannot be undone; and no will that self-determinedly apostatizes from God can be again the sound and strong faculty in reference to good, that it was before apostasy, except through the intervention of Divine renovating power. The moral bondage, therefore, like the moral blindness and the moral hardness, enters into the

---

* Confessions, VIII. 5.

sum total of human depravity, and goes to swell, and not diminish, the sum-total of human condemnation. All this is implied in Augustine's anthropology. Nowhere is there a more profound consciousness of the impotence of the apostate will, and nowhere is there a more heartfelt and humble sense of personal ill-desert, than is expressed in these Confessions. "In these spiritual things," says Augustine, "ability is one with will, and to will is to do; and yet the thing is not done. Whence is this strange anomaly (monstrum)? The mind commands the *body*, and it obeys instantly; the mind commands *itself*, and is resisted. The mind commands the hand to be moved, and such readiness is there, that command is scarce distinct from obedience. The mind commands the mind, its own *self*, to will; and yet it doth not will. It commands itself, I say, to will, and would not command unless it willed; and yet what it commands is not done. But it willeth not *entirely;* therefore, doth it not command entirely. For, it commandeth only so far forth as it willeth. The will commandeth that there be a *will;* not another's will, but its own will. But it doth not command *entirely;* therefore, what it commandeth does not take place." *

The overlooking of this *voluntary origin* of the bondage of the human will has led to much misrepresentation of the theological system of the greatest intellect of the patristic period. Friends, as well as foes, have charged him with fatalism. Milman's portrait of Augustine, for example, is in many of its features an accurate one, and the general coloring is laid on with an admiring and even an enthusiastic eye. But, Milman represents Augustinianism "as offering up free agency upon the altar of re-

* Confessions, VIII. 9.

ligion, and thereby degrading the most wonderful work of omnipotence—a being endowed with free agency." *
This statement would be true, had Augustine attributed the bondage of the human will to the creative act of God. But, in his theory, it is the product of a human act of free self-determination. *Self*-enslavement and *self*-ruin, are one thing; enslavement by the creative act, and ruin by compulsory force, are another. The charge of fatalism can, logically, be made only against the latter. The Latin father places all mankind in the first parents, and starts them with a created perfection—a holy will and an enlightened understanding. From this high vantage-ground, they fall by an act of self-determination as positive, and as free, as that by which any one of Adam's posterity exerts an individual volition. Augustine does not explain this, but he always postulates and supposes it. An opponent may charge him with holding a mystery that, in his own opinion, is untenable; but may not charge him with holding to a created sin, or to a perdition that is necessitated by God.

Such are some of the more salient points in the autobiography of Augustine. A moment's reflection upon them will evince that they are of the very highest order, and that such a religious experience as is here portrayed cannot be studied without profit. This book is worthy of being made a manual of devotion. It is not claimed to be entirely free from erroneous aspects of truth. No man wholly escapes the faults of his age; and the Confessions of Augustine exhibit some of the deficiencies of the Church of the fifth century. But, in reference to the permanent and everlasting elements of the Christian experience, the great main characteristics of the Christian

---

* Milman's Primitive Christianity, B. III. ch. 10.

life, here is certainly a bold and accurate, a clear and large utterance. We are confident that familiarity with this book, for even a single year, would perceptibly affect the person's religious experience. It would infuse into it the rare quality of vividness. There are no stereotyped phrases, no technical terms or forms. It is the life of God in the soul of a strong man, rushing and rippling with the freedom of the life of nature. He who watches can almost see the growth; he who listens can hear the perpetual motion; and he who is in sympathy will be swept along.

The revising of these Confessions has been a labor of love. As we have scanned the sentences and syllables, we have seemed to hear the beating of that flaming heart, which now for fifteen centuries has burnt and throbbed with a seraph's affection in the Mount of God. We have seemed to look into that deep and spiritual eye which gazed without shrinking, yet with bitter penitential tears, into the depths of a tormenting conscience and a sinful nature, that it might then gaze without dazzling, and with unutterable rapture, into the eyes and face of the Eternal. Our Protestantism concedes, without scruple, the cognomen of saint to this ethereal spirit. Our Christianity triumphs in that marvellous power of grace, which wrought such a wonderful transformation. Having this example and living fact before our view, we believe that Christ the Lord has all power, both in heaven and upon earth; and that there is lodged in his pierced and bleeding hands a spiritual energy that is able to renovate the mightiest and the most vitiated forms of humanity. The Cæsars and Napoleons, the Byrons and the Rousseaus, all the passionate spirits, all the stormy Titans, are within reach of that irresistible influence which is centred in the Redemption of the Son of God, and is accessible to the prayers and the faith of the Church.

www.ingramcontent.com/pod-product-compliance
Lightning Source LLC
Chambersburg PA
CBHW071226230426
43668CB00011B/1319